SHOTTERMILL
— its Farms, Families and Mills —

PART 1 – Early Times to the 1700s

SHOTTERMILL

— its Farms, Families and Mills —

PART 1 – Early Times to the 1700s

GRETA A. TURNER

Shottermill, its Farms, Families and Mills – Part 1

First published 2004

Typeset and published by John Owen Smith
19 Kay Crescent, Headley Down, Hampshire GU35 8AH

Tel: 01428 712892
wordsmith@johnowensmith.co.uk
www.johnowensmith.co.uk

ISBN 978-1-873855-39-3

Printed by CreateSpace

Publisher's Note

This is the first book of a two-part history of Shottermill and the area around – where the counties of Hampshire, Surrey and Sussex meet.

Although Shottermill is thought of today as part of Haslemere Town on the Surrey side of the River Wey, in earlier times it was essentially associated with a larger area covering both sides of the Wey valley as these books show.

They are the result of over ten years' research by the author who, with the help of archives in Haslemere Museum, three county record offices, local historical associations and elsewhere, has pieced together a compelling and readable history of the farms, families and mills in the area.

The second part of this history, covering the period 1730s to the early twentieth century, is published as a separate book.

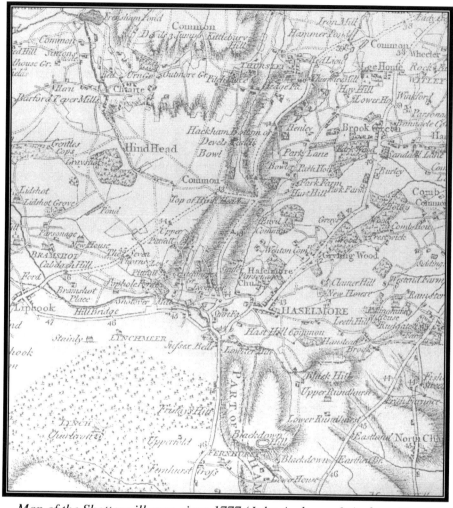

Map of the Shottermill area circa 1777 (John Andrews & Andrew Dury)

About the Author

Greta Turner read History and Archaeology at the University of Birmingham and worked for most of her life in London in the Library & Information Group of an International Chemical Engineering company. In 1976 she and her husband came to live in Haslemere, where she was Recorder of the local Archaeological Group for many years, served for a short time on the Council of the Surrey Archaeological Society, and directed the restoration of the Mediaeval Moated Homestead at South Park, Grayswood. After assisting in the transcription of the Diaries of James Simmons, paper maker of Sickle Mill, she continued in the 1990s to investigate the local Wey Valley's industrial past.

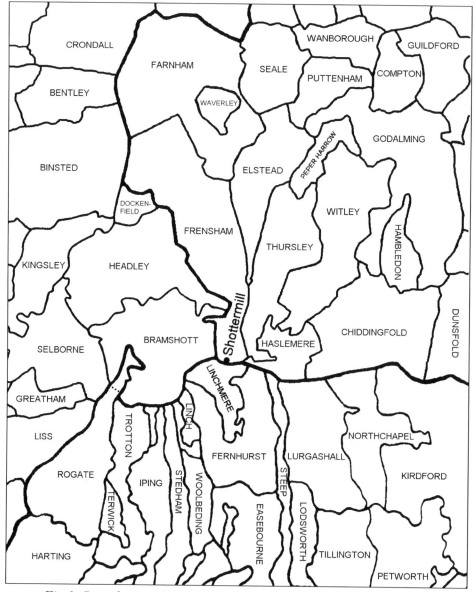

Fig.1: Boundaries of parishes surrounding Shottermill, circa 1851

Contents

ର୍ଯ ର୍ଯ ର୍ଯ

9

Illustrations

Maps

(drawn by the author)

Acknowledgements

I am grateful to many people for their assistance in the writing of this account: to members of the local history associations; to the various Record Offices for their help at problematic moments which certainly did occur; to Philip Brooks, J.W. Penfold, W.A. Sillick, W.J.D. Cooper, and James Simmons III, the Diarist, for their invaluable records; to E.E. Orchard for producing two volumes of the Diary; and also to the Haslemere Educational Museum which has allowed me to roam at will through its Archive. My particular thanks go to Carla Barnes for her information on Northpark, to Jeremy Hodgkinson, Chairman of the Wealden Iron Research Group, for reading through my ironworks chapters, to Professor Alan Crocker and Martin Kane for their fund of knowledge about the paper industry, to Austin Taylor for his information about the wider Baker family and to Peter Armitage for his business records.

I am much indebted to the owners of local properties of all ages for their kind reception and interest and often the production of deeds, photographs, etc; in particular to Miss Anna Roncaglia, Mrs Lockwood and Mr Appleby but also to many others too numerous to mention.

Most of the illustrations are taken from the Haslemere Museum Collection but some of the Linchmere properties were photographed by Mrs V.M. Queen who also helped garner early material.

Last but not least, my thanks and apologies to my husband who has borne years of neglect with only a reasonable amount of complaint.

Timeline for Shottermill

1086   **Domesday**

Manor of Farnham, held by See of Winchester to 20th century

Saxon Corn Mill, presumed pre-Domesday presence

c.1200   Priory of Linchmere & Shulbrede founded

1221   Market Town of Haslemere – Bishop of Salisbury grant

1285   Pitfold Manor created – de Bavents held to 1344

1300s   Shottover Corn Mill built possibly at this time – held by Priory of Linchmere & Shulbrede

1339   Saxon Corn Mill, last record – held by Pope family in 1300s

1345   Pitfold Fulling Mill – built by Pope family and held by them to 1520s

1348   **Black Death and slow recovery**

1373   Pitfold Manor held by Priory of Dartford (Kent) to 1536

1535/6   **Dissolution of Monasteries**

1535/6   Manor Linchmere & Shulbrede created out of Dissolved Shulbrede Priory – Montagues of Cowdray held to 1843

1535/6   Shottover Corn Mill held by Crown, Letters Patent issued

1566   Pitfold Manor bought by Montagues

1570s   Pophole Hammer built – owned by Montagues

1579   Pitfold Fulling Mill held by Payne family to 1631

c.1594   Pitfold Fulling Mill – possible change of use

late 1500s   Tanning/Tanhouse – Baldwyns, Bardens, Nappers associated

late 1500s   Smithy near Shottover Mill built by Bridays

late 1500s   Alien Ironworkers appear in Shottermill

late 1500s   Farnham Manor Records begin for local landowners: Combes to 1826, Paynes to 1640, Wheelers to 1636, Allens to 1646, Tribes to 1680, Sadlers to 1744

c.1600   Shottover Corn Mill leased by Payne

c.1600   Wheeler/Sturt [later Sickle] Hammer built – held by Wheelers to 1636

early 1600s   **Rebuilding of England, increasing prosperity**

1627   Middle Pitfold Farm held by Benifolds to 1765

1629   Tanhouse held by Nappers

1631   Pitfold Fulling Mill – Bardens occupy

1641   Shotters come to Pitfold – they hold Pitfold Mill and other properties to 1781

1642–1660   **Civil War and Interregnum**

1649   Sickle Mill – Hoads made sickles to 1712; Hoad daughters held to 1736

mid 1660s   Sickle Mill – Tamplins possibly working at

1668   Pitfold 'Manor House' built by Shotters

1674	Tanhouse & 'Cherrimans' – held by Cherrimans to 1767
c.1700	Shottover Corn Mill held by Edward Briday
1723	Shottover Corn Mill held by Fielders to 1805
1736	**Advent of Simmons family**
1736	Sickle Mill bought by Simmons: paper made to c.1860s, also corn milled to c.1780
mid 1700s	Turnpike Roads [local] built
mid 1700s	Broom-making local industry, first records
1750s–80s	Simmons Landed Estate acquired
1765	Middle Pitfold Farm bought by Bakers – first local connexion
1767	Tanhouse bought by Simmons, held by them to 1903
1776	Pophole – end of ironworking; Butler occupied from 1730s
1778	Shottover Corn Mill – Simmons held lease; bought in 1805
1781	Shotters of Pitfold sold land – end of local connexion
1781	Pitfold Mill bought by Simmons for papermaking
1788/90s	New Mill [paper] built by Simmons
1815	End of Napoleonic Wars – depression for years after
1830s	Emigration
1831	Pitfold Manor bought by Pritchard
1832–6	Simmons Landed Estate (except mills) sold to Bakers
1832	Shottover Corn Mill held by Olivers (with interruptions) to 1938
1840s	Pitfold Manor held by Bakers to 1880s
1841	St. Stephens Church built
1843	Manor of Linchmere & Shulbrede held by Earl of Egmont
1850s	Enclosures
1854	Sickle Mill bought by Appletons who made military braid; sold 1920
1859	**Railway arrives at Haslemere**
1880s on	Literary Community comes to Hindhead
c.1880	Trout Farm at Deepdene set up
1880s	Pitfold/New Mills leather industry revived by Thomas Gent; ended 1900
1890s on	Second influx into Shottermill of wealthy, professional people
late 1800s	Broom-making in decline
late 1800s	Start development of turn-of-century Shottermill population and housing increase
1896	Shottermill Civil Parish created
1900	Brickmaking on Clay/Wey Hill ended Hammer brickworks started up
1900 on	Decline/end of local mills
1903	Simmons Dynasty ended with death of James (IV) – property sold for housing
1933	Shottermill became part of Haslemere Town

[Dates here are approximate – details in text]

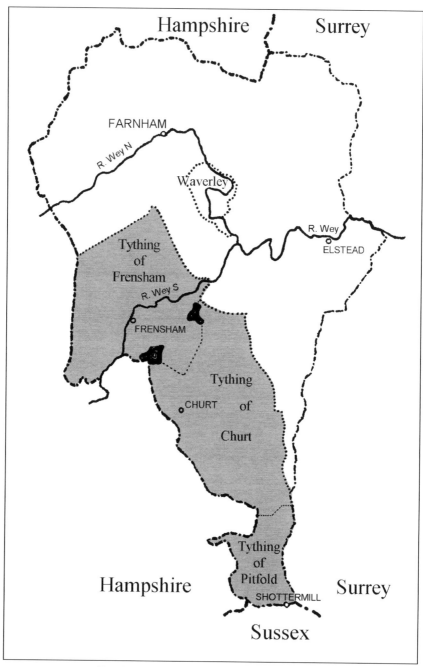

*Fig.2: Hundred and Manor of Farnham
showing the Tythings of Pitfold, Churt and Frensham
within the Parish of Frensham (highlighted)*

SECTION 1

Shottermill to the 1500s

-ooo0ooo-

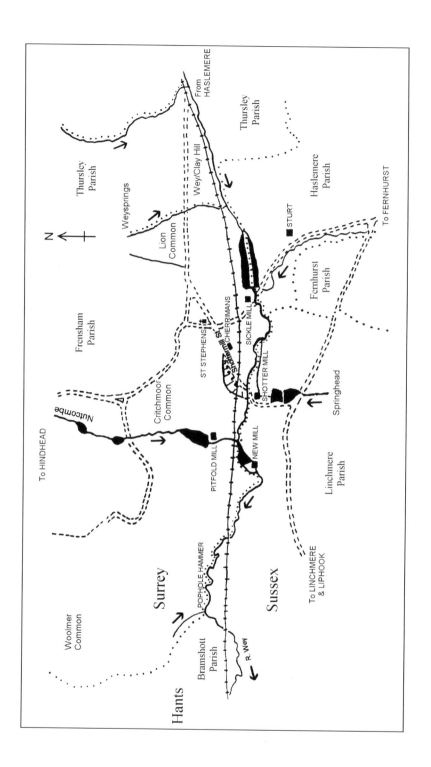

Fig.3: Water Supply System to the Wey Valley at Shottermill

Chapter One

Earliest Shottermill and The Saxon Corn Mill at Pitfold

Shottermill Today; Local Geography; Prehistory; Roman and Saxon Periods on the Sussex and Surrey Sides; Domesday 1086; Later Mediaeval Times to the 1500s; the Creation of Pitfold Manor out of the Farnham Manor Lands in the Tything of Pitfold; General Mediaeval Trends and How Far the Farnham and Pitfold Manors followed this Pattern; the Black Death, Slow Recovery and Emergence of Local Detail; Early Farms and Cottages in the Manor of Farnham; Early Farms and Cottages in the Manor of Pitfold; the Early Corn Mill at Pitfold and Lower Pitfold Farm; Later History of the Pope Family.

Introduction

The history of Haslemere has received a good deal of attention, first in *'Bygone Haslemere'* by E.W. Swanton & P. Woods, Newman, London 1914, and later in *'Haslemere'* by Dr G.R. Rolston, Phillimore, 1978. In neither book, however, is early Shottermill given more than a passing mention although by 1978 it had been part of Haslemere Town for about forty years. It was obviously regarded as peripheral to or even separate from the main Haslemere story and to some extent this was justified. Shottermill over the years had developed a strong sense of separate identity. In 1895 when it applied to become a civil parish in its own right, James Simmons (IV) of Cherrimans – an active member of the community and holder of many public offices – was reported, according to W.A. Sillick, the local *Herald* reporter for fifty years, to have dismissed the suggestion that Shottermill should become part of Haslemere as *'more than anything a joke'*.

This feeling was no surprise as Haslemere and Shottermill had different historical origins and development, were parts of quite different administrative units such as parishes and manors, looked for much of their history in different directions, often earned their livings in different ways and had a different social structure. Something of this separateness can still be seen in the character of the area between the boundary of the old Borough of Haslemere near Tanners Lane, and Wey Hill the start of Shottermill, which has been filled-in in a rather random way. This still gives the impression of a stretch of no-man's-land which is precisely what it was. It had also been for many years more than just the space between borough and hamlet. It was the source of the clay (Clay/Wey Hill) which had long underpinned a brick-making industry in Thursley parish and was an unbeautiful industrial area until 1900.

Interest in Shottermill was initially stimulated by the discovery of the Diary of James Simmons III, paper-maker of Sickle Mill, which covered the period from 1831–1868, the understanding of which necessitated a study of the earlier history of the various mills and farms he owned, and the identification of the many people he mentioned.

It soon became obvious, however, owing to the existence of Shotter Mill itself, the presence of other mills in the Shottermill area which are sometimes only loosely described, and the presence of the Shotter family known to be connected with iron-working and possibly with Shotter Mill, that an attempt to gather and examine as much documentary evidence as could be found might serve to clarify some of the associations. This study, therefore, starts in earnest with the first documentary sources around 1200.

It is clear from both the mid-nineteenth century Diary written by James Simmons III and earlier sources, that until the nineteenth century when its centre of gravity moved into Surrey, the focal point of the community which became known as Shottermill was the River Wey taking in both sides of the valley. To James Simmons III both the area in Sussex around Shotter Mill and the ponds as well as the area in Surrey up to Hindhead, known as Pitfold, whatever the administrative boundaries, was essentially part and parcel of the community *he* regarded as Shottermill. In this account, the *historical* Shottermill relates to the same area.

Some suggestions will be made as to why, in spite of this, the ancient name of Pitfold in Surrey should have been superseded by the equally ancient name of Shottermill which was originally in Sussex. The picture resulting from this study is not a balanced one as the records surviving for Surrey and for Sussex do not necessarily correspond either in time or in the information they provide and, as far as the Surrey side is concerned, local information is often buried in returns for larger units such as the parish of Frensham, the manor of Farnham and the joint tything of Pitfold and Churt of which Shottermill was only a part, and in which areas many of the inhabitants had no local connexions. Fig.2 shows the manor and hundred of Farnham, the tything of Pitfold and Churt and Frensham parish.

For the period up to the 1500s most of the sources are almost exclusively concerned with land and its holders, and these allow some insight into the structure and development of Shottermill. Not until the latter half of the eighteenth century do other sources become available, allowing other aspects of life to become visible. Mostly, people who did not hold land, pay taxes, leave wills or break the law, remained names without substance in the parish registers, and as most of the inhabitants of Shottermill were members of the 'rural poor', this applied to the majority of them. Local parish registers start from about the middle 1500s or 1600s depending on their early decipherability.

This account has tried to throw a little light on the structure and size of the community, the changes to this and its causes and effects; the houses it lived in; how it earned its living; the labour force and range of occupations; its standard of living; transport and communications; the religious bond; community concerns; and its education and leisure. It covers the period only up to about 1900, after which other sources are available. The ownership or occupation of property has been covered in some detail as much of it relates to families which have lived and worked in the area for some hundreds of years and whose descendants are still present.

Historians are very much dependent on diaries, letters and the like to put flesh on the bones but as many of the inhabitants of Shottermill were illiterate often until the middle 1800s and in some cases well beyond, little of that nature was found for the early period described in this book. For the later period described in the second book, however, the mid-nineteenth century Simmons Diary has been used extensively to illustrate typical middle-class attitudes on a variety of matters, and in particular on the church and education in chapters contributed by the late Dr W.R. Trotter, author of *'The Hilltop Writers'*.

Shottermill Today

Today, the *historical* Shottermill has been part of Haslemere Town for seventy years, but with a church and parish of its own, a population in 1991 of about 4,600 and considerably more[†] at the time of writing.[1] It lies now wholly in Surrey, extending from Hindhead to the County boundary which is marked by the infant Wey, although having lost a small part of its original extent around Hindhead. Its name comes from the presence of the old Shottover Mill which lies over the border into Sussex. Historically, on the Surrey side, Shottermill was part of the parish of Frensham and the manors of Farnham and Pitfold. On the Sussex side lay the parish of Linchmere and the manor of Linchmere & Shulbrede and a few acres of Fernhurst parish, now Camelsdale.

In Simmons' time, however, Camelsdale was not a community known to him as it was then purely agricultural land with only the odd house upon it. In their preoccupation with gaining a living, administrative boundaries never bothered the local population any more than it does today except perhaps from the point of view of local taxes, style and quality of housing, employment opportunities and inheritance of property.

Today, Shottermill is an area with much turn-of-the-century housing, some of it built for the needs of an expanding working class population during the late 1800s and early 1900s; other parts of it gentrified. There is

---

[†] Local Authority boundary changes make later comparisons impossible.

the usual collection of shops, schools, public houses, churches, filling stations etc – nothing out of the ordinary. Most, if not all of the older houses have gone and nowadays a portion of its population commutes from Haslemere station.

Twenty five years ago, the Births and Deaths column in the *Herald* never failed to include names which had existed locally for some hundreds of years. Today, after such a short interval, there are often none. During the second half and particularly towards the end of the nineteenth century, the Hindhead uplands were seen by the Victorians as a 'Little Switzerland' – an area of scenic beauty and clean invigorating air – a refreshing change from the summer stench of the London Thames and streets and regular outbreaks of disease caused by inadequate sewerage arrangements. The long summer vacation of the Houses of Parliament overlooking the Thames – the main sewer – was no accident.

The completion of the railway from London to Portsmouth with the first train going up the line in January 1859 put this delightful area within easy reach of persons wishing to spend the summer – or even longer – in more salubrious surroundings whilst still remaining in touch with London, and accounts mostly for the building around that period of many substantial houses some few of which still struggle to exist as private residences, with their large gardens and four floors, the top one of course for the servants. It also accounts for the naming of many smaller cottages as Rose, Blossom, Sunflower and April Cottage etc, a hangover from Victorian romanticism. With the coming of the railway – although not immediately – Shottermill lost what had been its essentially agrarian character. Many of the farms ceased to be working farms and their lands, as well as large amount of common and waste land which became available as a result of the enclosures in the 1850s, were sold off in plots for housing. Many of these houses were substantial and built or bought by a new type of moneyed gentry, often business or professional people. Shops and small businesses followed soon after. South of the river, however, in Linchmere parish relatively few such changes took place. Off the main roads, and not served directly by the railway, little if anything changed until quite recently and, even today, there is not a shop in the village.

Local Geography

From a height of almost 900 ft. at Hindhead, the land slopes down to the Wey and on the south rises again to Linchmere Ridge at about 600 ft. This area is greensand but on the valley floor in places the Wealden clay obtrudes.

Nowhere was this ideal farming land but the presence of the infant Wey to which the greensand released water in a moderately constant flow made the area ideal for small water-powered industries. Large rivers with tributaries and therefore subject to flooding and turbidity are not favoured for water-powered industries which require above all a constant but not necessarily high volume flow preferably of clean water. The river is the key to much of the history of Shottermill. The southern Wey rises on Blackdown near Cotchets Farm and at Chase Lane eventually flowing along Sturt Road behind the houses. Another stream flows down from the north and to the west of the Haslemere watershed to Foster's (Railway) Bridge and then along the King's road, and this stream, after being joined by yet another small stream emerging briefly at the bottom of Wey Hill by the Kingdom Hall of the Jehovah's Witnesses, flows into the eastern end of Sickle Mill pond. This latter stream is fed by a number of springs emerging a few hundred yards north east of Lion Green and known as 'Weysprings'. Much of this water system is now only visible intermittently as it is mostly piped and overbuilt. Last but not least is the spring-fed stream running down the Nutcombe valley which used to be the water supply for the old Pitfold Mill. This is now piped along part of Critchmere Lane as it runs through the housing below the Deepdene Estate and it joins the main Wey after passing under the railway near the old site of the New Mill and the present sewage works. The only water flowing into the valley from the Sussex side comes from the spring – Springhead – near Arnold's Garage into the Shottermill Ponds. This water system is shown on Fig.3.

On the Surrey side, a large area to the north of the river valley was known as Churt – a name derived from the Anglo-Saxon word Ceart indicating heath land covered with gorse etc On the Sussex side lay the cold clay of the Weald with its natural cover of hazels and oaks etc

Neither side was initially naturally wealth-promoting land, and if on the Surrey side the greensand uplands were more easily exploited they were in the long term less fertile. Apart from Wakeners (later Waggoners) Wells, on the higher parts there was little flowing water and wells are frequently referred to in the old literature, but there were a number of springs.

However, poor though this land might be on both sides of the Wey, it nevertheless provided other valuable natural resources such as stone for building and road-making; oaks for the tannin necessary to the leather industry; structural timber; underwood and coppice wood for hurdle and fence-making and for charcoal; clay for pottery and bricks and tiles; acorns for pigs – always a very important feature of the rural economy; 'fern' for animal bedding; and with fullers earth and iron ore not too far away.

The extensive heathlands to the north were invaluable for the products used for broom-making. The heathland turf was also used as fuel in the old massive hearths and references to 'turf houses' are common. James Simmons even used turfs which he dug from the common as a quick way of protecting his emergent potatoes and was indicted before the Linchmere manor court for this illegal abstraction.[2] Certainly in the middle eighteen hundreds when the censuses make it possible to ascertain people's occupations, and almost certainly for many years before then, there were sometimes as many people employed in heath and woodland husbandry as in farming, and this variety of occupational openings probably served the community well in times of depression.

That the Wey dominated the structure of the local community can be seen from the fact that the farms on both sides of the river looked into the valley, each farm having access to a stretch of the water, and also from the presence there over the last thousand years of at least one water-powered mill and often several.

Prehistory

Nothing will be said about the prehistory of the area, which is pretty well known. Field walking practically anywhere on the greensand will reveal in the form of flint artefacts evidence of the presence of the hunter gatherers of the Mesolithic (middle stone age) period and their successors, people of the Neolithic period and the first farmers, on the greensand itself and where it slopes down to and mixes with the edges of the Wealden clay.

Roman Period

There is certainly evidence locally for the existence of a native British population in the area in the Roman period. Within a moderate radius there is the villa at Chiddingfold, a tileworks near Fernhurst, a cemetery (and somewhere its settlement) at Haslemere, and in the immediate area the coin hoard found near the road from the Shottermill Ponds to Liphook not far from the turning off to Linchmere. This hoard dates to the late third century, a period of political instability and from which period other similar hoards elsewhere are known. It might well reflect the act of an apprehensive local inhabitant. Other finds have been made in the area generally at, for instance, Combeswell, Bramshott and Haslemere, of the odd Roman pottery sherd and coin. All these would have been left by the local native population who after the initial period of military occupation adopted Roman culture to some degree, and such finds can be found almost anywhere in the country.

Saxon Period

The Sussex side

After the departure of Rome in the early fifth century, the flourishing economy of Britain which had largely been dependent on its presence, began gradually to disintegrate. This period saw also the beginnings of the Saxon incursions as people looking for land on which to settle rather than as conquerors, and there is evidence in places in the initial period of amicable agreements to share land with the native Britons. There must have been local variations in this process, but the peasant may well have been largely unaffected, tied as he was to the land for his very existence, whatever the changes at a higher level.

It was the Saxons who gave the name of Andredesweald or the Great Forest to the area we now know as the Weald but the date of its penetration and settlement is still controversial although it is in general agreed to have been later than the Surrey side. On the other hand, it is now considered that its population, although still fairly sparse and localised, was greater than once thought. From the earliest times use must have been made of its timber and iron but equally early was its use for 'denning' or the seasonal grazing of cattle and in particular of swine.

Local areas of clearance and eventual settlement are indicated by place names such as 'hyrst' as in Fernhurst, by 'leah' as in Merdlegh (later le Mardle Heath) or Marley and 'falod' as in Hawksfold. The ancient name of Danley Farm – used in the Linchmere manor rolls until the nineteenth century – was 'Hogvogdens' or literally the den or clearing of the hog folk, which eventually developed into a farmstead. It is also possible that Camelsdale has a similar origin. On the Fernhurst Tythe Map of the 1840s[†] when many field names become visible for the first time, the two large fields rising from the Camelsdale road up the Ridge on the south side are seen to be called 'Camels Dene Wood'. It may be that this area was originally a place used by the people of Pitfold as a denn or seasonal pasture and 'Camel' a proper name possibly with an early origin. The mediaeval land parcel extending from the Wey across the Liphook road where the cottage called 'Rats Castle' now stands and on which New Mill once stood, was originally called 'Walshes', this sort of name as in Wales and Walton on Thames, being the term applied by Saxon incomers to strangers to them who in fact were the native Britons, who may have had a settlement on the Wey at this point. Certainly, there was a narrow strip of comparatively fertile land along both sides of the Wey.

The Surrey Side

The chronology of the Saxon advance along the river system on the north into south west Surrey is not well evidenced but a late seventh century charter (685) whereby King Caedwalla on conversion to Christianity gifted 60 hides of land called Farnham, two of these being specifically referred to as Churt, for the establishment of a church or 'monasterium', indicates that distinct folk group territories already existed. According to Blair, Caedwalla by this time is seen to be 'master of south western Surrey' and to him and also to Poulton, the picture is one of the Saxons settling in an orderly fashion into an existing framework so that there may well be in some places a degree of

---

[†] The Tythe Commutation Act of 1836 converted the payments of tithes due to the incumbent of the parish into an annual money payment. To facilitate this, maps were drawn containing details of the owner and occupier, land use, acreage and name of every field and building in the parish.

continuity with original places of settlement reaching back well beyond Saxon times.[3]

Also if, as now is accepted, one of the unnamed water corn mills mentioned in the Domesday Book as existing in the Farnham Hundred was on the Wey at Pitfold, then there must already have been present in pre-Norman Conquest times a community there for it to serve. The place names of 'Ceart' or Churt and 'falod' as in Pitfold indicate that there was early woodland clearance and that these clearances were probably pastoral rather than arable.

On the Surrey side after the Conquest lay the great manor of Farnham of which the area known as Pitfold formed the extreme southern part. Both manor and hundred (a division of a shire) extended from north of Farnham Town itself to the Surrey/Sussex county boundary on the Wey. The bounds of the Pitfold tything (which were divisions of a Hundred in which the inhabitants were mutually responsible for law and order) on the east side ran from immediately east of the Punchbowl Hotel at Hindhead down the Polecat valley and the eastern side of Lion Common which originally extended down to the stream at the bottom of Wey Hill, and took in Sturt Farm.

At no time did Pitfold tything include any part of Thursley parish of which a tongue included Wey Hill and much of the ridge to the south of Haslemere (see Fig.4). The Lion Common continued eastwards in Thursley parish to the top of Wey Hill and possibly beyond – on one occasion being described as taking in the *Crown & Cushion*.[4] Mostly, however, from around the later St. Christopher's Green down to Foster's Bridge it was more often described as Clay Hill. No explanation of the name of 'Lion' has been seen; only in the case of land near the junction of the Sturt and Camelsdale roads was a small area referred to as the 'roundlion' which may or may not have relevance.

On the western side from Hindhead the tything bounds took in a little of Kingswood, Wakeners (Waggoners) Wells and Woolmer Common continuing down to the Three Counties Bridge at Hammer. Most of this area was in the large parish of Frensham but the tything also included a small part of Haslemere parish around Sturt Farm. For well over a 1,000 years (with two short breaks) the manor of Farnham was owned freehold by the See of Winchester which was reputed to be the wealthiest see in England and the second wealthiest in Europe, only being surpassed by that of Milan. The Bishops of Winchester owned land from Oxford to the Isle of Wight and from Somerset to Southwark. They held the county of Hampshire entire.

By about 800 the Farnham church and lands had come into the hands of the See of Winchester and, after some possible interruptions, were back in its hands circa 850. Winchester held them at Domesday 1086 and thereafter. A charter of the tenth century (965) details the boundaries of this land and shows it to correspond with that of the mediaeval manor and hundred of

Farnham and it is in this latter charter that the first reference to Pitfold is found. Although according to Blair, this latter charter is a forgery, it does nevertheless contain the genuine tenth century bounds. A map and transcript of the 965 charter is given in Elfrida Manning's '*Saxon Farnham*'.

In this, the Farnham manor bounds, after proceeding from the Hogs Back to Elstead, go 'thence into hedge coombe' (Haccombe/Highcombe Bottom or the Punchbowl) and 'after that straight on to the wolf bank' (Woolmer in Pitfold) and then on to 'the (fen?) clearing' (perhaps the Lion Common) and 'after that west along the stream (ie the Wey) along the boundary of the lands of the South Saxons (Sussex) and the lands of the Bishop' (Surrey) and then 'up along the clearing to the trackway or gate of the pitfold'.

It has been suggested that this referred to a wolf pit, and that there were other wolf pits at Badshott and possibly Grayshott although the term 'wolf' could mean also an outlaw. The presence immediately to the west of the Farnham lands of the then great forests of Alice Holt and Woolmer make either meaning possible. After this the bounds go on to Whitmoor Bottom and Barford and eventually back to Farnham.

The manor of Farnham was huge and references to the location of the manorial tenants' holdings were always initially to the tythings of the manor which served to facilitate their identification. The affairs of the tything of Pitfold – small and sparsely populated – for both manorial purposes and for purposes of tax collection and law and order, were from a very early date included under those of the tything of Churt.

Fig.2 shows the manor of Farnham, the tythings of Pitfold and Churt and the historical parish of Frensham.

Domesday 1086

The Domesday Book described old English society under a new administration but otherwise little changed. Villages with their population and agricultural product value were grouped under the old Anglo-Saxon units of Hundreds. When the Domesday maps of Surrey and Sussex are placed top to bottom, there would appear to be a total dearth of settlement in the middle – the area of the Weald and also of the land up to Farnham Town – Farnham town itself appearing as the only settlement in the Farnham Hundred. The extreme southern part (Pitfold) is a blank.

If these maps appear to contradict the above remarks and to indicate that there was no local settlement, it should be remembered that the places marked were only the vills whose details were recorded and almost certainly, as far as the Farnham Hundred was concerned, the returns for whatever settlements were then in existence were simply grouped under the one heading of Farnham itself. The only thing which can be said with any certainty is that in regard to south west Surrey the population was much lower than that of the counties to the east – not more on average than a handful per thousand acres, although of course not spread evenly but comprising a number of small communities, mostly family groups.

Later Mediaeval Times to 1500s

The Sussex Side

On the Sussex side for the period from Domesday to the end of the Middle Ages – roughly the 1500s – and the Dissolution of the Monasteries, most of the documentary evidence relates to the Shulbrede Priory and the church of St. Peter.

Linchmere parish, later the manor of Linchmere and Shulbrede, ran down from the Wey to a point a little south of but not including Fernhurst village, and was enclosed by the much larger parish of Fernhurst. Fig.1 shows the local parishes. The Linchmere parish and manor boundaries were practically identical which was not always the case.

The Priory from which the manor took its name and which can still be seen, was founded circa 1200 by Sir Ralph de Arderne for canons of the Order of St. Augustine and was endowed by him with land. Some years later the Priory obtained the appropriation of the church at Linchmere which predated it. Between its foundation and its dissolution in 1536 the Priory had been gifted considerable lands and the Valor Ecclesiasticus of Henry VIII shows it to have been receiving rents from nineteen different places including Haslemere. In spite of this, however, it was never more than a small unimportant foundation notorious for its difficult access through the Sussex mud and certainly for much of its later existence seeming – in spite of its widespread holdings – to have been impoverished.

One item of interest referred to in a later Valuation (1608) of the Priory's undisposed-of property was the Churchyard of Old Haslemere. In 'Bygone Haslemere' p.39, Swanton traces back the ownership of the close known as 'Church Lidden' or 'the churchyard of Old Haslemere' which lies on the south side of Scotland Lane opposite Old Haslemere Field, now the Recreation Ground, to John Shudd in 1614. The late Valuation confirms this describing John Shudd as holding to himself and his heirs 'a croft of land lately a church yard containing by estimation 3 rods yielding 4d. p.a.'

Of more interest perhaps than Shudd's ownership is the fact that this old churchyard[†], presumed to have belonged to the period of Saxon Haslemere before the town was planted in its present situation circa 1221, is established as being once held by Shulbrede Priory. As consecrated ground, it is not surprising that it should have been associated with a religious foundation, but it is curious that this should have been Shulbrede Priory and not the church of Haslemere, in which parish it lay (see Fig.4).

[†] A note by John Wornham Penfold jnr recalls that James Simmons III had told him that human bones and fragments of coffins had been dug up there, but no trace of them has been found.

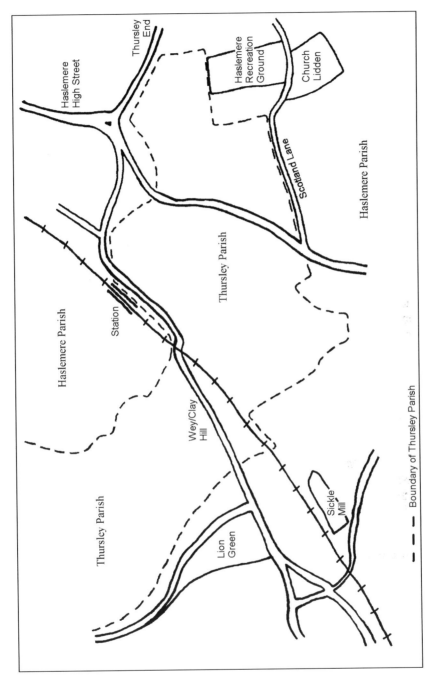

Fig. 4: Intrusion of Thursley parish into Haslemere

The Priory's history has been described by Arthur Ponsonby who made his home there in 1905, and whose descendants still reside there.[5] The records of the later Linchmere manor which begin in 1545 are, of course, much too late to give any indication of the date of permanent settlement in this part of the Weald but it is probable that the process was taking place in the 1100s and 1200s. Some of the farms appearing later in the manor rolls are recognizable by the late 1200s/early 1300s in the lay subsidies or tax returns in volume X of the Sussex Record Society. These returns list among others Phillip de Hurlonde (later the lands called Parrys & Hurlands of the Shotter family of Highbuilding); Johanne de Wlenchmere (probably of Linchmeres or Church Farm); Alic de Hacheshulle (later Hatch Hill which the Shotters later held with Parrys & Hurlands); Thomas de Stanlygh (Stanley Farm); Wulon de Merdleigh (Marley) and Matilda de Hauekfold (Hawkesfold Farm). Stanley which had been gifted to Shulbrede Priory by the Abbey of Dureford is mentioned as early as 1248.

Although there is nothing to describe how the Priory administered its Linchmere lands, at the Dissolution it can be seen that they were held for a money rent and were copyholds which in effect meant simply that a copy of the tenant's terms of obligation, the name of his holding and its size and rent, was given to him as proof of his right and title.[6]

Copyholders were tenants only of manorial land but such holdings were by custom a very strong sort of tenancy and copyholds could be bought, sold or mortgaged and in practice although not in theory, be willed away from the customary heirs. Any dealings of this nature required permission from and payment of a fee to the Lord of the manor but this rarely seems to have been refused. The manorial tenants if not in theory were in practice owners and by tythe map time in the middle 1800s they were called owners.

By Dissolution time all the farms present in the post-mediaeval period are already in evidence, and these will be described in the later chapter on Linchmere. In addition to the farms there were only two or three cottages, although these were more like smallholdings. Two or three other cottages which may also have existed at that time receive no mention as they were farm cottages, were counted as part of the farms which they served, and had no separate documentary life of their own. There may also have been a parsonage house near the church but this receives no mention at this date.

This is all that can be said about the Sussex side of Shottermill for the period up to the middle 1500s. Not until the end of the sixteenth and the early seventeenth centuries did additional cottage properties begin to appear and these will be detailed in the chapter on the Manor of Linchmere which succeeded the Priory. At the end of the mediaeval period there was nothing to suggest a cluster of houses round the church which might be called a village although Linchmere, at least, had a church as a focal point, which cannot be said for the Surrey side. That there was nothing else which could act as a local social or administrative centre is demonstrated in 1671 in the Linchmere rolls when the payment of annuity was instructed to be made in the porch of St. Peter's church. It was a typical dispersed community.

The Surrey Side & the Creation of Pitfold Manor out of the Farnham Manor Lands

There is considerably more information about the Surrey side for the mediaeval period up to the 1500s and this is contained in the great series of accounts known as the Winchester Pipe Rolls which contain the income and expenditure in all the Bishops' lands in exhaustive detail.

Anyone who doubts the mediaeval capacity for keeping sophisticated accounts down to the last pound of wool or bushel of grain should read the transcript made by Mark Page *'The Pipe Roll of the Bishopric of Winchester 1301–2'*, pub. Hampshire Co. Council, 1996. Unfortunately, these accounts deal with Farnham manor as a whole and it is difficult, therefore, to extract from them entries relevant only to the small part of that manor which lay in Pitfold. They do, however, include a record of fines (fees) paid in respect of land holdings, some of which may relate to Pitfold. Also, as explained below, after about 1285, the manor of Pitfold and about half of the land between Hindhead and the Wey was carved out of the manor of Farnham and was therefore after that date no longer of any concern to the Farnham manor authorities.

Access to the information in the Pipe Rolls has been made possible from the transcripts covering the Tything of Churt (including Pitfold) made by Philip Brooks in his book *'The Bishops' Tenants'*, 1983 (unpublished) copy of which can be seen at Farnham Museum. From these records some suggestions have been made as to the nature and whereabouts of primary settlement in Pitfold, the early history of Pitfold Mill and the local effects of the Black Death.

The first reference to the *manor* of Pitfold (as distinct from the tything of Pitfold) is seen in 1285 when it was carved out of Farnham manor, although the exact circumstances of this do not appear to be on record. In 1285, Edward I whilst at Woolmer granted the right of free warren to Adam de Bavent in all his demesne lands.[7] The rights granted to the de Bavents applied to a number of manors owned by that family which included Cocking and four others in Sussex, and others in Surrey, Kent and Suffolk. Pitfold was included in the list and the assumption must be that at this date, if not earlier, the de Bavents were already in possession of the manor of Pitfold.

Adam de Bavent and his son and grandson Roger were frequently in the king's service and in 1344 the young Roger granted most of his possessions, including Pitfold, and for reasons unknown, back to Edward III.[8] In 1362 Edward III granted the small manor of Pitfold to the Prioress and Convent of Dertford (Dartford in Kent). This priory had been founded by Edward III and was subsequently suitably endowed by him. The Valor Ecclesiasticus shows the Priory to have been awarded some of the other de Bavent manors. There were a number of grants of life tenure, surrenders and re-grants and some trouble including the forging of seals by Hawise the widow of Roger de Bavent, but from 1373 the manor of Pitfold was confirmed to Dartford Priory and remained in its hands until the Dissolution in 1536.

At the Dissolution in the Valor Ecclesiasticus or the great valuation of ecclesiastical property by Henry VIII, Pitfold manor was valued at 49/3d. At the same time the Priory of Shulbrede was valued at £17 for its Linchmere lands alone. Against a total value of £72 for all Shulbrede Priory's holdings, Dartford Priory's was £324. Pitfold manor was obviously of no great account. It is also unfortunately the case that the records of Pitfold manor, both during the mediaeval and post-mediaeval period (with the exception of a short period in the nineteenth century) are lost so that early information relating to this part of the Pitfold tything is available only spasmodically from the Pipe Rolls prior to 1285 and from a Minister's Account of 1549 which gives a picture of Pitfold manor at that date when after the Dissolution it was still in the hands of the Crown to which financial reports were made.[9]

The bounds of Pitfold Manor, very roughly, split the tything of Pitfold into two by a line commencing on the Wey immediately to the west of the later Shottermill cemetery at Sunvale and after going round the top of Critchmere Common made its way in a northerly direction towards Hindhead, leaving some land around and to the south of Hindhead as the Bishop's Farnham manor commons, and the land in the south east still in the Bishop's hands. Arguments and disagreements as to the whereabouts of this boundary as it approached Hindhead abounded and will be discussed further below. In general, the western and northwestern part of Pitfold tything comprised the manor of Pitfold and the southeastern part including Critchmere Common and Lion Common remained in Farnham manor.

Fig.5 shows the Pitfold manor boundaries up to the debatable line.

General Mediaeval Trends

and how far the Farnham & Pitfold Manors followed this Pattern

Because the pre-Domesday oral tradition gave way in the second half of the twelfth century to the written tradition, a good deal of information is available for the country as a whole in the mediaeval period and the general trends are well known. Briefly, this shows that, continuing the pre-Domesday trend, the population continued to grow dramatically – even spectacularly in some cases – and that the twelfth and particularly the thirteenth centuries were periods of prosperity until the population plummeted in the middle 1300s following the Black Death.

In general the increasing population had resulted in pressure on land and its consequent fragmentation. During this time of prosperity, sometime between 1160 and 1208 the planned town of Farnham was set up, probably one of several founded by Bishop Henry de Blois of Winchester, and other similar small towns with markets can be seen around this time. Blair writes 'The very regular plan of Haslemere may plausibly be associated with a market grant of 1221, following a reorganisation by the Bishop of Salisbury in which it superseded an earlier settlement at Peperhams'.[10] The mediaeval economy was essentially subsistence farming ie the object of a community was to provide for its own requirements with little or no reliance on surplus or money, and was in general cereal based.

After the Black Death which carried off a huge proportion of the population, disruptive features were set in train which were to change the face of mediaeval society. The shortage of labour increased the rate at which money wages were being substituted and increased the mobility of the peasantry in search of betterment. An attempt by the Crown to re-impose the wages and conditions of the period prior to the Black Death only resulted in a wave of social unrest culminating in 1381 in the Peasants Revolt.

How far do the Winchester pipe rolls show this general picture to have been true for the manor of Farnham and in particular for the Pitfold area? If anyone, looking at Lion Green and the nearby (but much later) church had imagined that this had originated as a nucleate village with a centre and open fields around, the pipe rolls soon show this picture to have no relevance to Shottermill; such villages only began to develop in the late Anglo-Saxon period in areas of dense settlement.

Philip Brooks after looking at the evidence in the Winchester Pipe Rolls was of the opinion that in many respects Farnham manor did not follow the general trends of population growth and fragmented land holding as described above. Compared with the counties to the east, Surrey and in particular this part of Surrey was less densely settled. Rather than land fragmentation as a result of population pressure, there seems to have been a process of accumulation into larger, more viable units, at least until the Black Death in 1348. From the references to rent defaults and vacant land in Farnham manor, the population, already comparatively low, seemed hardly to reproduce itself during the 13th, 14th and 15th centuries.

If there had been population pressure any vacant lands would have been snapped up promptly by other land-hungry men, but there is little evidence that this was the case. Even before the Black Death, from the end of the 1200s there always seemed to be land somewhere lacking tenants, particularly during the early 1300s – a period of poor harvests and famine – when land can be seen reverting into the hands of the Lord along with frequent reference to the lack of heirs.

Initially, from about the 1240s the pipe rolls show a large number of fines (fees) described as 'increase of rent' indicating the clearing and taking in of new land, these new assarts or clearings probably reflecting some increase in population and prosperity. However, these new lands were mostly small and were assarts used for grazing as there is no evidence for cropping. Rather there are many references in the 1200s to enclosures which indicates animal husbandry. There is reference in 1267 – not the first – to heathlands in Churt tything indicating that large areas of the original tree cover had been cleared.

By the late 1200s this process diminishes and is followed by a period of the steady exchange of small parcels of land as most people try to increase their lands to a more viable size, and overall, land seems to have been amalgamated into fewer hands, not more. In 1292[11] the first entry for a holding of two virgates is seen, larger than the normal holding of half a virgate (16 acres) which was deemed to be able to support a family. It is also noted that part of this process of amalgamation was the much re-marrying of widows, although there was nothing new in this. In times of subsistence farming in particular, husbands needed wives and vice versa if they were to survive and work the land whilst at the same time rearing useful children. Much of the farming process concerning the dairy, chickens and cheese-making was women's work, and in Bentley there is evidence that shearing the sheep was done by women who also often took part in the heavy work of the harvest. Farming was essentially a family business.

From about the 1290s the number of fines or fees for new lands decreased quite noticeably. In 1316 there are references to derelict land. From the late 1200s to the Black Death in 1348 there was always some land lacking tenants and the number of entries for the payment of fees begins to show a small decline. The period of famine around 1315 and after (as a result of poor harvests and a cattle murrain) is reflected directly in the rolls, particularly in allusions to a lack of heirs. With regard to the prosperity of the manor tenants, the first grant of a licence to demise, ie to sublet land, is found in 1224.[12] This was unusual as on the whole people held insufficient land and were too poor to exist on rents. Such licences do, however, become more apparent from the mid 1200s and become common in the fifty years preceding the Black Death, but after 1348 such grants cease abruptly and do not recommence until recovery set in around the early/middle 1500s, 200 years later, after which the landlord/tenant system became the normal order of things.

Reference has already been made to the Lay Subsidy (tax) returns for Linchmere where several of the Linchmere farms and families are in evidence. For the Surrey returns for the Tything of Pitfold and Churt in 1332 in the Surrey Record Soc. vol XI, they show payments being made by Adam Pope, John atte Sturt and a John and William both of Putfold. The most that can be said about these returns is that the difference between the largest payment of 5/6½d for the Churt farm of Ridgeway (an area of much greater fertility) and the smallest payments of 8d indicate that already there was wide divergence of wealth and there would also have been people not included as they were below the level of assessment.

A manor's demesne lands were those reserved for the support of the Lord and his household. In Linchmere manor the demesne land of the Montagues of Cowdray occupied a single large tract of land running up the centre of the manor, varying amounts of which were leased out by the Montagues from time to time and usually run from Shulbrede Priory farm. This had almost certainly been the Priory demesne previously. In the huge manor of Farnham, however, the Bishop's demesne lands were scattered and Brooks reckoned that wherever there were demesne lands there was a hall from which they were administered. In 1218[13] there is reference to halls at Seale, Tongham, Frensham, Pitfold and Churt and in 1235[14] there is an entry referring to carriage of timber from the hall at Pitfold to Farnham.

If the Bishop had demesne lands and a hall at Pitfold *(and this is by no means certain)* there is no clue as to its whereabouts or how long it existed. It might, however, provide a clue as to why when Farnham manor parted with some of its Pitfold lands to the de Bavents, the south-eastern part was retained by the Bishop. There is no doubt that the part the Bishop retained was the most productive and more settled part. According to James Simmons III at a very much later date, the land of his farm of Lower Pitfold (extending north from Critchmere Lane) was the best land around. Another very relevant point, discussed further below, is that the land the Bishop retained may possibly have contained the early corn mill at Pitfold. Mills were valuable possessions and not disposed of lightly, although Pitfold Mill, unlike some others, seems to have been a copyhold and not to have been held directly by the Bishop.

The Black Death and the Slow Recovery

The Black Death, or as it was more generally referred to at the time, the Great Pestilence, struck in the summer of 1348 and its effects as shown in the pipe rolls is striking. Estimations of mortality for the whole country range from a quarter to a half of the total population. Although the worst visitation came about in 1348 it was not the only one, there being further recurrences in 1361, 1374 and 1394/5. In fact plague was about until the 17th century but without the terrible initial impact. Also, before the Black Death occurred, in the early 1300s there had been severe harvest failures and epidemics of cattle murrain, due it is thought to a period of unusually cold and wet weather, and resulting in severe famine. The effects of the Great Pestilence therefore were not limited to a few unhappy years. Part of the fourteenth century was an unmitigated disaster.

Until the Black Death the pipe rolls list for the whole of Farnham manor during the previous fifty years about twenty fines or fees annually indicating changes of tenancy through normal exchange and mortality, but in 1348 and 1349 there was a huge increase in recorded fines. Initially the affected holdings were readily taken up by the survivors but the records over the next hundred years and more indicate that the local community showed signs of increasing poverty and difficulty. Brooks estimated that of all the manor, the Churt/Pitfold area was the one most badly hit and that probably its low population was the prime cause of its difficulty in throwing off the plague's effects which took the best part of 150–200 years.

The plague, borne by the fleas on the black rat[†], tended to affect denser communities more severely, but it is obvious that the more scattered family farms were by no means exempt. After the Black Death there are numerous entries recording rent defaults and fines which include frequent use of the phrase 'none of the blood survive'. Robo in his book '*Mediaeval Farnham*' pub. 1935, took this literally to mean that the farms and land in question were abandoned. Brooks, however, was of the opinion that more probably farms were run at a much lower efficiency and that many of the rent defaults and reference to the disappearance of an entire family did not indicate that there was absolutely no one left to pay the rent but more likely that the tenants refused to make payments for amounts of land where there were no longer sufficient people to work it. They were still producing but at a very low level.

Fines were frequently 'forgiven' but this was less an indication of manorial sympathy than the only practical option when payment simply could not be made. Many properties were undoubtedly abandoned and many changed hands. There were 150 years of defaults of rent and many of the fines show that the holdings passed to unspecified relatives rather than those in the customary direct line. Copyhold tenancies on both sides of the Wey were copyholds of inheritance about which there were specific rules. Many fines included a requirement that houses should be built, indicating that many of those existing in the more prosperous 13th century were now derelict. In 1440 almost every farm in Pitfold and Churt tything was in default.

There is also evidence that land parcels were split up and leased at reduced prices. In many cases the Bishop leased lands as and where he could but without issuing copyholds in the usual way which probably accounts for the statements regarding holdings on long or perpetual lease of the Payne family and the Wheeler family (of Wheelers Hammer, later Sickle Mill) in Pitfold when the Farnham manor court rolls commence around 1500, giving more detail. The Farnham manor court rolls (as distinct from the pipe rolls which contain accounts only) for the period prior to 1500 which would have given a better picture of everyday life were for some reason destroyed. From 1500 the Farnham manor court rolls do survive to the end of the manorial system in the early twentieth century although during this period their main function was to make a formal record of tenants' holdings.

Also surviving, but only from about 1600 are the presentments to the Farnham Hundred Law Court. This means that from the 1500s at least some

---

[†] The identification of the 'Great Pestilence' as bubonic plague is being increasingly questioned.

34

information about the part of Pitfold tything which remained in the hands of Farnham manor is available. The corn and fulling mills in Farnham manor were not exempt from the effects of the pestilence. In an article in the *Farnham & District Museum Society News Letter* of December 1990 p.66, Brooks summarised the reflection of the Black Death in these mills many of which became derelict. The corn mill at Pitfold disappeared at this time, but the fulling mill there, first heard of just before the Black Death, continued from that time without interruption.

Recovery was extremely slow. Not until the middle 1400s are references seen to the repair of mills and increasingly in the late 1400s to repairs of houses and barns and to the building of new ones. In the early 1500s licences once again began to be issued to dig fullers earth for the cloth industry. By the middle 1500s a steady replacement of old houses can be seen and around the end of the century and in the early 1600s existing houses undergo a process of enlargement and improvement. Also by the middle 1500s there is evidence that the landlord/tenant system was increasing and in a fair way to becoming standard practice.

In the middle 1500s a new heading entitled 'New Rents' appears and remnants of the waste where no common rights existed are being brought under cultivation, although 300 years later when Simmons advertised his Shottermill farms for sale, he included the information that, in the Tything of Pitfold and Churt, at least 5,000 acres of waste were still available; as late as 1788 the incumbent of Frensham parish estimated that only a fifth of his parish was cultivated.[15]

The entries from the middle 1500s in the Farnham manor court rolls show quite clearly a general resurgence of prosperity with new cottages being built on the waste, (although this process took, perhaps, a little longer in Pitfold) with the amalgamation of old lands into larger units and, significantly, once again the division of some lands between a number of sons, always a sign of prosperity.

Emergence of Local Detail

It is against this background of the long, painful period of recovery after the Black Death that some farms in Pitfold begin to have a continuously traceable history. Some of the old houses remaining such as Blossom Cottage (now Church Lane House), Lees Cottage, Buffbeards, Rose Cottage opposite Shottover Mill, and High Pitfold Farm are all Listed Houses dating mostly to the period of recovery in the 1500s (they cannot be dated more precisely) but some of them have documentary evidence indicating that the site was in use well before the date of the building presently existing. The Surrey Domestic Buildings Research Group is of the opinion that the 1450s would in most cases have been absolutely the earliest date possible which could be applied to the few mediaeval houses remaining.

As far as the Linchmere side is concerned, having no detailed record, there is only the despairing cry of the Prior of Shulbrede in a communication to the Bishop of Chichester in 1358 that he can get no one to work the land:

> 'the serfs and coloni of the Prior who were useful in carrying out their business have been taken away in the last wonderful pestilence which fell on the land of the Prior, nor can more be got, so that the land which used to be tilled by them and by the priests ... are made waste and useless.'

In Linchmere manor at the beginning of the manor court rolls in 1545, references to the decaying and dilapidated state of most of the farmhouses are constant and continue for some time.

Generally, the eventual recovery was of course much affected by the Dissolution of the Monasteries by Henry VIII in 1535 and the consequent redistribution of immense amounts of land, and the period from the middle 1500s is dealt with in a following chapter. In some cases the new owners of the monastic lands caused much grief and disruption amongst their tenants by throwing off the old copyholders and enclosing their lands for sheep, which required much less labour, or by the concentration of small holdings into larger, more economic units. Nothing of this nature seems to have occurred locally. In the first place the land was not essentially prime sheep country as was the Downs and most of Hampshire and secondly, much of this process was driven by economic necessity in that landlords were faced with fixed rent incomes from their tenants in a time of rising wages. On both sides of the Wey valley, the manor lordships of the Montagues of Cowdray and the See of Winchester seems to have been benign.

The Tything of Pitfold

Information in the Pipe Rolls

The pipe rolls begin in 1208/9 and initially they provide little information which can be used to say anything constructive about the Surrey side locally. In 1305[16] there is one of several entries describing, not unremarkably, that Pitfold supplied timber and also stone for Farnham Castle. There is in 1244[17] an entry recording the sale of a sheepfold and small house in Pitfold, references to Roger, Peter and Emma of Pitfold in the same year, and other references to William of Putfolde later in the 1200s for land, doing little more than confirming that a community existed at Pitfold. Other people holding and inheriting land in Pitfold appear from time to time up to the 1500s but many with no relevance to later known names. Such entries do, however, gradually begin to contain more detail so that it becomes possible to say a little about some of the inhabitants and farms there, but even so only in a few cases, and often with little certainty.

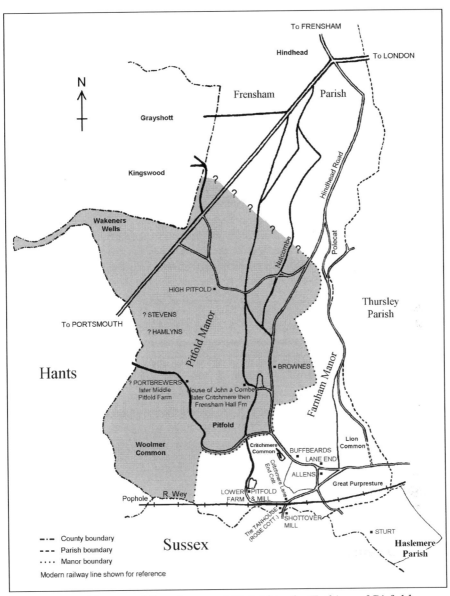

Fig.5: Manors of Farnham and Pitfold in the Tything of Pitfold showing the very early farms and cottages

All the lands of the manor of Farnham were initially held for a money rent and for an obligation of labour service although Bishop Aylmer de Valence in 1257 released many of his tenants from the obligation of bondwork and Brooks is of the opinion that for the Tything of Churt and Pitfold bondwork had been abolished earlier. Of the holdings in the Wey valley on the Surrey side, five are always described in the later manor rolls as 'bondland' indicating that they had been held from a very early date. They are Sturt Farm, Buffbeards Farm, Lower Pitfold Farm, Allens Farm and Lane End Farm. All these farms retained this description almost until the end of the manor court rolls. The rest of the known holdings were usually described as having been part of the waste or as 'purpresture' land. Purpresture was a Norman French legal term indicating land – usually waste – illegally encroached upon. When such an encroachment had occurred, in most cases it was recognized by the manor and made a copyhold in return for a rent but without any obligation of labour service. One such area was the 'Great Purpresture of Eighteen Acres' which lay between the Lower Lion Common and Sturt Farm. Another was the six, later ten acres which eventually became the Cherrimans land. The application of the Norman French term suggests that such areas were cleared and settled in the post-Conquest period but later perhaps than the bondland. Probably, therefore the area of primary settlement would have been roughly centered around the Lion Common and what is now known as Junction Place.

Because this was the area retained by the Bishops in the manor of Farnham after Pitfold manor went to the de Bavents circa 1285 it is possible to follow to some small degree the fortunes of some of these farms from an early date through the Pipe Rolls and then continuously through the post-mediaeval period from the court rolls of Farnham manor up to their end round about 1900. It is not possible, however, to do the same for the holdings in the manor of Pitfold. A few names and place names are given in the pipe rolls for the location of which a guess is hazarded but the absence of later information owing to the loss of the manor of Pitfold rolls, makes many remarks little more than guesswork.

The Farnham Manor Land in Pitfold Tything

Some Early Farms

The location of the early farmhouses in the manor of Farnham land in Pitfold tything, where known, is shown in Fig.5.

Sturt Farm

With regard to the farms in the area retained by the manor of Farnham, some of the earliest entries in the pipe rolls are found to refer to Sturt. Sturt is a word describing land between two streams, in the case of the local Sturt Farm these being the stream running from the east through the Sickle Mill pond and the stream running behind the houses on Sturt Road. It is not surprising, therefore, that the Sturt in Pitfold is not the only holding of this name, and although there are entries for people 'atte Sturte' in 1211, 1244 and 1268,[18] it is not until 1276[19] that an entry refers specifically to Robert of the Sturte paying for a small plot of land expressly in Putfold, although quite possibly the earlier ones were also for this land. (Pitfold over the centuries appears as practically anything from Pitfaud, Pytfaude and Putfold and Pitfall to Pitford and Pitfield to quote but a few).

In the same year Alice of the Sturte paid for land recovered from her brother[20] and in 1277 John de Wakeford paid for Alice and her land[21] ie he had married her. In 1277 Sturt passed yet again from Alice to Thomas Doncecod[22] but in 1325[23] a period of famine, it may have been the derelict land surrendered to the use of one of the Pope family. The Pope family which is generally considered to be remembered in the name of Pophole, was one of the local great surviving families and its members appear frequently in these early records. The fortunes of Sturt Farm during the period around the Black Death are not known but in 1420[24] a Thomas Pope married Cecelia widow of John Donstoc(Doncecod) and so may have got his foot in the door of this property again.

Only from the 1500s does the history of Sturt Farm become continuous when it is in the hands of the Wheeler family associated later with the Wheeler/Sturt hammer, afterwards Sickle Mill. In 1546 it was held by Richard Wheeler, inherited from his father William Wheeler of Haslemere parish.[25]

The Great Purpresture

As the first reference to the Great Purpresture does not appear until the 1500s, it is not possible to say whether it was an accumulation of small parcels or a single grant or at what date or dates such grant or grants had been made. In 1575 it was held by Henry Wheeler who had 'held it for a long time under perpetual lease', indicating that this might have been one of the land parcels leased out by the Bishop, but not as a copyhold in the regular manner, in the period after the Black Death, and there are hints that it had been in Wheeler hands earlier in the 1500s.[26] It never had a farmhouse of its own and until the 1600s seems to have been held by the tenants of Sturt Farm.

Buffbeards Farm

Little also can be said about the early days of Buffbeards Farm, which 16th century farmhouse still exists today a short distance to the west of the entrance to the Holy Cross Hospital, on the north side of the A287. The odd name by which it is still known was obviously a colloquial matter arising perhaps from the appearance of either the house or a sometime tenant. As such it had no meaning for the rolls and it is met with for the first time only in the late 1700s in the Land Tax returns. There is nothing to say for how long the farm had borne this name. Only its description as bondland indicates that the farm had a much earlier history. In 1564 William Baldwyn held it, this rolls entry referring to his inheritance from an earlier holder in 1546.[27]

Lower Pitfold Farm

Lower Pitfold Farm with its comparatively late seventeenth century farmhouse – built by the Shotters and much later known as Pitfold Manor House when it was occupied by members of the Baker family who held the Lordship of Pitfold in the nineteenth century – is now gone but remembered in Manor Close off the Critchmere Lane. This farm, associated from at least the thirteen hundreds with the old Pitfold Mill on Critchmere Lane, also now gone and overbuilt, will be dealt with below under Pitfold Mill. This farm and mill were associated from their first references in the pipe rolls with the Pope family whose name occurs frequently in relation to this and other of the Pitfold farms.

Allens Farm

Of the other two smaller early farms, only the Allens farmhouse still exists. This, until recently called Blossom Cottage but now Church Lane House, lies on the south side of the A287 on the corner of (St. Stephens) Church Road, opposite Holy Cross. Whilst not appearing especially old from the outside, Blossom Cottage contains within it features of its original construction as a small mediaeval open hall house of two bays (ie four walls and a roof only, no ceiling, and a smoke hole to cope with a central open hearth) and as a Grade II Listed Building is dated to the late mediaeval period.

Members of the Alleyn family can be seen in the Tything of Churt from the middle 1200s but they cannot in any way be attached to the Pitfold Allens Farm at this early date. In the returns of the Lay Subsidy of 1332, a William and Richard Allayn paid taxes in the Tything of Churt but again not necessarily for the farm at Pitfold. There were other Alleyns at Headley and around Haslemere; and in Haslemere, a Robert and William Aleyn paid taxes in 1524–5.[28] Whatever the connexion of the local Allens with these other Allens, some members of the Allen family were certainly living at the Pitfold Allens Farm in the middle 1500s from which date the history of this farm can be traced continuously. The Allens are first recorded as holding this farm in 1560.[29]

Lane End Farm

The last small early farm was the manorial parcel known as Curtis later becoming known as Lane End Farm but with the farmhouse now gone. It stood at the beginning of the A287 on the immediate west of Lion Green. The name Curtis seems to have derived from the Curtenesh or Courtinashe family which can be found in the area from the late 1200s, and although the length of their association with this particular farm from that early date is not at all clear, they and the Pope family were exchanging land specifically in Pitfold in 1440.[30] When John Pope inherited a messuage and half virgate in 1470[31] from his father, it was described as 'late of John Courtinashe' and in 1533 it is firmly identified as Curtis/Lane End Farm by that farm's description as previously 'Curtis once Popes'.[32]

Its history from 1533 is continuously traceable. In 1533 Alice Baldwyn held it.[33] Her family had a long association with the local tanning industry. Bartholomew Harding – a scion of the important Harding family of Frensham – inherited from her in 1540,[34] and in 1615 it passed from Alice the Harding heir to Thomas Combes.[35] From 1440 the Curtis family are no longer to be found in Pitfold but are still around in Haslemere in the 1600s and also in Chiddingfold. The Combes held this farm until the eighteenth century.

The Farnham Manor Land in Pitfold Tything

Some Early Cottages

In addition to the farms there were in the Farnham manor land in Pitfold tything a few cottages, for which also see Fig.5. The Lion Common was larger than it is today and the king's highway from Haslemere to Liphook and beyond went across it, dividing it into the Upper and the Lower Lion (now Haslewey) before descending through an area of waste past Shottover Mill. There is only one reference at this early time to a cottage on the Common's immediate edge and the records for the continued existence of this are less than clear as it reverted into the Lord's hands.[36] From its description it lay at the extreme southeast corner with the stream near the bottom of Wey Hill at its back and common on every other side.

The reason for this dearth of houses was, of course, that the Lion Common was surrounded on all sides by farm lands and the right to use the common was jealously guarded by the tenants of those farms. The only other cottages were three down by the Wey, all associated in the 1500s with the tanning industry and with the Baldwyn family. This family, first referred to in the pipe rolls in 1211 when they are seen to be accumulating small parcels of land, re-emerge in the 1500s after a gap of 200 years, thriving and well, and associated with Curtis/Lane End in 1533[37] and Buffbeards.[38]

In the middle/late 1500s (although the Farnham manor rolls are not entirely clear at this date and the Paynes also seem to be connected with these cottages) the Baldwyns held the two Tanyard Cottages.[39] A third 'lying near Shottover Mill' (Critchmere Lane End Cottage) and now gone under the railway embankment, was also inherited by Joanna Baldwyn from her father in 1562 when it was described as 'formerly Corts' – indicating that a house may have been there at an earlier date.[40] The Baldwins also held Deane Farm in the manor of Linchmere from 1545 to 1576 before disappearing from Pitfold in the late 1500s but continuing in Haslemere.[41]

41

The Pitfold Manor Land in Pitfold Tything

Some Early Farms

For the limited information on the Pitfold manor farms and cottages see Fig.5.

As far as the holdings in Pitfold Manor are concerned, there is nothing in the Pipe Rolls which enables anything certain to be said about them at this early date and before they ceased in the 1280s to be of any concern to Farnham manor, having gone to the de Bavent family. The Pitfold rolls not having survived, the earliest picture of Pitfold manor does not appear until it is described in a Ministers Account of 1549 to the Crown[42] in whose possession Pitfold manor was at that date and this 1549 document does in some cases refer to dates earlier in the 1500s.

There is land in the Tything of Churt described in the Pipe Rolls as '*atte Combe*' which probably indicated valley land, and may have been in High-combe or Haccesham in the Punchbowl. Pitfold Manor lands did not extend into the Punchbowl. However, later references to land in Pitfold manor known as 'a Combe' were the lands of 'John a Combe' centered on what was later known as Critchmere Farm and then Frensham Hall Farm and which are described in the 1549 Ministers Account as the place where 'the Pitfold Manor Courts were used to be held every two or three years'.

This statement implies that the land called 'a Combe' had occupied for some long time (the first date is 1509) an important position in Pitfold manor. It certainly occupied the central part of the Pitfold tything and it had on its eastern side another parcel called Combers or Cumberrys, held in 1549 by Richard Person, but later – up in fact to the nineteenth century – quite clearly owned and occupied by the Combe family who are one of the families with the longest local pedigree.

It is possible, though with no real evidence, that the name 'Nutcombe' may have been a corruption of Northcombe, lying as it does between Combe at the south end of the Pitfold valley and Highcombe in the Punchbowl to the north. It was formerly known as Pitfall Bottom.

Other land referred to in the early Pipe Rolls was that called '*atte Cruche*' or land where there was a cross. Crosses were not uncommon. If any of the early pipe roll entries did refer to land in Pitfold tything they would have indicated the land around Critchmere Common (now Deepdene), Critchmere being a corruption of Crutchmoor meaning a cross on 'moor' or poor land. In spite of the Deepdene/Critchmere land being an area full of springs and later ponds, the original name never derived from any connexion with a mere except, of course, that its very watery condition was probably the reason for it being described as moor or poor land in the first place.

For other small Pitfold manor farms the information comes principally from the 1549 Ministers Account, and little can be said about them except that they appear to have occupied the area in the west and southwest of Pitfold tything, eventually being combined to constitute the farm of Middle Pitfold in the 1600s. Only the fact that the family names, by which these holdings are still known at a much later date, appear in the Pipe Rolls in the 1200s and 1300s indicate that they may well have had early beginnings.

The first of these holdings was known as *Portbrewers*, a family name first seen in 1236 and as Portebras in 1273 and 1379. Members of this same family are also seen from time to time in the rolls of Bramshott manor of 1339, 1341 and 1379 when a John of Pitfold has common rights for the few animals on his holding. The Bramshott entries mostly concern fines for illegal use of Bramshott Common so that it would seem reasonable to assume that Portbrewers was in the western part of Pitfold manor and too close to Bramshott Common for its lure to be resisted. After the 1300s this name is no longer met with and does not survive locally today, and in 1549 the land was held by Thomas Warner. Copy of the early Bramshott manor rolls was kindly given to the writer by Laurence Giles, of the Bramshott and Liphook Preservation Society.

Another holding was *Hamlyns or Hamblyns* about which also nothing is known except, like the above, it was a tenement and half virgate still being referred to as such in 1667 although not identifiable.[43] In 1549, it was held by Henry Paine.

The last amongst the holdings destined to become Middle Pitfold Farm was *Stevens*. The name of Stevens occurs frequently in the Pipe Rolls but with no identifiable connexion with Pitfold but the holding of 'Stevens' is described in the Ministers Account of 1549 when Pitfold manor was in the hands of the Crown for a period after the Dissolution, as being held by Edmund at Legh alias Stevens, inherited from his father William atte Legh in Headley. Various references to people atte Legh appear in the Bramshott rolls, one in 1333 as being fined for illegally grazing his sheep in the Lord's wood. This may possibly be the same Headley family as that described by Blair[44] when Richard atte Legh over a period of 40 years from the 1290s built up a considerable Downland estate of arable and sheep pasture. It is possible that the Stevens' land parcel in Pitfold formed at this early date part of this estate and part of the sheep grazing lands. The family atte Legh were still accumulating land in Bramshott manor in 1465.[45]

Because the location of none of the above holdings is known, it is uncertain which of them, if any, survived to become the site of the Middle Pitfold farmhouse, although there is a hint in some much later accounts of James Baker of Stilland Farm, Northchapel, that it may have been Portbrewers.

The last well-known farm in Pitfold manor is of course *High Pitfold* itself. It was probably held in the late mediaeval period by the Wakeford family who first appear in the Pipe Rolls in 1277. Thomas Wakeford held it in 1549. The Wakefords also appear in the Bramshott rolls for illegal use of the Lords common in the 1300s, when John Wakeford is described as tenant of Pitfold manor.

The large assart or woodland clearance adjacent and immediately to the north of the farm was known as 'Wackfords', one of the very few informative field names surviving in this area, and was usually associated with High Pitfold Farm. The Wakeford family still exists locally after 700 years. There is nothing in the rolls to identify this farm until the 1500s which is the Grade II listed date of the present farm building. Almost certainly however, it had a history going back to a period considerably before this. The Wakefords held land in Haslemere in 1486[46] and are listed in the Haslemere Hearth Tax in 1663.

The 1549 Ministers Account refers to holdings in Pitfold which are called variously *Combers/Cumbers/Cumberrys*, names which often stem from an association with wool combing or shearing; and in one of the rare surviving documents for Pitfold manor – a 1727 rental – the duty payable on property changing hands is expressed in terms of sheep. All tenants are required to provide 'one shipp' on these occasions.[47] Whilst this Pitfold manor rental is of a comparatively late date, almost certainly it reflects a custom stemming from a much earlier period.

There is no evidence, apart from this, to show how preponderant a part of the farming economy sheep husbandry was. The best evidence comes from entries in the early manor court rolls of neighbouring Bramshott which, like Pitfold, comprised a fertile strip along the Wey but was otherwise mainly greensand, where numbers of sheep ranging from a handful to occasionally fifty were a constant cause of complaint on account of their illegal pasturing on its Commons. Local inventories of the early post-mediaeval period show that most of the tenants of the Wey valley farms had only a few sheep. Thomas Person in 1570 had 27; in 1623 the Quennells of Hammer Farm had £4 worth, and Mother Mitchell of Pitfold had amounts of canvas for baling wool in her workshop, but nowhere are they found in huge numbers.

Sheep were kept essentially for their wool and skins for parchment. All the early inventories show people to have had wool about the house, and Brooks noted that no-one, at least at the high table, seems in the very early period to have eaten mutton although doubtless somebody did when eventually the sheep died. That wool and cloth played an extremely important role in the mediaeval economy is well known and its local importance is shown by the number of fulling mills in Farnham manor which was blessed with a multitude of small streams and fullers earth.

Fulling was the process of degreasing and thickening of woollen cloth by beating it in a solution of fullers earth and although originally carried out by treading or walking (hence the name Walker) it soon became mechanized, the beating hammers being water power driven. There are many references in the Pipe Rolls from their commencement to fulling mills and to fullers, and of course to the building of a fulling mill at Pitfold in 1345.[48]

There was a sheep and cattle fair at Farnham as early as 1232.[49] On the whole from the evidence in early post-mediaeval inventories, it would seem that locally everyone had a few sheep but no one had a great many, the Pitfold economy being then as later a mixed economy, probably much of the cereal produced being barley.

The Pitfold Manor Land in Pitfold Tything

Some Early Cottages

The last item of information provided by the 1549 Ministers Account of Pitfold manor is that apparently only three cottages existed, one being Brownes – possibly now the site of Brownescombe on the A287; one called Develyns of which the location is unknown but which seems to have been part of the land of John a Combe; and a tenement and a few acres held by a Nicholas Combes which he had inherited from his father John a Combe and lying near High Pitfold. Bearing in mind that one of the tenants listed in 1549 (Henry Paine) is charged 1/2d rent for a garden only, it would seem reasonable to assume that the list is an accurate reflection of affairs on the ground.

There is nothing from any source to suggest that in the mediaeval period there was any huddle of cottages round Lion Green, in the Nutcombe valley, at Critchmoor, on Woolmer or around Waggoners Wells. It is not until the end of the 1500s and into the 1600s that new cottages begin to appear, and this will be dealt with in a later chapter. There is no evidence on the Surrey side as a whole for the beginnings of a village. However, there is no doubt that the Wey valley could be said to constitute a community of loosely connected units. None of the farms were large and none of the farmhouses were separated from each other by any distance and, in fact, most of them were linked by the king's highway from Haslemere to Liphook.

Almost certainly there were on both sides of the valley illegal or temporary structures. There would have been workers in the woods – hurdles for instance were necessary from the moment land was cleared. Charcoal burners moved about as their work required, living in temporary hovels and meriting no mention. Heathland products were extensively used and may have supported an itinerant way of life requiring no permanent dwellings.

Unlike the Sussex side, there was in Pitfold not even a church, the parish church of Frensham being not only seven miles away but also separated from Pitfold by an area of heathland which until almost the beginning of the twentieth century constituted a very real barrier to communication contributing in some degree to the backwardness and isolation of the Wey valley community. Certainly its inhabitants tended to look in any direction other than the north. It is difficult to appreciate today when Frensham and

45

Farnham are so easily reached just what a barrier this was, as is illustrated by the episode of Catherine Simmons' wedding in 1847 when on returning from Frensham Church across the heaths, some of the party including both Simmons and Penfolds whose families had lived in the area for generations, managed to get lost.

Before leaving the mediaeval period, a few local names appearing in the Pipe Rolls and still present in the area are mentioned. Among these is Isabel Wakener who is recorded as holding land in Headley in 1309. It is very likely that this lady's family name is connected with the land which presently goes by the corrupted name of Waggoners Wells. In 19th century documents this name is still Wakeners. The ancient meaning of 'well' very often indicated a spring rather than what is understood by a well today. The ponds at Waggoners Wells (not part of Pitfold tything lands) are not natural but were probably constructed by Henry Hooke, Lord of the Manor of Bramshott, in the early 1600s as pen ponds to augment the water supply to his ironworks at Passfield.

Other local names appearing early are: Glaysers (Thomas was repairing Farnham castle windows in 1409), Bedells, Chaluner or Chandlers, Cuper or Coopers, Hardings, Hylde Chutter (Hilda Chuter), Luffs, Brownes, Kenes (Keens), Grevetts, Philps or Philips, Boxalls, Vallers or Vollers, Upfolds, Figges, Madgwicks, Michinalls (Micheners), Bicknolds, Bristowes, Morers (Mooreys?), Warners, Haywards, Stevens and Tribes, to name but some.

The Early Saxon Corn Mill at 'Pitfold' and Lower Pitfold Farm

In the Domesday Book of 1086 the Farnham Hundred is recorded as containing six mills ie water corn mills, although none of these are named. One is now clearly identified as being at Pitfold and there are pipe rolls entries relating to such a mill at Pitfold between 1235 and 1339. The mill's presence in the Domesday Book means that it must have already existed in pre-Conquest times, and it presupposes that there was then in Pitfold a sufficiently large corn-producing community for it to serve. After 1339[50] all references to this corn mill cease but only six years later, in 1345, a fulling mill at Pitfold is built by John le Pope.[51]

The earliest mention of the corn mill, described as existing in the time of King John, circa 1200 (but written at a date later than 1200), appears in the Register of Bishop Pontissara (Bishop of Winchester 1282–1304) when it is described as 'Poppehale Mill', a name which is assumed to have derived from the presence of the Pope family who were associated with mills and land in Pitfold for 300 years.[52] It has also been assumed that the mill in Pitfold was at Pophole on or near the site of the much later hammer. The possibility exists, however, that the 'Poppehale mill' might not necessarily have been in the place *now* known as Pophole, but a few hundred yards upstream on the site of the slightly later Pitfold fulling mill on the bend in Critchmere Lane.

Entries in the pipe rolls in 1235 and 1244 refer merely to Gilbert of Pitfold and his mill but this, of course, merely meant that it was somewhere in the tything of Pitfold. It was not a specific location but obviously it would have been somewhere on the Wey, and Pontissara's description of the bounds of Alice Holt and Woolmer forests, in which the corn mill appears, proceeds (with no further detail) from Grayshott to the mill of Poppehale in the Wey valley and thence to Chiltley (near Liphook).

Significantly, however, references to the corn mill continue to appear in the Pipe Rolls amongst entries relating to holdings of the manor of Farnham (1313–1339) during the period when the area which included the location *now* known as Pophole had become part of the manor of Pitfold and was held by the de Bavents (1285–1344). These are: 1313 – Fine paid by Adam le Pope for a messuage, virgate and [corn] mill in [tything of] Churt from John his brother,[53] and 1339 – Fine paid by John Wakeford for Agnes la Pope & her messuage, virgate and water mill, which she had inherited from her husband Adam.[54]

The boundary separating the two manors is not defined at this early time but there is nothing anywhere to indicate that it had changed, and the Pophole area was undoubtedly Pitfold manor land in the 1500s and after. *Neither at this early date nor at any future time do any of the other lands in the manor of Pitfold ever appear amongst records of the manor of Farnham.*

Also, there are entries in the pipe rolls referring to the Pope family's fulling mill which suggest that it might have been on the same site as the earlier corn mill, and there is absolutely no doubt that this fulling mill was built near the bend in Critchmere Lane. The Pitfold (fulling) mill occupied this site until the 1970s when it was demolished, and its continuous descent there is traceable in the records from the 1300s to the 1900s. In 1384 in the pipe rolls Thomas Pope held the fulling mill and a virgate of land once ('quondam') of Adam Pope. The above Adam Pope[55] had held the corn mill in 1313,[56] inheriting it from his brother John, the previous holder. The word 'quondam' was used frequently and significantly to link entries pertaining to the same holding but made many years – sometimes generations – apart.

The first descriptions of the corn mill locate it merely at Pitfold, and it may be that its location in Bishop Pontissara's Register as being at Poppehale was not a precise one. Members of the Pope family held land all along the Wey valley. They held Lower Pitfold Farm (Popys/Poppies ie Pope's) almost certainly the virgate of land referred to along with the mill in 1384 and possibly the land referred to in 1284 as being held by Alice, widow of Thomas Pope;[57] they held other land (location not known) called Popes Reeds; and they held in the Sussex Lay Subsidies of 1296 and 1340 a parcel on the Sussex side belonging to Shulbrede Priory called Pophole, now the land of Hammer Farm. Poppehale may have been, therefore, a term covering a long stretch of the local Wey valley. The term 'hale' may have referred to the Popes' homestead or it may as in the description of the Pitfold manor boundary in the late 1500s refer to a wooded valley. In this document the greenway leading from 'hyndhed to Shottover myll' (down the Polecat Valley) is called 'myll hale'.[58]

It is not unreasonable to suppose that the corn mill should have been situated in that part of Pitfold which was retained by the Bishop in his manor of Farnham; it was probably the most productive and first settled part. There is no way that either location can be definitely proved but there is another possible explanation for these apparently inconsistent records. In the Valor Ecclesiasticus under the returns for the Priory of Dartford which held the manor of Pitfold at that time, there is an entry to show that the Priory paid 3/4d to the Bishop of Winchester 'for the collection of rents of the manor of Pitfold'.[59] It may be, therefore, that there had been some sort of long-standing arrangement of mutual convenience between Dartford Priory (and the earlier de Bavents) and Winchester, and that this may have related to the corn mill, accounting for the mill in Pitfold manor lands appearing in the Farnham manor records.

Lower Pitfold Farm

The farm or the messuage and virgate long known as Popys (Pope's) is associated with the fulling mill from the early 1300s and possibly from the late 1200s[60] until the 1830s when farm was sold but the mill retained by James Simmons III of Sickle Mill. The land of Lower Pitfold Farm lay on both sides of Pitfold mill, its western edge constituting the boundary of the Farnham and Pitfold manors. The Popes seem to have held it until the early 1500s as by 1537 it was in the hands of the Payne family.[61]

Later History of the Pope Family

The later history of the Pope family in Pitfold is of interest as they seem to have been one of the great survivors of the difficult period after the Black Death. For whatever reason, no more is heard of the corn mill after 1339 when widow Agnes la Pope along with her messuage, virgate and water corn mill was snapped up by John Wakeford.[62] Widows with a mill and farm to run could not and did not remain alone for long. The fulling mill, however, continued from 1345 onwards in the possession of the Pope family with little apparent interruption until 1520[63] when it was recorded as having fallen into decay, the then Thomas Pope licensing it to Thomas Bedyll for ten years on condition that he repaired it. After this it was used for various other products more or less continuously until the end of the nineteenth century, although still obstinately always described as a fulling mill.

It would seem that members of the Pope family seized such opportunities as presented themselves in the post Black Death years when farms became vacant, although they had started this process of expansion in the period of famine before the Great Pestilence. In 1325, a messuage and virgate – almost certainly Sturt Farm – was surrendered by Thomas Donsekod to the use of William Pope the fine or fee being remitted because it was derelict.[64] In 1384, Thomas Pope the Younger paid a fee for a messuage and two virgates from John Hurlebat which was a holding that became known as Popes Reeds, somewhere in the Tything of Churt but its exact location unknown, in this case none of the blood surviving.[65] In 1393, William Pope paid for a messuage and half a virgate of purpresture land from John Derynal, again location unknown,[66] and in 1420 Thomas Pope is found paying for the newly widowed Cecelia Donstoc,[67] the Popes still apparently maintaining their interest in Sturt Farm. In 1470 John Pope purchased a messuage and half virgate late of John Courtenesh (Lane End Farm),[68] and they are shown in the 1549 Minister's Account for Pitfold to have held Brownes, a cottage in Pitfold Manor, sometime before that date.

The last reference to a member of the Pope family comes in 1522 when William Pope the son of Thomas paid a fee for Popys or Lower Pitfold Farm,[69] by which time they had leased the decayed fulling mill. There are no further entries for them in Pitfold but they can be seen in Haslemere. In 1486 Thomas Pope was listed in a Rental as holding property there; in 1505 Thomas Pope held Popes Farm and in the 1524/5 Lay Subsidy, a Richard and Thomas paid taxes in Haslemere.[70] They are remembered in the name Popes Mead at the bottom of West Street.

There seems to have been only one hiatus in the long occupation of Pitfold Mill by the Popes when in 1421 Thomas Tanner paid a fee for Joan, widow of William Pope, together with her mill and land,[71] and eight years later in 1429 John, son of Thomas Pope, paid for the mill and land 'and a mill pond and one acre with racks on, formerly of John Luff and Thomas [blank] who had no heirs'.[72] The blank here is unfortunate. Was it Tanner or Pope? If Tanner, Thomas may have been one of the Haslemere Tanner family who, as tanners round about this time, appeared more than once in Haslemere courts for selling their skins at too great a profit. The presence at the mill of 'racks' in the field adjoining promotes the thought that the mill might then have been concerned with processing skins rather than with fulling cloth, although in fact racks could have been used for either process.

Brooks noted that in 1257 the water mill at Standford (Headley), described in the rolls as a fulling mill, was held by Henry the Tawyere.[73] Two hundred years later it was in the possession of a man described as a cordwainer, ie a person producing fine 'Cordoba type' leather. Brooks continued that the basic process of 'tawing' or impregnating fine white leather with an alum based substance and that of impregnating cloth with fuller's earth, have sufficient features in common to make it possible that some so-called fulling mills were in fact given over, totally or partly, to the production of white leather.

As far as Pitfold mill is concerned it can be no more than a suggestion at this date (the late 1400s) although later on the mill is certainly connected with the skin dressing industry and was 'converted' (undefined) round about the 1570s. As already mentioned, the official description of the mill remains always a 'fulling mill' until the 19th century, long after it was well known to have been used for various other purposes for many years.

The fulling mills in the manor of Farnham reflect the manufacture of woollen cloth which had from the 13th century formed a staple industry of south west Surrey centered on Godalming, Guildford and Farnham and the surrounding villages. In 1301 Waverley Abbey was supplying wool to the Flemings. The building of the fulling mill at Pitfold in the middle 1300s demonstrates the increasing importance of the weaving industry although from the evidence, many such mills became derelict and suffered severely during and after the Black Death. Their repair in the early 1500s enabled them to play their part in the final period of prosperity of the cloth industry in this area before it finally decayed in the middle 1600s. The fulling mill at Catteshall, about which much is known, closed down some time in the 1650s.[74]

References in Chapter One

[1] Waverley Census Factsheet, pub 1993 and 2003.

[2] Diary of James Simmons III 2.2.50.

[3] Blair, J :Early Mediaeval Surrey, Surrey Arch. Soc. 1991. Poulton, R :Saxon Surrey, eds J & G.D. Bird, Archaeology of Surrey to 1540, Surrey Arch. Soc. 1987.

[4] Thursley Census 1861

[5] Ponsonby, A: The Priory and Manor of Lynchmere and Shulbrede, Wessex Press, 1920.

[6] PRO.SC6/H8.3674.

[7] PRO.Chart.R.13 Edwd I, No.23

[8] PRO.Pat 18 Edwd III, pt 2, m.30

[9] PRO.E36.169

[10] Blair, op.cit. p.56

[11] HRO.11M59/B1 159314

[12] HRO.11M59/B1/159279

[13] Ibid.159275

[14] Ibid.159284

[15] Ward, W.R: Parson and Parish in Eighteenth Century Surrey – Replies to Bishops' Visitations, Surrey Record Soc. vol. XXXIV, 1994.

[16] HRO.11M59/B1/159321

[17] Ibid 159287

[18] Ibid 159271, 159287 and 159450A

[19] Ibid 159303

[20] Ibid 159303

[21] Ibid 159304

[22] Ibid 159304

[23] Ibid 159338

[24] Ibid 159422
[25] HRO.11M59/E1/ 108/5
[26] Ibid 111/6
[27] Ibid 110/5 and 108/8
[28] Rolston, op.cit. p.108.
[29] HRO.11M59/E1/109/8 & 110/1
[30] HRO.11M59/B1/159436
[31] Ibid 155835
[32] Ibid 155877
[33] Ibid 155877B
[34] Ibid 155883B
[35] HRO.11M59/E1/117/4
[36] Ibid 119/9
[37] HRO.11M59/B1/155877B
[38] HRO.11M59/E1/110/5
[39] Ibid 111/4, 111/7 and 113/2
[40] Ibid 110/3
[41] WSRO.Cdy 264, Nos. 52, 71, 92, 103, 112, 120, 138, 162
[42] PRO.E36/169
[43] Has Mus. LD.5.246
[44] Blair, op. cit.p.82–3
[45] BL Add Ch 26567 4 Edwd IV
[46] Woods Mss, Loseley Rental 2 Hy VII 1486
[47] Has Mus. LD. 5.258
[48] HRO.11M59/B1/159350
[49] Farnham & District Museum Soc.J. 12, No.6, 2000, p112
[50] HRO.11M59/B1/159350
[51] Ibid 159355
[52] Surrey Record Soc.No. IX, London 1917, 450
[53] HRO.11M59/B1/159328
[54] Ibid 159350
[55] Ibid.159391
[56] Ibid.159328
[57] Ibid 159306
[58] Has Mus.LD.5.234
[59] PRO.E.344/6 f23b
[60] HRO.11M59/B1/159306 & 159328
[61] Ibid 155880
[62] Ibid 159350
[63] Ibid 155866
[64] Ibid 159338
[65] Ibid 159391
[66] Ibid 159400
[67] Ibid 159422
[68] Ibid 155835
[69] Ibid 155867
[70] Rolston, op.cit.pp.31 & 108
[71] HRO.11M59/B1/159423
[72] Ibid.159429
[73] Farnham Mus. Newsletter vol.6. No.6. June 1982
[74] Crocker, A & G, Surrey Arch Soc. Research Volume No. 8, 1981.

SECTION 2

Shottermill from the 1500s to the 1700s

The Sussex Side

-ooo0ooo-

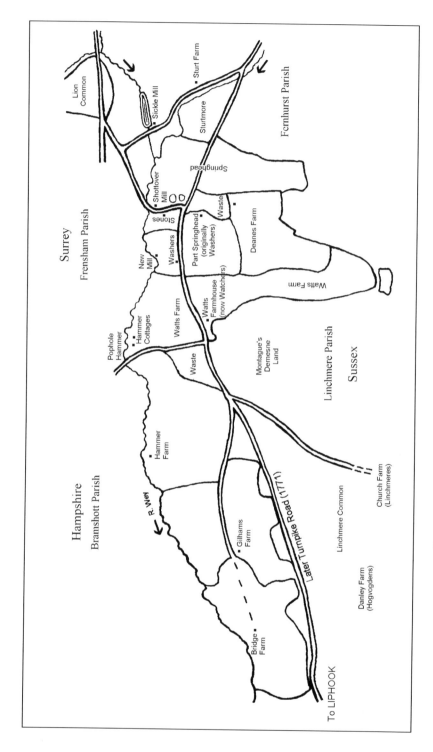

Fig. 6: Early Farms in Linchmere Manor bordering the Wey

54

Chapter Two

From Priory to Manor of Linchmere and Shulbrede

From Priory to Manor; the Montagues and their Tenants; the Cash Economy; the Relationship between the Sussex side and Haslemere; the Iron Workers; Everyday Life; the Church; the Poor and the Aged.

This period associated initially with the end of the Wars of the Roses and Tudor times was, in effect, only part of a long process changing into higher gear. Nonetheless, it marks the end of a time in which custom was everything to a time of change. It sees the end of the power of the great nobles and ecclesiastics based on private armies of retainers owing a feudal obligation of service, and the rise of a new class of gentry whose wealth and power was based in many cases on the purchase of the dissolved monastic lands and on changes in agricultural economy. This process was emphasized by the English system of primogeniture where the eldest son took all and the younger sons, after an equally good upbringing and probably with equally high expectations, had to make good as best they could, providing a constantly reinforced and mobile 'middle class'. Many turned to trade, for which the later contempt did not exist at this time, and education became increasingly necessary to success in life.

It also saw the rise of a more modest but no less important class of independent and substantial farmers, essentially a peasant aristocracy, who called themselves yeomen, men who regarded themselves and who were regarded by others as enjoying a status above most of their neighbours. Their distinction was economic and they were, locally, copyholders with land in secure and stable tenure. Land held even on a modest scale meant power and wealth. Lastly, the period marked a change in the systems of production where a surplus and profit and a cash economy began to become the accepted norm replacing a subsistence economy.

After a period of stagnation, the population began to increase and once again land hunger can be seen, as also an increasing divergence of wealth between landholders of varying degrees and landless labourers and un-employed retainers who were no longer cared for by manorial and monastic establishments. Today, the age of the Tudors is often seen as a golden age, but in fact during much of the earlier 1500s there were high taxes and high prices, debasement of the coinage, the decay of many towns as the only real industry of this period – the cloth industry – moved out into the (cheaper) rural areas, and at the end of the century there was an episode of climate-related, near agricultural disaster. In this period of rising prices, the yeoman copyholder who paid only a nominal quit rent was able to sell his produce at much above previous prices.

The landless wage earner, together with those bereft of employment, had to meet the increased cost of living and suffered accordingly. Many labourers were made redundant by landlords who had to make the most efficient use of the land at a time when their incoming rents were still static by custom. For the first time central government had to make provision for the 'deserving' poor. Trade, from the stimulation of rising prices and the repeal in 1571 of the act prohibiting lending money on interest, rapidly increased in the 1600s in particular when the trading hegemony of the Dutch ended.

From Priory to Manor

The Montagues and their Tenants

At the Dissolution in 1535 Shulbrede Priory and its immediate surrounding lands in the parish of Linchmere were granted by a charter of Henry VIII to Sir William Fitzwilliam, High Admiral of England, afterwards created Earl of Southampton. On Southampton's death his estates passed in 1543 to his half brother Sir Anthony Browne of Battle Abbey whose heirs beame the Viscounts Montague.

The priory lands in the parish of Linchmere became the manor of Linchmere and Shulbrede and the Montagues made their principal seat at Cowdray near Midhurst. The manor affairs were run from Cowdray House. At this time the lands of the manor comprised about 2,000 acres with the Montagues' great demesne farm of about 300 acres running up the centre. The written records for these lands – the rolls of the Courts Baron of the Manor of Linchmere – exist from 1545, the date of Anthony Browne's first court, until about 1900 in an almost unbroken sequence.

The Linchmere manor court rolls comprise three bound volumes but as they did not surface until long after Arthur Ponsonby had written his account of Shulbrede Priory, it has been possible to enlarge upon his chapter dealing with the manor's tenants after the Dissolution. In particular, it has been possible to throw additional light on some of the possessions of the priory and manor, the Shottover corn mill, the hammer at Pophole and also on some of the manor's most prominent families, in particular the Shotters. Only the farms and tenants in the northern part of this manor abutting the Wey are strictly relevant to the history of Shottermill, but a summary of the entries in the rolls from 1545 to 1890 covering *all* the holdings of the manor can be seen in the Haslemere Museum Library.[1]

The Montagues of Cowdray held the manor in the direct line until 1793 when the last male heir was drowned in a boating accident on the Rhine at the age of 24. In that same year Cowdray House was destroyed by fire and sadly many of its records either went up in flames or subsequently mouldered away in the ruins, with little or no attempt at rescue by the unhappy family.

Ruins of Cowdray House

In view of the fact that the Montagues had had a close connexion with the local iron working sites such as the hammer at Pophole and the furnace at Northpark, this loss meant that many questions relating to the local iron industry will probably never be answered. What has been assembled so far is covered in the chapter on Pophole Hammer. The fire also meant that the court rolls of the manor of Pitfold which had been purchased by the Montagues in 1566 may have also gone up in flames at this time and at all events they are lost.[2]

The Montagues were initially a Catholic family but in spite of this they managed to retain the favour of Elizabeth I and both she and Edward VI were entertained lavishly at Cowdray. In 1585, in fact, Montague was one of the two Roman Catholic Lords who were part of the Commission appointed by Elizabeth which tried Mary Queen of Scots and found her guilty of treason. After this, however, the family became gradually impoverished (relatively speaking) being implicated in the Gunpowder Plot (Guy Fawkes had been a footman in the Montague household fifteen years previously) and having its estates sequestered during the Civil War as a result of its adherence to the Royalist Cause.

During the late 1700s and the 1800s the rolls begin to show the gradual diminishing of the Linchmere manor holdings some of which were sold off as freehold properties, although the manor of Linchmere and Shulbrede was, of course, only a small part of the Montague possessions which also included locally lands in Linch, Fernhurst, Verdley, Lodsworth, Easebourne, Lurgashall and Tillington, Woolavington, Buddington and Pitfold. On the death of the eighth Viscount the last male heir, the title became extinct and the estate passed to his sister the Hon. Elizabeth Mary Browne who had married William Stephen Poyntz of Midgham, Berks.

They acted as joint Lord and Lady of the Manor until Poyntz' death in 1840 when the estate was divided between their three daughters, one of whom married the Hon. Frederick Spencer, later Earl Spencer (of the family of Diana late Princess of Wales, and possibly explaining the presence of an early but unimportant document relating to Pitfold manor in the Spencer Archive in the Northampton Record Office). In 1843, as the sisters quarrelled, the estate was sold to the sixth Earl of Egmont and in 1909 it passed to Sir Weetman Pearson who was created Lord Cowdray. In 1999 the Cowdray Estate sold the Commons of Lynchmere, Stanley and Marley to the Lynchmere Society.

William Fitzwilliam, later Earl of Southampton, and Anthony Browne to whom the manor of Linchmere eventually passed were typical benefactors of the Dissolution. Anthony Browne a gentleman originally of no wide lands nonetheless had impeccable connexions in that he was the half-brother of William Fitzwilliam who had been 'an intimate friend from childhood' of Henry VIII.[3] He himself was esquire of the body to Henry VIII, master of the horse, and named guardian of Prince Edward and Princess Elizabeth, all his influence emanating directly from the Crown. At the Dissolution he was granted manors and lands including Battle Abbey and on the death of his half-brother, who had held many high posts, he inherited the latter's Cowdray lands.

This chapter deals with the manor of Linchmere which, apart from a few possessions in other parishes, was co-terminous at that time with the parish of Linchmere. In the nineteenth century there were exchanges on the east side with the parish of Fernhurst, but the 1846 Linchmere Tythe Map represents near enough the old boundaries obtaining at the Dissolution.

Much of the information about Linchmere manor during this period comes from the manor court rolls which enable the history of the farms and their holders to be described. During this period the rolls are mainly concerned with making a formal record of the manor tenants and their holdings; the manor no longer controlled the lives of its tenants in any detail, apart from its requirement that manorial custom be adhered to. These customs included the order of copyhold inheritance through sons and daughters, the right of widows to continue to hold their late husband's property for a nominal fee so long as they lived sole and chaste (their widow's bench), and a tenant's obligation to swear fealty to the Lord, to

58

participate in the manor court which dealt with small customary infringements, and to pay the Lord a heriot or death duty.

The concern for widows' upright lives was probably more to do with the security of the claims of children of a first marriage. Where a daughter inherited, her rights were officially assumed by her husband but her agreement was required to any decision to sell etc. Manorial tenants were, however, not necessarily always the occupiers of the land they held. As the descent of copyholds was by inheritance this meant that sometimes they went to kin who already had livelihoods elsewhere. As time went on, therefore, the holders and actual occupiers diverged, and so long as a tenant sublet his lands to a suitably responsible person, the manor did not take much interest in the sub-tenant, the manorial tenant remaining liable for the fees and obligations to the manor. Whilst, therefore, the names of the manorial tenants are known, the names of those who occupied and worked the land are not necessarily known.

For much of the early post mediaeval period, however, in Linchmere, many of the copyhold farms remained in the hands of local resident families. Name changes often only indicated inheritance, for example, by married daughters. When farms were bought by new men, for example the Butlers who came from Ireland and bought Stanley Farm and the Maidmans of Dorking who bought Springhead Farm, in the middle and late 1600s, they came to live and farm there, although there were also instances of investment purchase by outsiders, particularly in relation to the farms of Springhead, Washers and Deanes in the Wey valley.

When copyholders bought, sold, sublet or mortgaged their holdings, payment of a fee was required by the Lord but permission by the manor does not ever seemed to have been refused. The reversion into the Lord's hands of the hammer at Pophole, dealt with in a following chapter, was obviously done by agreement and involved financial compensation by the Lord of the manor. There are a number of wills and inventories of the late sixteenth, seventeenth and early eighteenth centuries left by Linchmere parishioners from which something can be gathered about how people both rich and poor earned their livings, how they farmed and what sort of houses they lived in. The rolls also contain a considerable amount of interesting financial information which shows how people managed their lives, or in some cases failed to do so.

There is an extensive Cowdray Archive at the West Sussex Record Office at Chichester but much of this concerns the land transfers, leases and financial affairs of the Montagues. Personal documents emanating from inhabitants of Linchmere in this period are usually wills and inventories but these show nevertheless that, whether aware of it or not, they were living in the early modern period. They were farming for profit, their living standards were rising, they knew how to make money work for them, literacy was increasing slightly and the church to some extent had less respect.

If the picture in the late mediaeval period seems to have been one of stagnation following the Black Death and a sluggish recovery, it is also evident that from the middle 1500s to the middle 1600s the population was growing, although in general much of this was in towns. One very striking thing, however, when looking at the Linchmere parish registers which commence in the middle 1500s, is that they indicate a much greater evidence of mobility of the inhabitants than might have been expected.

The peasantry had never been totally immobile and many of the surrounding early parish registers show that, besides local concentrations, the same family names occur widely throughout Surrey, Sussex and the eastern part of Hampshire. Families disappearing from one area can usually be found in another, not too far away. Partly on account of the movement of younger sons of all classes and the urgent need of everyone to find a means of livelihood in changing circumstances, people were dispersing. Whilst in the manor rolls there are names of copyholders like Shotter, Hoggesflesh, Baldwyn, Boxall, Quennell, Cover, Hopkyn, Chalcraft, Farnden, Hayward, Collins, Bedyll, Ede, Theyre and Harding who were in evidence in Priory time and who continue to the end of this chapter and in some cases well beyond, new names also appear and continue, some of these belonging to the iron workers.

There are also, however, in the Linchmere parish registers 1570–1600 about thirty names in addition to those known to be of local long-standing, which remain only names. Nothing is known about their holders except that they existed. If these unfamiliar names are compared with those equally unfamiliar in the period 1650–80, it can be seen that very few of them are the same. There seems to have been a transient section of the population – perhaps comprising farm and domestic servants and casual labourers – notoriously mobile. Some are described as being 'wandering' folk. No comment of this kind can be made about the Surrey side as the Frensham parish registers are not legible until the middle 1600s.

There are two early documents for the manor around the time of the Dissolution which show there to have been about twenty farms. The first was the official return of the possessions of Shulbrede Priory in 1536[4] and the second the list of manorial tenants drawn up for Anthony Browne in 1545.[5] The farms along the Wey valley and most relevant to Shottermill were Bridge, Gilhams, Hammer, Watts, Washers, Stones, Springhead and Deanes, for which see Fig.6. All are described in some detail in a subsequent chapter and some brief reference is made to others in the south of the manor but of special interest.

It is these land-holding families who constitute the bones of the local history. These were the people who sometimes specified, and received, burial in the chancel and not in the churchyard; who acted as churchwarden and were concerned with arrangements for the poor; who acted as officials of the manor and parish – as bailiff or steward and constable; who were the collectors of state taxes; who were sometimes (but not always) literate and left wills. These were the people who in many cases were able to live off their rents, who acted as pledges and were described as 'persons of credit' and in some cases as gentlemen.

These were the tax payers and employers. It is these men who acted as tythingmen or the equivalent and were called upon to act (sometimes very frequently) as members of Grand Juries which decided if there was a case to be answered (viz. the recent Clinton hearings in the U.S.). It was these men who were active in money lending, particularly to their less well off neighbours, often using their profits to acquire more land; and finally it was these men who were into corn milling, fulling, malting, tanning and iron-working or whatever commercial opportunities offered.

These were the men who most influenced local affairs. These were the men who, involved in trade, had contacts with the outside world, in particular London which was increasingly an important market affecting its hinterland. Some of them are described as gentlemen a title which, unlike that of Esquire, had no legal connotation. The term 'gentleman' seemed to indicate a superior status acknowledged and conferred by friends and neighbours and could be awarded to persons of means based on commerce as well as land, although gradually the holding of land came to be seen as essential, and by the 1800s it was a courtesy title applied widely.

In the Linchmere rolls, almost all copyholders until the 1700s were described as yeomen or husbandmen. The status of gentleman was not seen to be conferred on anyone in Linchmere parish in the early part of this period until a Roger Shotter Gent. quitclaimed Diddlesfold manor in 1697;[6] another is so described in his will of 1735, and William Shotter of Fernhurst was termed gentleman in 1571.[7] The Shotters had a coat of arms and were therefore properly entitled but there were almost certainly others in the parish not seen. On the Surrey side, the Paynes were described as gentlemen in the early 1600s.

Few landholders seemed to be without some sort of secondary source of income from a commercial or small industrial enterprise, and many cottagers had a trade or craft. Even large landowners such as the Montagues were quick to take advantage of the potential profits they could see arising out the iron industry.

An important way of supplementing incomes from farming and rents, lay in timber. There are many agreements surviving for the seventeenth century in the rolls to show that timber products comprised an important and in most cases a carefully managed resource, although there were always instances of felling being carried out without the manor's permission. In 1570 Richard Farnden of Springhead Farm was fined 12d for cutting down a single beech. In 1609 Thomas Person of Watts farm was indicted for an illegal episode of 'lopping' when he confessed that it was not for the first time. Another large-scale illegal felling exercise on Stanley Farm is described in the chapter on

61

Pophole. In 1618 Roger Shotter of Pitfold purchased Shottover Fields up on the Ridge from Springhead Farm of which they had originally been part, and some time after came to an agreement with the manor for the timber to be felled and sold.[8] In 1632, in a similar agreement with John Farnden of Springhead 'to fell and coale (charcoal) all woods, underwoods and trees' on Springhead, it is specified that 'sufficient and competent roots of all sorts of trees ... are to be left standing and growing'.[9]

Doubtless this condition whereby trees were to be coppiced was applied to most such agreements. A Cowdray map of 1650[10] entitled 'Montagues Demesne Coppice Lands' shows that much of Montague's demesne lands running up through the middle of Linchmere parish was dedicated to this use. In 1667, the Homage delivered a special message of thanks from Montague for the making of fences or the planting of quickset hedges by his tenants, as they were obliged by custom, round certain of his coppiced lands. They were freed thereafter from any further responsibility.

As far as the small men were concerned, particularly the craftsmen, only in towns could they find sufficient custom to support themselves entirely by the exercise of their craft. In a scattered rural community the crafts followed were those essential to any agricultural community, such as wheelwrights and carpenters and smiths, and were mostly combined with a smallholding.

Seen in the Linchmere rolls and parish wills and inventories are Blaise Briday of Stones who built the smithy near Shottover Mill in 1590; Richard Michener of the smallholding called 'Covers' who in 1632 was also a bricklayer; George Willard yeoman of Goldhorks who in 1634 also ran a wheelwrights business; William Hayward of the Popmore smallholding who in 1654 was a millwright; Thomas Steed who, holding a cottage and a few acres near Bridge Farm, built himself a malthouse in 1670; and finally Henry Rasel (of an unknown Linchmere dwelling) who in 1640 was a tailor. Although there always seemed to be a surprising number of tailors about, Henry Rasel at least had not made his fortune. His inventory showed him to have died with only 1s in his purse, to have had no luxuries and to have wasted nothing. His canvas bed was filled with hulls and his coverlet was made up of tailors shreds. On the other hand, perhaps reflecting the improvement in living standards, there were other tailors – Joseph Mills of Eashing amongst them – who were able to invest in local property, in this case Washers.[11]

The Cash Economy

The removal of barriers to credit transactions was an important factor in the development of a cash economy. In mediaeval times, usury was a sin. It was unlawful for a Christian to lend money at interest. It was, however, no sin to *borrow* at interest so this problem was usually happily settled by recourse to the Jews. It did, however, severely inhibit trade and in 1571 this prohibition was removed and later only the levying of interest over 10 per cent remained illegal. This enabled money to be loaned and borrowed with facility and borrowing on the security of land and property became widespread.

The Linchmere rolls in particular give a great deal of information on mortgages, the amounts, rates and dates of repayment or forfeiture being meticulously entered. Initially a property might be surrendered for a specified sum on condition that if the money was repaid within a specified period usually a year then the surrender would be void and the borrower would retain his property, and in the 1600s forfeitures were not uncommon. Later, however, it became acceptable that so long as the interest continued to be paid regularly both sides were satisfied, and in fact in the seventeenth century the courts gradually established that mortgages could not be terminated at the whim of the mortgagee. Anyone requiring his capital back would sell his loan at a discount.

For most of the period the interest rate was 4% or 4½%, or if unlucky, 5%. People took to this like ducks to water and soon practically everyone had access to credit by raising money on their property whether large or small. Cottagers were no exception. Taking out a mortgage was often done to raise cash on a short term basis, for example when a will left property to a number of children. That way cash could be raised and the terms of the will satisfied without breaking up the property. Most of these mortgages were repaid within a fairly short period.

Another reason for small, short term mortgages seems to have been the requirement for cash when a copyholder needed to pay the Lord his fee on inheritance, a period of twelve months being normally allowed for this to be done. Although the ancient quit rents on copyholds remained unchanged until the end of the manorial system, the fees levied by the manor on alienation by sale or inheritance increased substantially. In 1555 the admission fee to Bridge Farm was 33/4d, in 1865 it was £88.10s. and in 1626 the fee for Parrys & Hurlands was £20 and in 1785, £90.

The inventories show that most people managed to get along without having very much cash in their pockets, and even in the mid nineteenth century James Simmons III was not above doing the odd bit of barter when convenient. In 1839 on the sale of some paper to Mr Pewtress of the Iping paper mills, he took in part exchange a tun of bleach and a horse.[12]

Wills show that however modest the circumstances, the testator very often instructed that moneys left in trust for widows and minors should, until they inherited, be usefully employed or invested, although never specifying how or in what.

In the 1600s in Linchmere mortgage money was raised from a whole variety of people. Some were undoubtedly the local better off yeomen but others came from further afield such as Francis Jackman of Thursley End, Haslemere, Joseph Mills of Eashing, William Marles of Chiddingfold, John Fludder of Yateley, Hants, James Woodyer of Compton and other persons in Bramley, Lodsworth and Shalford. In some cases the amount of money raised indicated the monetary value of the property, but this cannot always be assumed. In the middle 1600s for example, Springhead Farm and Washers were each mortgaged for sums around £200, and Stones, later Mill Tavern, for £60.

The Relationship between the Sussex Side and Haslemere

Just what the relationship was between Shottermill on both sides of the Wey and Haslemere during this period is not easy to determine. As described above, some of the credit raised on the Sussex side came from outside the area but not very often from Haslemere.

During the 1600s and early 1700s as far as can be seen, only two Haslemere families, the Uptons who were maltsters, mercers and glovers, and the Fielders bought land locally on the Sussex side. In 1675 the Uptons purchased Deanes Farm and in the 1670s Sturtmore which comprised about 20 acres of freehold land in Fernhurst parish abutting the Haslemere parish Sturt Farm on its western side.[13] The Fielders bought Shottover mill.

Perhaps this was due to the fact that much of the Linchmere manor land during this period remained in local family hands for long periods. People like the Shotters, Quennells, Butlers, Chalcrafts, Willards and Collins etc held their farms for periods between 120 and 300 years, but even in the early 1700s it was outsiders like the Simmons (who came from Worcestershire), the Benifolds of Bramshott and the Bakers of Northchapel who took advantage of land sales or financial difficulties to accumulate local estates. Not until the later 1700s and the early 1800s can money be seen to come from obviously wealthy tradesmen and shopkeepers in Haslemere such as Thomas Sayer, butcher, Edmund Greenfield, shopkeeper, and Caleb Withall (possibly a sawyer).

Apart from land, there was little in Shottermill in the 1600s to attract people from elsewhere looking for work, beyond the tanyard and the mills and at no time would these have employed numbers of people beyond what the local population could satisfy. Rather, as expected, the picture is that of younger sons seeking work in Haslemere Borough. There are references to members of the Quennell, Shotter, Combes, Hall, Kingshott and Jennings families pursuing the trades of butcher, mercer, tailor, maltster and carpenter there, although correctly identifying individuals from the parish registers at this time is difficult, as one thing which is very apparent is that people (with only a few exceptions) went to the most convenient church, not necessarily their own parish church, to be married and to register births and deaths and these churches were undoubtedly Haslemere and Linchmere.

The long and difficult journey to Frensham church over the heaths for the local Frensham parishioners seemed to be avoided wherever possible so that on the face of it there seemed to be more contact between the inhabitants of Pitfold and Linchmere than even with Haslemere. Probably the most frequent point of contact between Shottermill people and those of Haslemere would have been the market.

One question, which is touched upon neither by Swanton nor Rolston, is where the Haslemere yeomen farmers took their corn to be ground. There was, of course, no mill in the Haslemere Borough itself as there was no appropriate water supply. The nearest mill was Lowder mill up Bell Vale Lane, but little is known about this mill after the Dissolution until the 1700s when it was both a corn and grist mill. A court case in 1690 shows that a member of the Hall family which had mills at Godalming and Eashing was taking corn from Haslemere to mills there for grinding. Thomas Hall the younger deposed that Moses Gammon of Haslemere was indebted to his father for the carrying of 115 loads of wheat to his father's mill.[14] How far Shottover corn mill took business from Haslemere is simply not known.

The Iron Workers

Members of one particular group of families increasingly to be found in Linchmere and Pitfold (and also Bramshott parish) were the descendants of the iron working families who first appeared in the late 1500s. Most of these families seemed to have survived in some numbers, particularly the Hoads and Bridays. As work at the hammer at Pophole may have been intermittent in the 1600s, and as the furnaces at Northpark and Imbhams went out of operation in the middle 1600s and the hammer at Sickle Mill in the early 1700s, they are seen increasingly in other employment in Haslemere.

What the local attitude was to the presence of alien iron-workers in the late 1500s and 1600s, can only be guessed at. As they were Huguenots, having fled Catholic persecution in France, there would have been no religious divide, and several of them became churchwardens of Linchmere parish. They were not present in the local area in huge numbers in the 1600s and seem to have been absorbed without trouble. Nonetheless, for a long period many of them can be seen to have stuck together through intermarriage, in wills as witnesses or devisees, as mortgagees and as financial pledges for each other.

Everyday Life

The great interruption of what, otherwise, was probably a life of a moderately even tenor, was the Civil War. The Linchmere manor court records cease between 1640 and 1645 and many of the Farnham manor records are missing between 1640 and 1660. Farnham Castle was important strategically and changed hands several times. In July 1648 the Parliament gave orders for it to be demolished and the Farnham manor records sometime about that date cease abruptly.

Most of the fighting seen in Surrey and Sussex centered about Farnham Castle, although Arundel Castle, Midhurst and Chichester were also involved. Nearer home, the Quennell iron masters of Lythe Hill and the Imbhams furnace made 'gunns and shotte for his Majestie's stores' and raised a small Royalist force but this was quickly dealt with. The third Viscount Montague, who was a Roman Catholic, suffered much for his devotion to the Royalist cause. In 1643 his estates were ordered to be sequestered and the following year all his goods, plate and treasure were seized and sold. Cowdray itself was garrisoned and the House, narrowly escaping total destruction, remained in possession of the Parliamentary troops until the Restoration.[15]

At the beginning of the troubles, in 1641, any man fit to have office in the Church or Commonwealth was required to sign the Oath of Protestation to maintain and defend the true Reformed Protestant Religion. Possibly the only man in Linchmere parish not so subscribing was Thomas Ayling, a Popish recusant. Sandwiched between Farnham and Cowdray/Midhurst most likely most people in Linchmere parish just paid their taxes (the collectors who were local men are named) and kept their heads down. The Surrey side returns are not available.

Although the manor court was chiefly concerned with making a formal record of its tenants, it is the penalties listed at the end of each court that put a little colour into the daily goings on. On average the manor court met twice a year. Most of the complaints were for the usual mundane things, allowing property to decay, not keeping ditches and fences in order, cutting down trees without permission and abusing the common land with overgrazing or digging holes to remove stone, loam etc and poaching.

This abuse of manor land was not confined to the lowly inhabitants. Montague, as shown in the Bramshott rolls, regularly cut down trees in Bramshott manor and Henry Hooke, Lord of the Manor of Bramshott, was indicted more than once for digging and removing clay from Linchmere manor land. Besides overloading the commons with various grazing animals, one of the most prominent complaints was about free-ranging pigs and a fine of up to 12d per pig per offence was levied if they were caught un-ringed and doing damage to commons. Unringed pigs could turn grazing land into a ploughed field in a very short time. It was also necessary by maintaining the 'railes' or fences to keep them out of the churchyard. There is record elsewhere (although not in Linchmere) of lately interred parishioners being in danger of suffering premature and unexpected resurrection.

The commons were, of course, not common to all but only to manorial tenants. They provided, amongst other rights, additional facilities for the pasturing of anything from geese to horses, and their rights were jealously guarded, although not always with success. Between 1640 and 1651, for instance, William Hughes of Bramshott was repeatedly indicted for pasturing his animals on Linchmere commons until in 1651, exasperated, the Linchmere Homage made a special announcement that he would be fined the large sum of 40s. After this, no more is heard of him but eight years later his son Richard was at it again.

The Church

Other sources illustrating everyday life were the Churchwardens' Presentations to the Chichester Archdeaconry between 1620 and 1670 about misdemeanours which came under church law.

Most of them relate to the period prior to the Civil War. On the whole they show that in the years subsequent to the Reformation the church had lost its way. It was no longer as well attended nor as well respected as hitherto. The physical fabric was no longer supported by parishioners' donations as had been the mediaeval custom, many incumbents were absent or neglectful, and some proportion of the parishioners, by reason of continued adherence to the old popish faith or an increasing leaning toward Dissent or sheer disinterest, did not attend church regularly.

These records refer to the usual problems such as bastardy, witchcraft, rows about wills, cohabitation etc, but two things are outstanding. One is the poverty of many small village churches. Of the many wills consulted, relatively few in the 1600s show that the mediaeval custom of gifts to the parish church was still common although in 1584 Alice Baldwin left 4d apiece to Frensham and Haslemere churches and John Balden left between 2d and 5d to all the local churches. More often they contained donations to the parish poor such as Thomas Person of Watts Farm who, not a wealthy man, in 1570 left 2d to the Linchmere poor.

In the later 1600s it seemed to be the habit of more wealthy members of the community such as Edward Rapley who in 1651 left the poor of Linchmere 10s., and Ralph Tribe who in 1668 left the Pitfold poor 5s. By far the majority of wills ignored this earlier custom, and after the Dissolution it was no longer possible to leave moneys to chantries for the saying of masses for the souls of the dead.

Often in the small Chichester Diocesan churches there seemed to be no bibles, vestments, altar covers, books of homilies and cannons, pulpit cloths or 'comely surpluses' (sic). The very fabric of some churches is described as ruinous or as 'so undecently and beastly kept … that through the pigeons dung and other filth … the people are not able to endure the ill and noysome smell'. There are complaints about the ministers themselves who neglect their duties and do not perform services regularly. 'He doth not say neither the lettany nor the ten commandments hardly once within the yeare …. [He] preacheth not hardly one tyme in five yeares. He doth not catechise.'

The sidesmen, churchwardens and clerks were not always much better, being neglectful and unlettered, and they and others not above making lewd suggestions to the minister about where he should put portions of his anatomy, and calling him a 'shittbreech' and a 'turd' and 'most swinishly vomiting'.

As for the parishioners, not all did their Sunday duty, and are indicted for 'selling meat, ale, carting, carrying wood and broome to a limekill[n] … and playing cricket in the churchyard on Sunday', bringing their dogs to church and 'singing' (possibly an alternative version or singing in a church where congregational music was not approved of). Some are not admitted to services because they cannot say even one of the ten commandments.

There is much reference to sexual laxity for example by the two characters who 'doe suspiciously resort under hedges and ditches'; the 'impudent queane' who has more than one bastard; and another 'incontinent person, a gadder up and downe, a common carry tale, a maker of lyes, one that hath contracted herself to one or two knaves and is married to none'.

The other problem was the liability of the ale house to distract persons calling in to refresh themselves before attending church, innkeepers and other individuals 'keeping tipling in their houses in divine service time'. And lastly, as already mentioned, complaints about the churchyard fence 'which lies downe to the ground and the bodyes of the dead are dayly ready to be digged uppe of the hogs'.

None of these colourful presentations by the Chichester Diocese church-wardens, however, have reference to Linchmere parish which seemed to have conducted itself in a sober and upright manner. There were only two complaints, one concerning widow Jane Collin of Reeks, Reynolds & Fridayes who had wilfully absented herself from the obligatory Easter communion, and another concerning Roger Chalcraft the younger (of Danley Farm) who (sinfully) refused to live with his wife.

Perhaps the absence of a village nucleus in Linchmere and the apparent lack of an alehouse, to which there is no reference at this date, was in part responsible, although not too far away in Fernhurst in 1642 the alehouse there was suppressed and Jeffrey Goodyer, the keeper, bound over for good behaviour.[16] The only other things that can be said about Linchmere Church is that on a couple of occasions it ran out of parchment needed for the parish register; in 1621 it had no pulpit cloth or cushion and in 1687 there was wanting a booke of homilies, canons, articles and a table of degrees prohibiting marriages.[17]

The Poor and the Aged

There are at this date few local references to the treatment of the poor. In 1637 the parish, which was responsible for them, had rented a tenement from William Shotter for 'some poore people who were wanting dwellings', paying him 20s per annum. The parish, however, neglected to pay William his rent so that in 1647 he took the Churchwardens and Overseers of the Poor to Court for the arrears of the last two and half years.[18]

Paupers would mostly have been the old, sick and widows, but they would have amongst them from time to time persons struck by unforeseen misfortune as in the case of Jane West of Fernhurst who whilst returning from Ireland was taken at sea by 'Turkish Pyrats' (who infested the Irish Sea) and who returned to her native parish bereft of everything except the clothes she stood up in.[19] Further provision for housing the Linchmere poor seems to have been made in 1672 when Roger Shotter, Walter Butler, John Shotter and Robert Woodman were granted the copyhold of a parcel of land and a cottage by the manor for 'the inhabiting of paupers'. The location of neither of these dwellings for the poor is known.

It was advantageous to no one that aged widows should be thrown upon the parish and, as far as landholders were concerned, widows were entitled to keep their late husband's lands (their bench) so long as they lived 'sole and chaste'. Often parents with land or a house made these over to their children in their lifetime in return for an annuity, although on some occasions a cautious note is heard as in the 1672 will of Robert Woodman of Redwater/ Woodmancote. He left Redwater to his son but also specified a £6 annuity to his wife which his son was to pay. She was also to have meate, drinke, lodging and houseroom. If, however, Woodman added, any difference should arise so that the mother should 'mislike her board and usage', then the son was to pay her an increased (unspecified) annuity.

In another will of 1633, when Richard Michener of 'Covers' left it to his son, he specified that he should pay his mother '£3 yeerely and the keepeing of one Hogge with halfe the peares and apples growing upon the aforesaid lands to feed him, and ground yerely to sell or sowe a peck of beans with the Lofte over the Hall and the Little Roome of[f] the Chimney end'. This and other annuities of this size indicated that a widow could live on this sort of money, although around the same date similar provision required from their sons by the Shotters of Pitfold was £20 p.a.

Of the many wills looked at, only a very few were signed in the 1600s, and these by people from the upper yeoman stratum such as the Shotters, Rapleys, Combes and Quennells. Unusually, however, in 1645, Rose the wife of Thomas Hoad an iron fyner, signed her name.[20] Not many women of modest status were literate.

References in Chapter Two

Note: where references for rolls entries and inventories are not given – see 'Copyholds of Linchmere Manor' in Haslemere Museum Library.

[1] Turner, G.A. The Copyholds of the Manor of Linchmere and Shulbrede 1545-1890, 1998.
[2] There is a collection in the Haslemere Museum of a few Pitfold Manor documents.
[3] Dict.Nat.Biog.
[4] PRO.SC6/H8/3674 of 1536
[5] WSRO. Cdy 264
[6] Feet of Fines, Ssx Rec.Soc., vol 19, p128
[7] WSRO. Albery & Lucas papers
[8] Has.Mus.LD. 5.327 of 1635
[9] Has.Mus.LD. 5.370
[10] WSRO.Cdy MS 1635 of 1650

[11] L'mere Manor Rolls, 1671

[12] James Simmons III Diary 1.4.39

[13] Has.Mus.LD. 5.426

[14] PRO.Court Exchequer 2 Wm & Mary, Mich 25, 1690/9

[15] Trotter, Torrens: Cowdray, its early History, 1922

[16] WSRO. Ssx Record Soc. vol 54, Quarter Sessions Order Book

[17] Sussex Record Soc. Vols. 49 and 78

[18] Ssx Rec.Soc. vol 54, Quarter Sessions Order Book

[19] Ibid

[20] WSRO. Mf 187

Chapter Three

The Farms and Farmhouses in the Manor of Linchmere

Farming Practices; New Farming Techniques; The Wey Valley Farms of Bridge, Gilhams, Hammer, Washers als Watchers, Stones, Springhead and Deanes; Signs of Prosperity – Building Improvements; the Shotter Family Holdings of Parrys & Hurlands (High Building), Shulbrede Priory Farm and Watts.

Introduction

When the Linchmere manor rolls begin in 1545 there are seen to be something of the order of twenty farms in existence, already there under the Priory as they were listed in the Ministers Account of 1536[1] which itemised the Priory's Linchmere holdings. Although there is nothing to say how the Priory had administered its lands, by the late Middle Ages almost certainly they were held for a money rent and under the new Montague ownership nothing much changed. At the Dissolution most of the landholders were paying a quit rent and were described as copyholders.[2]

In 1536 many of the farms were described as being of a virgate of about 30 acres; later, in the rolls they were more often described as having 50 acres, but probably both these figures were notional as by Tythe Map time (1846) most of them were considerably larger without any obvious explanation for this subsequent to 1545. The fields have the typical appearance of being formed by the gradual pushing back of woodland. Further details of the history of the farms and copies of the inventories may be seen in the 'Copyholds of the Manor of Linchmere and Shulbrede' (unpublished) in the Haslemere Museum Library.

For these farms a number of inventories between the late 1500s and early 1700s have survived. The rooms and their contents are listed but only in some cases is it possible to compare the same house at different periods. Inventories were made by relatives or neighbours and vary widely in quality as at no time were the appraisers aiming to be estate agents. In 1623 Alice Willard of Goldhorks seems to live in a house described as 'in decay' with only one downstairs living room (the hall) but three lofts. By 1661, Goldhorks had a living room, a 'parler', a best and another lodging chamber, a kitchen, drinkhouse and milkhouse and a cheesepress room. In 1623,

Hammer Farm seems to comprise only a hall and sleeping chamber; in 1674 there is also a cellar, a brewhouse and various lofts. Highbuilding, the Shotter house which bears an extension date of 1687, is very different from (presumably the same) house Eden Shotter lived in a hundred years previously. In 1586, Eden Shotter's house contained only a living room, a sleeping chamber and a kitchen. By 1689, it also had a milkhouse, a washhouse, a brewhouse, cellar, pantry, garret and various 'lofts over.'

Often rooms in the house were used for storage of apples, cheeses, bacon, butter, malt and wool, and also grain in addition to that stored in the barns. The furniture is usually described in similar terms ie boxes, chests and cupboards and there is no way of telling if the quality varied. Bedding certainly varied from feather beds with curtains and valences to borden beds filled with hulls or flock, some of the latter being in houses with no reference to chairs so that they may well have acted as daytime seating. Seating was often on forms or joyned stools although later in the 1700s there were fashionable caine chairs at Highbuilding. Tableware was universally of pewter and brass (although the Shotters at Bridge Farm had some silver ware) and the kitchens were full of heating, cooking and preserving utensils made of iron including one reference to a 'podge of blacking' leaving no doubt as to the work involved on the kitchen range. Everyone had preserving and salting troughs etc Both the Shotters of Highbuilding and Bridge Farm possessed clocks, but apparently no one else.

Farming Practices

The local economy was based on mixed farming. It is difficult to tell how many acres of any particular crop were produced as this varied according to the time of year in which the inventory was made. In winter the fields would be bare. From the amounts of cereals produced however, particularly if the Shotter inventories are looked at, it is obvious that the days of subsistence farming were long past and that crops were grown for sale and profit, although there is nothing at this time to indicate where they went. It is, however, possible to tell what they grew and the main crops were cereals of all description – wheat, oats and barley and on occasions rye, also pease and always hay and tares for fodder.

Everyone had a few animals. In 1586 Eden Shotter had 12 cattle but the largest number a hundred years later in 1689 was only 25 kept by William Shotter at Highbuilding, most of the milk being used for cheese and butter. Everyone had a few pigs and poultry and most people had both horses and oxen, along with ploughs and harrows specified for use with either draft animal. Oxen whose feet were better adapted to Wealden clay were seen to be in use to the late 1700s. The number of sheep kept varied widely. At Hammer Farm in 1623, Roger Quennell had about 20–30; in 1674 James Quennell kept 84. In 1689, John of Bridge had 99 but elsewhere they are usually visible only in smaller numbers.

Most people had an orchard and bees were commonly kept. The brewing of ale for home consumption was universal, and many houses contained wool and spinning wheels. There is also reference to flax spinning wheels and to hemp although there is no evidence for the growth of flax locally. It is also interesting to note that in valuing their farmyard equipment, dung was always specifically mentioned as a valued commodity. If the value of animals and crops is set against the total value of the estate in the inventories it is easy to see that this is where the main wealth lay, usually comprising about two thirds of the estate's value.

As an aside, it was a long time before the 'vans' appearing in most of the 1600s farmyards were recognised as fans (for winnowing) in Sussex speak.

New Farming Techniques

Although the 'agricultural revolution' did not really come about until the eighteenth century, new ideas were pouring forth in books and pamphlets in the seventeenth. There is little sign in the inventories, however, that many of these had penetrated Linchmere parish.

Marling had been used on the clay since earliest times but the more efficient use of lime can be seen. Fuel and chalk for kilns appear regularly. Whether rotation of arable and pasture was being practised cannot be gleaned from the inventories, but there is no sign of root crops. Perhaps the most obvious improvement can be seen in the widespread growing of clover hay.[3]

One crop which appears regularly is French wheat – possibly, it was first thought, an innovation, but this was probably the name for a type of naked wheat resembling and often known as French barley which took less nutriment out of the ground and was traditionally grown.[4]

Personal Finances

The inventories show it was quite possible to get along without much cash in hand, the usual amount being around £2–£3, although increasing slightly as time went on. One of their most interesting features is the light thrown upon the finances of the Linchmere parishioners. They show that, after the freeing of access to credit, people large and small put any spare money they possessed out to loan.

Most of the following examples are for persons not closely connected with the Shottermill end of the parish but they serve to give a flavour. The Shotters were pre-eminent in this field, having money out on bond on occasion to the tune of £200–300, but small men like Henry Lanaway a husbandman of Lynchmere Cottage down the hill from St. Peter's had £44 out on loan out of total estate of £56; Roger Cover, another husbandman, had £51 out on loan out of a total estate of £57; Thomas Hoade a fyner at the Hammer, had £42 out upon bond out of a total estate of £51; and lastly William Etherington, husbandman, also of Lynchmere Cottage, had £50 out on bond out of £62. Wills also usually specify that money/land left in trust for minors or widows should be made to work or usefully invested.

The Wey Valley Farms

Below are brief summaries of the farms along the Wey on the northern border of Linchmere manor which are most relevant to the history of Shottermill. Their later history appears in the next book in the chapters on the Simmons family which came into possession of some of them. Fig.6 shows the location of the farms in the Wey valley.

All manorial properties had early names which in the absence of maps and many important roads were of a descriptive nature eg 'Aldermarsh near Pitfold Hatch' (now Lynchmere Cottage down Linchmere Hill from St. Peter's) or 'Linchmeres' (now Church Farm) or were given the names of early holders such as the Danleys and Gilhams. They are described by these names in the rolls practically until they end in the late 1800s. All pictures are of the present and much altered farms.

Bridge Farm *(manorial name Waterhouse)*

This was held by the Bedylls at the start of the rolls which refer back to its existence under the Priory in 1516. Its lands lay between the Wey and the present Liphook road. In 1572 it passed to the Covers, Nicholas Cover having married a Bedyll daughter. The Cover family held this farm until 1623 when Richard Cover sold it to Roger Shotter senior of Shulbrede Priory although various members of the Cover family remained there as Shotter under-tenants for some time. It was one of this local family, Nicholas Cover, who was called to give evidence regarding the hammer at Pophole in the 1598 Tythe Dispute.

Roger Shotter senior of Shulbrede Priory Farm in 1635 willed this farm to his youngest son John who probably went to live there sometime in the 1630s at about which time the property became known as 'Bridge'. Roger senior also left to John many of his personal possessions presumably as John had only just attained his majority, was still living with his father and had yet to set himself up in a home of his own. This purchase on John's behalf had originally been made as early as 1623.

The farm was described in 1659 as a farmhouse, two barns, a stable, garden, orchard and 40 acres. Its ancient name of Waterhouse is not difficult to account for as the farmhouse lies close to the Wey and a bridge there gave access to Hewshott and Bramshott. The house the earliest part of which is dated to the 1400s[5] was the subject of manorial complaints in 1612 and again in 1622 when it was described as 'falling down' and 'in decay'. Its repair seems to have been the work of Roger Shotter senior who applied in 1623 to the manor for wood to repair it. His initials, along with those of his son John, I.S (Iohannis) are still to be seen in the dining room panelling with a date of 1631. Stonework from the Priory can also be seen there, not at all surprising in this case as the Shotters farmed from the Priory at this time.

The house which is large is mostly brick and tile hung and some of the original timber frame can still be seen. The Shotters held Bridge until after the end of the period dealt with in this chapter, although even at an early date this branch suffered from a lack of direct heirs. It eventually went in 1773 to a Shotter nephew, Thomas Combe of Frensham parish, but until then the John Shotters seem to have been resident at Bridge. The above first-mentioned John died in 1656 and his son in 1689 after which Bridge went to the latter's nephew, John, son of his brother William.

The 1689 inventory of John Shotter shows the farm to have been a prosperous one the household goods including items of silver and a 'Clocke upon the Staires'. His assets came to £336, of which £100 was due to him upon bond. There is no doubt that the holders of Bridge at this period were of a high status and lived in some relative style. Their sleeping arrangements showed the Shotters to have had, contrary to other descriptions of borden beds and canvas sheets, a feather bed equipped with curtains and a valence. This inventory also shows quite clearly that essentially their wealth stemmed from their crops and animals. Although described as having 40 acres, in fact Waterhouse/Bridge was extended by the purchase by Roger Shotter of Shulbrede in 1627 of 13 acres of Chithurst – the name of the holding, now Gilhams, next door to the east – which small parcel became an integral part of Bridge.

Gilham's Farm *(manorial name Chithurst/Chidhunt and var.)*

This farm had been held by the Cover family in Priory times – it was their ancestral holding. The lands of this farm also lay between the Wey and the later Liphook road. The house shows clearly several periods of addition from fairly small beginnings, and was also the subject of complaints from the manor concerning its decayed condition between 1610 and 1625.

There seems to have been a plethora of Covers in the Linchmere parish register at this time who might, as kin, have inherited but for whatever reason something goes amiss in the middle 1600s (not at all clear from the rolls) and in 1637 the Thomas Covers, father and son, surrender this farm to Lord Montague 'with all rights for him to do as he pleases'. In 1659 a widow Cover seems to recover part possession but this farm is next seen in a Cowdray estate map of 1771[6] as part of Montague's demesne lands which he leases out.

Gilhams Farm today

Present in Linchmere parish in the 1600s was the Gilham family, one of whom was a parish churchwarden, and it was probably one of these Gilhams – a Montague leaseholder – who left his name to the farm by which it is still known. Another of Montague's leaseholders may have been Edward Rapley.

In 1682 the manor court indicted Rapley for the 'overflowing of the widow Quennell's ground … in watering of his medow called Chithurst the said widow to have her Quittrent discharged till Mich[aelm]as one thousand six hundred eighty and eight and to be allowed for the said overflowing 10s per annum'. This entry – the only one of this nature seen in the rolls – almost certainly alludes to the operation of 'watermeadows' along the Wey whereby riverside meadows were artificially flooded to promote early and vigorous growth of grass. Rapley was obviously flooding his Gilhams meadows and throwing the water back on to the land of the Quennell's Hammer Farm upstream. It is significant that whereas widow Quennell was compensated, Rapley was not fined.

Hammer Farm *(manorial name Pophole/Pophalle & var.)*

This farm lay east of Gilhams and in part abutted Hammer Lane; it comprised a virgate of land. The records of the Quennells who held this farm do not begin in the rolls until 1560 but from another source, the Ministers Account of 1536[7] it would seem that they were in fact there at that earlier date.

Reference to this Linchmere land parcel with the manorial name of Poppehale can be seen as early as 1296 in the Lay Subsidy. These Quennells, who were without doubt related in some way to the Quennells of Lythe Hill who operated the ironworks at Imbhams, were *not* connected with the hammer at Pophole, and Pophole Hammer was *not* built on this manorial land parcel called Pophole. Reference in the Linchmere manor rolls to the land parcel called Pophole are always to the land of what later became known as Hammer Farm.

The farm, as shown in two seventeenth century Quennell inventories, was a fairly modest one. When held by Roger Quennell in 1623 it was worth £30 and had a few sheep, a few acres of rye and oats, and a half part of five stalls of bees. In the time of his grandson James in 1674, it was valued at £71 and had only a few acres of wheat and rye but a considerably larger number of sheep.

In 1674, James in his will leaves £20 apiece to his two daughters when they become 24 or be married, and 20s to his son Thomas (who would of course have inherited the farm as well) when he became 21. The rolls show in 1654 when James Quennell was admitted to Pophole for £8, he could only manage £5, promising to pay the rest later. In 1670 he raised £84 on the farm and again in 1671 he raised £105 and finally in 1675 he mortgaged the farm to Walter Butler of Stanley for £30. All this money was repaid fairly promptly but James was either having trouble managing or he was making improvements.

In 1622, the house and the farm fences were 'decayed'. The Quennells held this farm until Thomas, the last Quennell, died in 1741 when it passed to his eldest kin, William Cover of Bramshott, whose son sold it in 1767 to the Lashams who retained it until about 1846. It ended up in the hands of William Chalcraft of Bramshott who enfranchised it in 1864.

A somewhat rusty sword was found in one of the farm's outbuildings which was identified at Guildford Museum as a 1788 pattern of the Surrey or Sussex yeomanry trooper's sword. Further details of this manorial parcel are given in the chapter on Pophole Hammer.

Watt's Farm *(manorial name Linchmeres Wattmans and Elliotts)*

Watt's Farm lay on the east side of Hammer Lane and was the land on which Pophole Hammer was built in the late 1500s. Relevant to the Pitfold Shotters, it is described later below.

The holding on the east of Watt's Farm was:

Washers alias Watchers *(modern name of farmhouse is Rats Castle)*

Rats Castle today

Washers farm which ran south from the Wey, straddled the present Liphook Road and extended for a little way to the south of it up the Ridge. The farmhouse of this holding is now known as 'Rats Castle'.

The present building is dated by the DoE List of Buildings of Special or Architectural Interest for West Sussex to the 1700s, but documentary evidence shows that a building of some sort was certainly there before the 1700s, the rolls indicating in the 1600s that it was in an extremely decrepit state. It is now stone clad and has a tile hung extension. Unlike most of the other farms, this holding never acquired a modern farm name as it became divided in the late 1700s, the northern part being bought in 1781 from the Maidmans by William Simmons (paper maker of Sickle Mill) who built New Mill there where its land touched the Wey, and the southern part across the Liphook road being absorbed into Springhead Farm, so that it lost its identity.[8] Only 'barns and buildings' remained on its southern part across the Liphook road and these are now gone and built over.

On first meeting with it in 1537, Washers was in the hands of the Hopkyn family. Widow Agnes Hopkyn married Thomas Person of neighbouring Watts Farm in 1588, losing her rights to her widow's bench, but her sons inherited and after them it passed via various married female descendants until about 1650, and then through a number of short term absentee holders (seemingly investors) until in 1699 it was acquired by Richard Maidman, yeoman of Dorking. Richard Maidman and his son also bought Springhead Farm and came to reside locally.

In 1571 and '72, when a house of some description was certainly there, it seems to have passed for a short period to two of the iron workers, Charles Pelham and James Barden. Another would-be tenant was a John Allen who endeavoured to purchase Washers in 1651 on the basis of a mortgage of £160 supplied by Francis Jackman of Haslemere. This attempt failed and in 1655 John Allen admitted that the sum had not been paid. The Allens, although disappearing from Allens Farm (Blossom Cottage now Church Lane House) in Pitfold round about this time may have held the 50 acres of land called Allens between Marley Heath and Carpenters Heath, Fernhurst, later known as 'Lower Farm'. It may be that these Allens and those of Pitfold were the same family.[9]

In most cases great care was taken that the names and descriptions of manorial properties should remain identical from one conveyance to the next partly to avoid argument but also because the copy of the rolls entry describing the property was the copyholder's proof of title. In 1654 in connexion with the cottage and garden near Linchmere churchyard, Stephen Rapley who was in possession, was ordered to go away and find his copy of court roll showing his right and title before the Homage would recognise his claim and formally admit him. In the case of Washers, however, its description wandered. Starting off life as Walshes, it became in turn, Wallshes, Walshes again, *Coldwashers*, Washes and Washers, until in 1699 it became (by clerical error) Watchers. After this it was always referred to as Washers alias Watchers until the end of the rolls.

The house presently bearing the name 'Watchers' (Dexam International) acquired this name many years later by accident when a late nineteenth century owner of Watts or Watses Farm thought that that name (Watts) was short for Watchers whereas in fact it was short for Wattmans – full manorial name Linchmeres Wattmans & Elliotts. The name as seen in a local article has, unfortunately, almost certainly nothing to do with the romantic suggestion that it took its name from its use as a place where smugglers kept a look-out for the excise men.

The name of Coldwashers applied to this property in 1637 is of interest if only to speculate about the reason why this term should have come into the mind of clerk of the rolls as he wrote. It may have had something to do with the skinning or tanning industry at Pitfold Mill and the Tanyard opposite the farm's border on the Wey at this time, which would have certainly have involved much cold washing. In 1788 William Simmons bought Springhead Farm which by then included the rest of Washers.

Stones *(manorial name Stanes)*

The next property along the Wey was the small farm called Stanes or Stones, still known in recent times as Stoney Farm and being the land around the Mill Tavern. It again was held originally in the 1500s under the Priory. It was held by the Harding family between 1520 and 1585, during which time a part of this property was taken back into the hands of the Lord because waste had been committed by the abstraction of a cartload of hay from a croft in the land without licence and against the wishes of the manor, the last entry of this sort of manorial interference recorded.

In 1585 it was sold to Blaise Briday, the Linchmere ironworker about whom more is said in the chapter on Pophole Hammer. The Bridays held Stones until 1647 after which it passed through the hands of the Boxolds, the Collens of Linchmere (of Reeks Reynolds & Fridayes) and eventually to Thomas Combes of Combes (Critchmere Farm later Frensham Hall Farm). From 1766 until the end of the rolls it was in the hands of the Stillwell family of blacksmiths.

Stones/Mill Tavern

There are, however, two interesting rolls entries for Stanes. First, in 1649 and again in 1651 the building on this land is described as 'Shotter Mill Inn' although not described again as an inn or tavern until the middle 1800s when it became the 'Railway Tavern' (now the 'Mill Tavern'). This was at a time when the land was mortgaged to James Napper of the nearby tanyard, and later its land was in the occupation of Thomas Cherriman, also tanner at the tanyard. The old timber-framed part of the house is still visible, as shown on the left.

Whether the name of Stones emanated from the stony character of its land or whether it had something to do with the presence of Shottover mill opposite and its millstones, is not known.

Springhead Farm (manorial name Shottover)

Springhead farm lands ran from the present Liphook road south over the Ridge. It also included the land immediately to the east of Shottover Mill, part of which is now the Camelsdale Recreation Ground. Its farmhouse, by the spring, lay on the south side of the Liphook road and its manorial name presumably arose from its proximity to Shottover Mill.

Referred to in documents in the 1500s, it had obviously existed from a very early date. The earliest part of the listed house is dated to the 1400s. It was held until about 1650 by the Farnden family, a Thomas inheriting it from his father Richard in 1577 which is the date of the death of Richard Farnden, the Rector of Linchmere. Thomas, who died in 1610, left behind him an inventory which, although severely mutilated, indicates that at this date Springhead was by no means the magnificent farmhouse and great barn existing today. The house seemed to comprise only a hall with a chamber over, an inner chamber and a kitchen and Thomas Farnden's estate amounted only to £12.15s, with no reference to any farm crops or implements other than one ox.

Like most of the other farmhouses, in his widow's time there were several complaints that her house was in decay and falling down. Eleanor, Thomas's widow, died in 1637 at the ripe old age of 97. Widows in the rolls are conspicuously present. For women the childbearing years were obviously the most dangerous but if these were survived there seemed to be little to stop them achieving a respectable old age. As far as men were concerned, untroubled by child-bearing complications, the crucial years seem to have been the fifties. When, as did happen on occasion a man achieved a century, if he did not get royal congratulations he was usually awarded a respectful mention in the parish register.

Springhead Farm

After the death of John Farnden, Eleanor's son, in the early 1650s saddled with a mortgage, the farm seems to have been held as an investment by the Butcher family of Bramley until it was bought by the Maidmans who came to reside in the area in 1699. During this period, in Eleanor's lifetime, 12 acres of this holding, Shottover Fields, which were at the extreme southern end of this property were sold in 1618 to Roger Shotter, son of old Roger of Shulbrede, and henceforward were always counted as part of Watts Farm. This small additional acreage was up on the Ridge and seems to have been bought for its timber.[10]

The part of Shottover just to the east of Shottover Mill was mortgaged by Eleanor's son John in 1648. It seems that the last Farnden was in need of money. On John's death a further mortgage on the whole of Shottover is recorded as not repaid. This entry also contains the only hint seen regarding the possibility of money troubles emanating from the turmoil of the Civil War. In 1651 it is recorded that the redemption of the mortgage on Shottover/Springhead should be made 'without fraud or further delay and also without any further deduction or reprizes whatsoever concerning the Parliament, the warre, quartering of souldiers or otherwise'.

Purchased in 1699 by the Maidmans, in 1788 Springhead was bought by William Simmons of Sickle Mill. The great barn was probably built by his son James III.

Deanes als Deanehouse

The last farm looking into the Wey Valley is that known as Deanes or Deanehouse. This is not Dene or Deans farm which lies on the Midhurst road near the *Sussex Bell* which was not Linchmere manor property, but a small farm lying on the slope of the Ridge on the south side of the valley, tucked away behind Springhead. It is one of the few farmhouses still showing its timber construction and unfaced by stone.

At the start of the rolls the holders were the Baldwyns, others of this family seen earlier in Pitfold where they were tanners. Alice Baldwyn and her son William were both dead by 1576 after which this little farm was held by the Boxalls for about a hundred years. By the end of their tenancy, the direct heirs having failed it was inherited by William Boxall yeoman of Badshott who was nearest kin.

The land of this farm lay on both sides of the track over the Ridge from Springhead to Linchmere and during the next twenty years these two halves were sold off separately, one half to Stephen Willard of Goldhorks, and there is much talk of re-siting the great and small barns. In 1675 both parts of the farm, once again reunited, went to William Upton of Haslemere.

Throughout the first half of the 1700s the Uptons were maltsters, glovers and mercers of Haslemere and in the middle 1700s a number of untimely Upton deaths resulted in this farm being sold to the Simmons family of Sickle Mill, papermakers, when James I bought it for his son James II in 1763.

Originally a small farmhouse it now consists of a timber-framed part and another tile-hung cottage at right angles with an enormous chimney stack which almost dwarfs the house.

Signs of Prosperity – Building Improvements

Not mentioned in every case, in fact practically all the farms in Linchmere manor received in the late 1500s and early 1600s complaints from the manor about the condition of the buildings.

A perfect example is the complaint about Washers/Rats Castle where Alice Hopkyn's house in 1593 was deemed to be 'defective in doorways, windows, boards and lofts' and she was allocated timber to make good. In 1610 and again in 1627 there are, however, further complaints about its condition and the apparent lack of immediate response is typical.

It was, of course, extremely detrimental to the value of the manor if the manor tenants allowed their houses and lands to deteriorate which was easy enough where the manorial tenants were not the occupiers. Usually the process of improvement seems to have involved much nagging over a prolonged period before repairs were effected.

As described in the first chapter, with the slow recovery after the Black Death, it may well be that many of the farmhouses then existing belonged to an older tradition of relatively impermanent timber construction. Many of the Linchmere houses are now seen to be stone-clad or tile-hung but there is nothing in the rolls to indicate when this took place other than that the complaints by the manor about their neglected state seemed to have ceased by the mid 1600s. Contrary to the use of structural timber, which required the Lord's permission to be felled, there is no sign in the rolls that use of stone needed to have the manor's agreement. Probably stone, being widely available on the greensand, was to be had for the taking. There was also available, the stone from the dissolved priory buildings and bits of these can be seen to be incorporated in several farmhouses.

Linchmere manor was not alone in being in this decayed state. The early 1600s are often known as the period of the Rebuilding of England reflecting by that date more settled and prosperous times. The same almost certainly applied to the Surrey side but the Linchmere rolls are more explicit in this respect. It is likely that most of the old houses and farms now existing stem architecturally from around the 1600s although many of them will contain features pointing to an earlier existence.

The Linchmere Manor Farms outside the Wey Valley

These are Church Farm, Stanley, Danley, Reeks Reynolds & Fridayes, Goldhorks and Redwater and the two smaller properties of Covers and Causey End. Their details are in the Haslemere Museum Library, but they are insufficiently relevant to the history of Shottermill to warrant comment here except to say that Church Farm was in the hands of the Rapley and Baker families who purchased Shottermill property in the 1600s and 1800s, and that Stanley Farm was owned by the Butler family one of whom operated Pophole Hammer in the 1700s.

The Holdings of the Shotter Family

Below are summaries of Parrys & Hurlands & Hatch Hill (Highbuilding & Northpark), Linchmeres Wattmans & Elliotts (Watts Farm by Pophole Hammer) and Shulbrede Priory Farm all of which were held or leased by the Shotter family. Shottover Mill and its relationship to the Shotters is dealt with in the following chapter.

High Building & Northpark
(manorial names Parrys & Hurlands & Hatch Hill)

The holding called Parrys & Hurlands, together with Hatch Hill, which lie on the Linchmere/Fernhurst border and where Northpark furnace was later erected, had undoubtedly been in Shotter hands in the early fourteenth century when a Shotter and the Hurland land were mentioned in a Lay Subsidy. Thomas Schotere and John atte Hurland reported on oath the returns for Edward III's Nonae tax in 1341.

High Building today

This farm was also one of the larger ones. Its farmhouse is now known as Highbuilding and was an enlargement in 1687 of an earlier building which can be seen on a map of Montague's demesne coppice lands of 1650.[11] The present house is of high-quality stone. This holding remained in Shotter hands until 1793, and in 1536 is described as a two virgate farm. It does not really come into an account of the farms in the Wey Valley but it is important in establishing the Shotter family as being one of the longest enduring families of standing in the area.

The Shotter family is sometimes seen as being chiefly associated with Shulbrede Priory, conveying the impression that the Priory was the main and original Shotter property. This, however, was not the case. The ancient and original Shotter holding was Parrys & Hurlands, a Shotter (and a younger son, Roger, at that) only inheriting the leasehold of Shulbrede Priory Farm in 1587 and living there for about fifty years.

The records of Parrys & Hurlands, particularly those dealing with the setting up of Northpark iron furnace in 1614 by Lord Montague and Sir Thomas Gray, help to define the relationship of the Shotter family to the iron industry. It has been suggested that the Highbuilding Shotters were iron masters. The agreement in the 1626 rolls entry shows, however, that as manorial tenants of the land being used, their main involvement lay in receiving from the Montagues the cash benefits of the ore removed and compensation for any damage done. The agreement (repeated at every conveyance until the late 1700s when the furnace at Northpark had ceased working) stated:

'That the Lord of this Manor his heires and assignes shall from time to time hereafter at his owne will and pleasure without doeinge any more hurte or prejudice to the said Robert or the said landes than needs must, have free and quiet liberty at convenient times to dig have and take the Myne and Iron Oare in and from the said coppyhold lands Except only in the twoe meads there called the greate meade th[e]other Farnest Land meade payinge to the said Robert his heires and assignes in Levy of the spoile and damage to the land in digginge and takeinge thereof after the rate of vi d the loade for every parte and parcel of the said Myne there to be digged had and taken and filling up the Myne pitts in such sorte as by or through the defaulte thereof noe losse of cattell may ensue. And that the furnace built upon or neare the coppyhold landes called Hatchhill with all easements thereto for laying the coles and Myne there and otherwise and the cottage there built shall be kept and continued there as heretofore they have beene to and for the use and benefitt of the Lord his heires and assignes without yielding or paying any thinge therefore'.

There is no suggestion in this agreement that the Shotters had any further participation in or other form of profit from the working of Montague's furnace at Northpark.

The rolls open in 1545 with these lands being held by Phillip and Eden Shotter. If the inventory of Eden, widow of Phillip, in 1586, is compared with that of William a hundred years later in 1689 and with that of William's son's in 1706, it can be seen that the Shotters seem to have done very nicely out of the above arrangement. Whereas Eden in 1586 left £43, William in 1689 left £320 and in 1706 his son William left £588, although it should be noted that this branch of the Shotters also held land elsewhere from which they derived additional income.

They were for the most part lenders rather than borrowers and from the time of the building of the Northpark furnace became increasingly wealthy although in 1610 William's house had been, like most others, the subject of complaint about its decayed state and in 1615 he was threatened with forfeiture for having felled timber on his lands without licence. His indignant reply that he had had permission must have been accepted as no more is heard of this.

This branch of Shotters was descended from William, Eden and Phillip's eldest son, but they like the John Shotters of Bridge Farm, suffered from lack of direct issue and the holding descends through a nephew Robert. The last holder, a William Shotter, sold these lands in 1793 to Anthony Capron the Younger of Moor, Easeborne. On this occasion William is described as of Farnham where, as an attorney, he had acted during the latter half of the eighteenth century as Clerk of the Castle at Farnham and Steward of Farnham Manor.[†] A Shotter family tree is given in the chapter on Pitfold.

The Shotter inventories are given below[‡]:

Inventory of Eden Shotter late Wife of Phillipp Shotter of Lenchmore taken 27 March 1586/7 — Appraisers John Chalcroft William Ede & ... Willyard

	Parrys & Hurlands
	£ = s = d.
In the Chamber	
Imprimis: A bedsted & one old fether bed with a bolster two pillowes a payre of shetes a payre of blankets a coverlett also bedtester with [all] belongeth theretofor	1=13=04
Itm: an olde bedsted & a flockbed with all things belonging therto prist at	13=04
Itm: her apparrell that is two gowns iii peticots ii smoks a cap & two panes[skirts] two payre of shots [illegible insert] with ...? other lynen prist at	3=00=00
Itm: iiii cofers prist	6=08
The hall	
Itm: one bord two table clothes one form two chers a paire of cussions? and a joynd stole prist at	4=00

[†] The last William Shotter of Highbuilding, as an attorney and official of Farnham manor, was very likely not resident there full time. On his death in 1797, having no issue, he left the bulk of his estate to his partner (his wife's nephew), James Trimmer, on condition that Trimmer changed his name to Shotter, which he did. James Trimmer/Shotter followed William as Clerk of the Castle of Farnham.

[‡] If, in the inventories, the sum of the individual items does not correspond exactly with the total given, this is probably due to the difficulty in identifying accurately digits in documents which, after some 200–300 years, are often frayed and mutilated.

Itm: fyve platers ix pewter disshes two erdn dishes iiii pewter   16=00
    sassers iii saltsellers one dossen of spoones & three
    candellstickes prist at
    The Kitchen
Itm: iii smeall & braze pots one caldren iii littell braze panns   1=16=08
    vii ketteles one braze, a grid yron one andyron a paire of
    potthoks with a potthanger one brewing vat one kefer a
    powdring trough two...? iii baks with dishhes and ...? and a
    ladell prist at
Itm: iii payrs of baks prist at
Itm: xxii pound of woole prist at
    In the barne
Itm: iiii bussheles of rye prist at
Itm: viii bussheles of malt prist at
Itm: xii bussheles of smeale ots prist at
Itm: ...? haye? prist at
Itm: two old forkes prist at
Itm: iii akers of rye being...? upon the ground prist at   1=10=00
Itm: iii akers of otes prist at   16=00
    The Cattell
Itm: one cupple of oxen prist at
Itm: two sters
Itm: iii kyne
Itm: ii heffer   2=06=00
Itm: v smeall bollocks   4=10=00
Itm: iiii mangers   11=00
Itm: xix ewes and a lame   4=00=00
Itm: xii tyges [teggs]   1=12=00
Itm: ii hogs   10=00
Itm: vi piges   10=00
Itm: v hens and a cock   2=06
Itm: one mare   1=00=00
Itm: the plowe irones & cart with all th'appartinances   1=00=00
    appartaning to the plowe and cart with two sythes one axe
    and a byll ii agers and one shovell prist at
Itm: her purss with   3=04
Total   43=12=08

Inventory of William Shotter Yeoman of Linchmere taken 30 July 1689
Appraisers were John Shotter, Roger Shotter, Richard Luff, Roger Luff
and John Willard

Parrys & Hurlands/High Building

£ = s = d.

Imprimis: his wearing apparrell & money in his purse   26=00=00

Itm: in the Kitchen five tables one forme & severall other goods	*4=00=00*
Itm: in the Hall one table two joynt formes one clock & severall other goods	*6=16=00*
Itm: in the Milk House one cheesepresse a salting trowe three kivers & other goods	*1=08=06*
Itm: In the Washhouse four potts & other goods	*1=02=06*
In the pantry one frying pan & other goods	*1=10=00*
In the Hall Chamber two bedsteddles one feather bedd linnen & woollen & other goods	*17=07=08*
Itme: In the little chamber over the Seller one Bedd & bedsted & severall other goods	*3=10=06*
Itm: in the Garrett 22 bushells of wheat & nineteen pound of woole	*3=02=06*
Itm: in the Roome over the Pantry one bed & bedsted	*1=00=00*
Itm: over the Hall ...? bushells of malt	*1=10=00*
Itm: in the Roome over the Seller 2 bedds & other goods	*3=11 =00*
Itm: in the Brewhouse one furnace severall kivers a stone trowe & other goods	*3=02=06*
Itm: for cheese bacon & pewter	*11=10=00*
Itm: in the Milkhouse 19 milk treas & other goods	*1=06=00*
Itm: for forty acres of pease barly oates and wheat	*70=00=00*
Itm: for 20 load of chalke & 1400 of faggotts	*8=10=00*
Itm: for 20 loads of hay & clover	*20=00=00*
Itm: for one load of wheat	*5=00=00*
Itm: for two load of sacks	*10=00*
Itm: for four acres of seed clover	*3=00=00*
Itm: for five hoggs	*6=00=00*
Itm: for five calves	*5=00=00*
Itm: for tenn cowes & a bull	*32=10=00*
Itm: for two oxen	*8=10=00*
Itm: for a fann	*10=00*
Itm: for five horses	*22=10=00*
Itm: for three sheepe	*1=00=00*
Itm: for tenn young bullocks	*19=00=00*
Itm: for five load of wood	*1=00=00*
Itm: for timber boards	*1=00=00*
Itm: for carts dungpotts & other lumber	*14=00=00*
Itm: for straw	*10=00*
Itm: for lime & dung	*3=12=00*
Total	***320=01=04***

Inventory of William Shotter Yeoman of Linchmore taken 8 Nov 1706 Appraisers John Shotter, John Wakeford & Edward Rapley

	£ = s = d.
Imprimis: his wearing apparell & money in his purse	18=00=00
Itm: in the hall chamber one feather bedd one boulster twoe pillowes twoe blanketts one quilt cutains & valence & one bedstedle	9=00=00
Itm: twelve caine chaires valued att	2=15=00
Itm: twoe flagg bottome chaires one chest one small iron back one paire of andirons fire pann & tongs	14=00
Itm: nyne paire of sheetes five dozen & a halfe of napkins five paire of pillow coates five table cloaths & one Holland sheete	12=05=06
Itm: in the kitchen chamber three feather bedds three boulsters three coverletts thirteene blanketts twoe pillowes one bedstedle curtains and valence two halfe headed bedstedles matts & cords & all thereunto belonging	11=05=00
Itm: one presse twoe chests one trunk seaven chaires & one joynt stoole	1=14=00
Itm: thirteene paire & one sheets being course	5=06=00
Itm: one clock and some lumber	1=10=00
Itm: in the chamber over the sellar one table twoe old bedstedles twoe old chests and some lumber	10=00
Itm: in the garretts one paire of andirons & ... old iron ...?	15=00
Itm: one mault querne	18=00
Itm: one old bedstedle two old flock bedds four blankets twoe sheetes & all thereunto belonging and some lumber	2=00=00
Itm: in the kitchen twoe pie [pair] of andirons twoe paire of tongs one fire pann one slice three pothangers one iron trift [trivett] three paire of gridirons one iron back one fender four spits one tosting iron & some other small iron things	2=01=10
Itm: four iron potts one iron kittle three iron dripping panns & iron mortars & pestles	1=14=00
Itm: one iron jack	12=00
Itm: one pair of iron ...?	6=00
Itm: seaven & twenty pewter dishes three pewter candlesticks & twoe pewter porringers	4=05=00
Itm: twoe dozen of pewter plates	1=02=00
Itm: one old table & frame one forme ten old chaires and some lumber	1=03=00
Itm: one brasse kittle four brasse skilatts one brasse warming pann and one brass chafing dish valued att	1=04=00
Itm: in the milkhouse twenty one milk trayes twoe with panns three cheese presses twoe churns three buckets & some other things that belongeth to the deary	3=06=00

Itm: in the Brewhouse twoe brasse furnaces one brewing vate   *4=01=00*
   and seaven kivers valued att

Itm: five old tubbs one kiver some lumber valued att   *11=00*

Itm: in ye Brewhouse chamber some lumber   *1=03=06*

Itm: in ye Pantrey twoe frying panns three searches [strainers]   *14=06*
   one powdring tubb and some other lumber

Itm: in the hall one table & frame & twoe formes   *1=06=00*

Itm: one oval table one paire of andirons fire pann & tongs   *2=17=00*
   one iron back twoe old chaires & three joynt stooles

Itm: in the Cellars one ...? one ...? dish sixe barrels five   *4=07=00*
   kilderkins five virkins & sixe old stands

The goods without doors five hoggs & eight piggs   *10=00=00*

Itm:one hogg one sowe & sixe piggs   *4=00=00*

Itm: twoe oxen   *7=15=00*

Itm: nyne cowes   *21=00=00*

Itm: one old horse & twoe mares   *9=00=00*

Itm: three calves   *3=15=00*

Itm: three steers & twoe heifers   *10=00=00*

Itm: tenn weathers   *3=17=00*

Itm: sixe ewes & nyne teggs   *3=11=06*

Itm: sixe paire of cart harnesse & other harnesse &   *4=04=00*
utensils thereunto belonging

Itm: twoe waggons & wheeles one dung pott & wheeles   *9=03=06*
& cart ropes

Itm: three yoakes & three chaines   *16=06*

Itm: three plowes   *3=00=00*

Itm: twoe horse harrow & one oxe harrow   *1=02=06*

Itm: one thousand of faggotts   *2=10=00*

Itm: old wheate straw valued att   *15=00*

Itm: wheate valued att   *44=00=00*

Itm: oates barley pease & tares? valued att   *33=10=00*

Itm: hay valued att   *18=00=00*

Itm: one grindstone & stoning ...?   *4=00=00*

Itm: sacks poakes & baggs valued att   *2=00=00*

Itm: one vann one bushell one halfe bushell & other utensils   *1=00=00*
   belonging to husbandry

Itm: dung   *3=10=00*

Itm: one halfe load of wheate valued att   *2=11=00*

Itm: due to the deceased upon a mortgage   *280=00=00*

Itm: due to the deceased for rent after taxes & repaires   *4=11=00*
deducted

Total   ***588=15=01***

Shulbrede Priory Farm

It was a junior branch of the Shotter family – the Roger Shotters – who were connected with the Shulbrede Priory Farm which occupied the centre of Linchmere manor. This was part of Montague's demesne land varying parts of which were leased out over its history. Some of the demesne land the Montagues always reserved to themselves and these were the woods and coppice lands which were of great value in an age when timber was the most important structural material and in great demand and also when the fuel requirement of the Wealden iron works was at its height.

Shulbrede Priory

Shulbrede Priory Farm had almost certainly been previously the Priory demesne farm. It does not figure in the rolls as not being a copyhold, it was no concern of the Homage. Its leasing was a private matter between the Montagues and the leaseholders so that the records are intermittent. As recounted in Arthur Ponsonby's History of the Priory, one of the early leaseholders was Richard Shorye who in 1587 left the remainder of his lease to Roger Shotter, his son-in-law.

Roger who was eulogised on his death in 1639 in the Linchmere parish register as 'an expert Chirurgian [who] cured in his life time multitudes of impotent poore people of foule & dangerous sorances at his owne proper charges', was a younger son of the Phillip and Eden of Parrys & Hurlands. Roger married into the family at Shulbrede Priory Farm (Alice, Shorye's daughter) and, although a younger son, obviously did sufficiently well for himself and his family as to be able to purchase for his three sons copyholds of their own in his lifetime. In 1615 he was Montague's bailiff.

Watt's Farm (manorial name Linchmeres Wattmans & Elliotts)

As seen under Waterhouse/Bridge above, that farm was bought by Roger of Shulbrede Priory for his youngest son John in 1623, but previously in 1610 he had bought Watts Farm, on which land Pophole Hammer was by then built and operating for the two elder sons, William and Roger.

The first recorded tenants of Watts Farm were members of the Theyre and Pereson/Person families, but in 1610 it was bought from Thomas Pereson by Roger Shotter senior of Shulbrede. He did not, however, purchase the entire farm. That part on which Pophole Hammer was at that date working, was returned into Montague's hands and the details of this arrangement are given in the chapter on Pophole Hammer. This farm was to be held by the two sons jointly, William the elder for his life only and then by Roger and his heirs, Roger being a minor at the time. This supposes that William had a livelihood elsewhere but if so, its whereabouts are not known although it is possible it was in Bramshott parish. (The Bramshott rolls refer in 1711 to a William Shotter as holding Dounhurst and Wakefields). At all events William died in 1620 and from then on Watts or Watses Farm as it was known locally descended through the five generations of the Roger Shotters of Pitfold until 1781.

After old Roger of Shulbrede's death in 1639, the Shotters were no longer connected with Shulbrede Priory Farm except that one of the daughters married John Ellyat who seems to have been there in 1653. Roger Shotter, the son who held Watts Farm after his father's death, moved into Pitfold and he and his descendants' fortunes are continued in the chapter on the Surrey side and Pitfold. During the whole of this period the rolls show this and other of the lands of the Pitfold Shotters to have been sublet.

One of the tenants of Watts Farm in 1685 may have been John Chilsum who is described in 1662 as being of Pophole Hammer. He certainly lived in a house of some size, his inventory describing it as having a hall, a hall loft, two chambers, a garrett, a buttery, bakehouse, cellar, milkhouse and brewhouse. It is not known whether he was actually a hammer worker. His rent was £6 p.a. He died owing about £14 to his four daughters who, from the presence in the house of four linen wheels and two woollen wheels, might have contributed more than a little toward the family upkeep.[†]

[†] In the early 1700s the Chilsum family had moved into Bramshott manor when the Bramshott bailiff distrained Jane, one of the daughters, for fealty for her cottage

In the absence of the volumes of the Linchmere rolls in Arthur Ponsonby's day, he assumed that the holding of Linchmeres Wattmans & Elliotts became divided up into one called 'Linchmeres' and another called 'Wattmans & Elliotts'. In fact this was not so. 'Linchmeres' was the quite different holding later known as Church Farm. The reason for Linchmeres being tacked on to Wattmans & Elliotts had probably originally been to distinguish it from another farm held by Wattman in Haslemere, near Stedlands.

In 1781, on the death of the last Roger Shotter of Pitfold, Watts Farm was bought by James Simmons II. The suggestion has been made in the chapter on Pophole (which see for more detail) that the farmhouse from which Watts land was worked after the early 1600s, now called 'Watchers' [Dexam], was newly built around that date and that the old Watts farmhouse became one of the 'Hammer Cottages' which were surrendered to Montague along with Pophole Hammer.

References in Chapter Three

[1] PRO.SC6/H8/3674
[2] Ibid
[3] Taylor, C: Fields in the English Landscape, London 1975
[4] Thirsk, Joan ed: The Agrarian History of England and Wales, CUP. 1967, vol 4, p.170
[5] WSRO. DoE List of Buildings of Special or Architectural Interest for West Sussex
[6] WSRO.Cdy Ms 1660
[7] PRO.SC6/H8/3674
[8] Land Tax & divison of quit rent
[9] WSRO. Lucas & Albery Papers
[10] Has Mus.LD.5.327
[11] WSRO.Cdy Ms No. 1635

next to Pophole Hammers. This is probably the house now called Chelshams on the corner of Sandy and Hewshott Lanes.

Chapter Four

The Shotters and Shottover Mill

The Shotters and Shottover Mill; Various Renderings of the Shotter name; the Early name of Shotter Mill; the Connexion between the Shotters and Shottover Corn Mill; the Start Date of Shottover Mill; its function; the History of Shottover Mill.

The main question concerning Shottover Mill is its relationship, if any, to the Shotter family. This is a question to which there is and probably will never be any definite answer, but as much information as could be found about the very early Shotters and the early mill is given below. The names of the Shotters and Shottover mill and the land parcel called Shottover (Springhead Farm) were examined to see if there was evidence of a common derivation.

The Various Early Renderings of the Shotter Name

All the early mentions of members of the *local* Shotter family seen are listed below:

1296	Lay Subsidy – These returns include a payment of tax by a Philip de Hurlond. No Shotter is named but Philip may well have been an early Shotter as their ancestral holding was Parrys & Hurlands, and Phillip a family name.
1332	Lay Subsidy – there is named a John atte Hurlond and a Richard de Schotor.
1334	Bramshott Rolls. Thomas de Shotter is fined for having pigs in the Lord's woodland.
1339	Bramshott Rolls. Richard de Schotover is fined for illegally pasturing animals in the Lord's pasture.
1341	Thomas Schotere of Lenchmer parish is witness to the valuation of the tythes for Edward III's Nonae Subsidy. (Ponsonby pp.48 and 134/5).
1380 & 1382	Bramshott Rolls. Robert Scherter – entries re a life tenement and a debt.
1408	Robert Sherter vicar at Firle West (near Brighton) – WSRO.MP.2709

1417/18	John Sherter vicar at Firle West (ibid)
1421	John Shortere vicar at Faring West (ibid)
1431	John Shottere of Romsey holds manor of Embley (Feudal Aids ii 373) (ibid). His grandson was a Professor Doctor of Theology.
1441 &	a William Shorter is described as Secular Acolyte and then
1442	ordained secular deacon appointed to the title of Shulbrede Priory. (Extract Bishop Praty's Register, Ssx Rec. Soc vol. IV pp.193/4).
1524	Lay Subsidy. William Shotover appears under the heading of Easebourne Hundred as paying tax but there is also a note that he was of Farnest (Fernhurst).
1524	Lay Subsidy. A Robert Shotover pays tax.
1536	Robert Shoter holds lands in Fernhurst (probably Hatch Hill) and Robert Shottover holds Parrys & Hurlands in Linchmere. (PRO.SC6/H8/3674 Ministers Account)
1544	Will of Robert Schetyer of Lynchmere parish. (WSRO.STC/1/5/f.45b.)
1571	William Shotter of Fernhurst (WSRO Albery & Lucas papers). See 1524 above.
1580s	(and possibly earlier) in the Surrey Musters for Churt Tything, a number of Shotters are listed – always Shotters. (Sy. Record Soc. vol. III).

In the 1580s & 90s, the Shotters of Cooksbridge in Fernhurst are Shotters. The Roberts of 1524 and 1544 above are the same although referred to both as Shotover and Schetyer, and are for Robert of Parrys & Hurlands. The Rolls confirm his death and inheritance of his widow Philippa in 1545 and the admission of their son Philip and wife Eden in 1564. The Robert of 1536 for Parrys & Hurlands, is Shottover, but the same Robert for Hatch Hill is Shoter.

In the Linchmere Rolls the Shotters are occasionally in the early years referred to as Shottovers but from 1586 on, when the clerk of the rolls changes, they are always Shotters. At same time as some of the Shotters are referred to as Shotovers in the rolls, ie for the first forty years, in papers emanating from the family *during that same period*, eg Robert's will of 1544 and Eden Shotter's inventory of 1586, *they call themselves Shotters*. They also are invariably Shotters in the Linchmere parish register.

In some Fernhurst deeds, the story seems to be the same. In the Sussex Assizes records between 1577 and 1600 they are always Shotters (with the one exception of a Richard Shotyer in 1590). In these Assize records, it is noticeable that they are, with one exception, always on the right side of the law, indicting various persons for robbery, rape, and seditious utterances.[1] In conclusion, therefore it seems reasonable to suggest from the above evidence that the original name of this family was Shotter or some version of it – but rendered variously in an age when there were no spelling conventions.

Whether *all* the early Shotters are related is not known.

Suggestions for the use of Shottover rather than Shotter are given below. The Schurterre family which was connected with the Chiddingfold glass industry, according to Rev. T.S. Cooper in his exhaustive History of Chiddingfold (unpublished, copy in Haslemere Museum Library) became Shorters.

The Early Name of Shotter Mill

By contrast, *always* in the Linchmere rolls (with only two clerical slips in 1623 and 1639) until the 1800s, and in other legal documents, Shotter Mill was described by its official designation of 'Shottover or Shotover Mill'. It had obviously become shortened to Shotter Mill (as was the district) by the 1600s when it is referred to as such in parish registers. Most probably its name was shortened by the local people quite simply because 'Shotter' was easier and quicker to say.

The origin of its name, however, was undoubtedly 'Shottover' and not 'Shotter' and may well have derived from its mode of operation. Overshot wheels were the most efficient mode of operation and in the late 1800s when the Olivers replaced the wheel at the mill with a turbine, it is still described as having an overshot wheel with an 11 ft drop.

The Connexion between the Shotters and Shottover Corn Mill

Shottover Mill had without doubt been a possession of Shulbrede Priory – there is plenty of documentary evidence for this in the records of the Court of Augmentations. At the Dissolution it was, however, excluded from the manor of Linchmere and Shulbrede and it did not, therefore, appear in the court rolls in the normal way of things as did the manor land parcels. Nonetheless, there are many entries relating to it for other reasons, one of these being that as a prominent and well known landmark it was used as a point of reference by which the location of other manorial holdings could be described.

The ancient house (parcel of Farnham manor) now gone, but which stood at the old entrance to Critchmere Lane was always described as 'lying near Shottover Mill' and this was in the Farnham rolls which normally described locations on the Surrey side with reference to features in Pitfold. It is possible, therefore, that the name of Shottover mill, better known and more often used than that of Shotter family, was used mistakenly for members of that family, particularly in the 1300s and 1400s when for instance the Lay Subsidy returns[2] might well have been made by people without intimate local knowledge. Approximations and weird renderings of proper names in early documents are legion. In the Dissolution documents we find examples such as Poppam for Pophole and Aldershott for Aldermarsh at the bottom of Linchmere Hill.

It may be, of course, that the connexion with or confusion of the two names stemmed from the fact that the Shotters had indeed had at some time the lease of the mill. The number of monks at the Priory was never very large and Shottover mill would certainly have been leased out as were the others. If so, it must have been in mediaeval times as, during the whole period covered by the Linchmere rolls from 1545 to about 1900, nothing whatsoever has been seen to connect the family with the mill or the Shottover land parcel (Springhead Farm), and there is nothing in the early references, for example the above entry of 1339 in the Bramshott rolls, to indicate with certainty whether the Shotter connexion was with the mill or farm. At no time in the Linchmere rolls from 1545 on, is the tenant of Shottover/ Springhead Farm also the holder of the Shottover mill, although reference to the mill in the rolls is probably not without gaps.

There is no present answer to this question. There are, however, at the PRO collections of documents emanating from the Court of Augmentations (not seen) which apparently contain unindexed some pre-Dissolution leases. If anything relating to pre-Dissolution Shottover Mill has survived, the answer may lie there.

The Start Date of Shottover Mill

It is not known when Shottover Mill was built and started working. The reference of 1339 in the Bramshott rolls to Richard de Schotover may have been either to the farm or the mill but in either case it might well indicate that Shottover Mill was operating at that date and, if so, its presence may have had something to do with the disappearance of the corn mill at Pitfold in the mid 1300s. The first reference by name to its existence in the 1500s certainly postdates its startup.

What Sort of a Mill was it?

The function of Shottover Mill has, unfortunately, been the subject of mis-information over a long period when it has been wrongly described as an ironworks and even a shot mill.

Known during comparatively recent times as Shotter Mill, the local presence of the Shotter family, the mill's situation in the heart of the Shottermill area which contains other mills sometimes referred to as 'of Shottermill', the known existence of a hammer locally and the known but undefined connexion of the Shotter family with iron-working have all conspired to make Shotter Mill the Shotter *Iron* Mill and its ponds hammer ponds. Before presenting the documented history of the mill, therefore, some comment is made on the historical references.

The primary culprit was Dallaway who published his great two-volume tome entitled '*History of Sussex*' in 1815. Here (vol. I p.304) he says 'Shottover or Shotter iron mill in this parish [Linchmere] was anciently held from the priory by a family so named who retained it for several generations' and continues 'Shotter Mill with an adjoining estate was sold by William

Shotter Gent to Anthony Capron, Gent. of Midhurst in 1793.'

The manor rolls establish quite clearly that this mill and estate sold in 1793 by William Shotter to the Caprons was the ancient Shotter-tenanted estate comprising Hatch Hill and Parrys & Hurlands on which the iron mill known as Northpark furnace operated intermittently from the early 1600s to about 1776. Dallaway's remarks that the Shotters had held these lands for many generations from the Priory and later manor are perfectly true except that they are not the lands associated at any time with or near Shottover Mill.

These remarks were repeated, amongst others, by Canon Capes in his *'Rural Life in Hampshire among the Manors of Bramshott'*, pub. MacMillan 1901, where he says: 'Shotter Mill derives its name from the iron works which were long carried on there and not abandoned until 1776. A family named Shotter held them in old time under Shulbrede Priory'.

The *Victoria County History for Surrey*, vol II, 1905, also quotes Dallaway and states that 'Shottermill … belonged to Shulbrede Priory and was an iron mill', quoting Dallaway's source PRO Land Revenue Office vol. 3/197 f.87, 1608, (which was in fact incorrect and should have read Land Revenue vol. 2/197 f.87 — LR 3 does not contain relevant material).

Arthur Ponsonby was more cautious and, whilst saying nothing much about Shotter Mill, correctly identified the land and mill concerned in the sale in 1793 as Northpark, and Swanton and Woods in a footnote (p.223) identify Shotter Mill as a corn mill (although this at a much later date when it was in no doubt), but the incorrect association was continued in Dr Rolston's book on Haslemere, where he describes going past Cherrimans to 'Shotter iron mill in Lynchmere parish', and it also served perhaps to inhibit a careful examination of Straker's comments in his book *'Wealden Iron'*, pub. Bell, 1931.

Straker again quotes Dallaway but goes on to describe the 'Shottermill Forge' (hammer) as being in Haslemere parish and one eighth of a mile *SE* of Shottermill Church. He continues, 'The pond is still in water, and the picturesque group of dilapidated mill buildings seems to have served for many uses'. Clearly Straker's Shottermill Forge was Sickle Mill (or the forge/hammer in the Shottermill district) which *is* an eighth of a mile SE of the Church and *is* in Haslemere parish, and not Shotter Mill itself which is neither.

Around any ironworks evidence of its existence always remains in the form of its characteristic detritus. Straker confirmed that forge cinder was to be found plentifully round his 'Shottermill Forge' which is true for Sickle Mill. It is not true, however, for Shotter Mill where the absence of forge cinder has always needed an explanation. There are a few forge bottoms at Rose Cottage opposite Shotter Mill, but these were often used for construction purposes and therefore wandered. The latest edition of the Wealden Iron Research Group's Gazetteer confirms that Shotter Mill should no longer be considered as an iron mill, nor the ponds hammer ponds.

History of Shottover Mill

When the possessions of the dissolved Priory of Shulbrede passed into the hands of the Earl of Southampton and afterwards Anthony Browne (later the Viscounts Montague) and became the manor of Linchmere and Shulbrede, Shottover Mill was not included in the manor lands but was reserved to the Crown and issued under Letters Patent. This was not unusual as it was a quick and painless way for the Crown to make money.

It meant, however, that the holders of the mill did not appear in the manor rolls except when, as was frequently the case, they incurred penalties for the illegal use of the nearby manor common and waste when their names and details of the offence were presented by the Homage to the manor court. Otherwise information on the mill comes from the records of the Court of Augmentations which was set up in 1536 specifically to administer the immense amount of property of the lately dissolved religious houses. This Court was in existence until 1553 when its records reverted to the Exchequer.

The mill at this early date is usually described simply as a mill or sometimes a water mill, but such a term (without qualification) usually denoted a corn mill. In the Latin, used up to the mid 1700s, the terms for corn, fulling and iron mills were not the same and were used specifically. Certainly the term 'molendinum' (means for grinding) and 'fabrica ferria' (iron works) would never have been applied loosely and incorrectly. In the former case the term 'mill' indicated not a building but a pair of millstones. In the lease given below,[3] Shottover mill is described as having two mills or two pairs of stones under one roof, which it still had in the 1800s. On no occasion was Shottover Mill ever referred to as a 'fabrica ferrea'. (However, somewhat illogically, a fulling mill was described as a 'molendinum fullonicum').

In the property of Shulbrede Priory listed in the Valor Ecclesiasticus the compilation of which heralded the Dissolution process, among the rents an entry appears for the lease of a mill in Coutershall (Coultershaw) near Petworth (53s.4d); and another for rent from a mill in Lowdell (Lowder) 2s; and for rents of lands and tenements in Wellynchemer (Linchmere) which totalled £17. 6s 5d. There is no mention of Shottover Mill, but probably the mill, being in Linchmere parish, was included in the total Linchmere parish rental which was not itemised. Coutershall and Lowdell appeared because they were in other parishes all of which were listed separately. However, in the Ministers Account of 1536 to the Crown[4] where the Priory's Linchmere holdings are itemised in detail, there is still no mention of Shottover mill, although all the other manorial holdings are listed giving the name of the holding, the tenant and the rent etc As the total rental for the Priory's Linchmere lands in this latter document is less than the above £17.6.5d. it may be that Shottover mill whose rent was £3 had already been withdrawn from the Priory's lands.

There is, however, in this 1536 document reference to a fulling mill, rent 20s, leased out to Thomas Quennell (Pophole Farm itself was held by *John* Quennell). It is not known where this fulling mill was. It is possible, but extremely doubtful that it was Shottover mill itself. In the later details of the holders of the Letters Patent and the leases which start in 1548, only 12 years after the Ministers Account, Shottover mill is always named and is never described as a fulling mill. This reference to a fulling mill amongst the Priory's Linchmere landholdings is never mentioned again. It may be that the Quennells had a fulling mill along the stretch of the Wey passing through their farm. If so, no remains now exist according to Laurence Giles of the Bramshott and Liphook Preservation Society and Adrian Bird of the River Wey Trust who are extremely familiar with this stretch of water.

This entry relating to the fulling mill was the last entry on the list of the Priory's Linchmere holdings, being immediately preceded by another relating to the lease of some Marley waste to George Mose. The Mose family and Marley waste also never occur again in the Linchmere manor rolls (being at one point specifically excluded from belonging to Linchmere manor) and it may be that neither entry is for Linchmere, but for some property of the late Priory held elsewhere as the document goes on to list all the Priory holdings in other areas such as Yapton, Rustington and Farnest etc etc

With regard to Shottover mill the first known holder of Letters Patent for the mill was one Henry Shereley who held it for a term of 21 years from 1548/9, rendering a payment to the Crown of 60s. per annum.[5] After him came Thomas Smyth who held Letters Patent for a period of 21 years from 1565.[6] The clear yearly value of the mill is given as 60s. and the fee for the lease is £12 or the equivalent of 4 years rent.

After Smyth, George Scales held the mill under Letters Patent for a period of 40 years from 1583.[7] Also from the Calendar of Particulars for Leases, a mill in Linchmere is leased to Richard Russell in 1582–3. He may have been the first of Scales' under tenants as he appears in the early Linchmere rolls (below) as offending at Shottover mill by failing to control his water supply between the spring (at Springhead) and the mill. Russell is succeeded by Thomas Payne of Pitfold.

Valuations of dissolved monastic property continued to be taken for a considerable period after 1536 as the Crown continued to scrape up the last possible cash return, and one late Valor (Valuation) exists for 1608 for the remaining properties of Shulbrede Priory still undisposed of at that date.[8] It is to this 1608 survey that a lease is appended which describes Shottover Mill and the rights accruing to it in detail and shows that Thomas Payne of Pitfold then had the lease of Shottover mill from George Scales. This original document is shown and given in transcript overleaf.

Transcript of Lease

Thomas Payne claims to hold by virtue of letters patent under the Seal of the Exchequer issued to a certain George Scales given the 17th day of May in the 25th year of the reign of the late Queen Elizabeth. [1583]

Lease of a Mill called Shotover Mills in parish of Linchmere

All that messuage and mill or all those two mills built together under one roof called or known by the name of Shottover mill otherwise Shotover mills with all their appurtenances and all and singular the house buildings grounds orchards gardens common waters water courses weirs banks ponds fishponds fisheries suits sokes amercements of tenants wastes heaths profits commodities gains emoluments and hereditaments whatsoever appertaining to the said mills or in whatever way respecting or belonging to the same as usual heretofore for rent reserved in the same letters patent reserved leased found used known accepted occupied or

101

reputed to exist

> *To have and to hold to the said George his heirs and assigns from the day given in the letters patent to the end of the term and for a term of 40 years by payment annually of*
> *Annual value of the lease £20*
> *In witness of which the aforesaid jurors have affixed their seals and Names or marks on the day and year aforesaid namely – Richard Moath, Nicholas Bell, Henry Hobbs, Francis Collins with others named above*

The holders of the Letters Patent were not pursued beyond this point as nothing relevant appeared in the Calendars up to Charles II and by the later 1600s it is obvious that the mill, a corn mill, was held freehold. Other references to the mill appear in the Lists of Penalties with which the meetings of the Linchmere manor courts concluded. They are detailed below and show quite clearly that there was never any great hurry to acknowledge the manor's complaints and pay the fines. There are, unfortunately, no accounts for this period.

The first complaint appeared in 1584[9] when it was presented that (the above) Richard Russell, tenant of Shottover Mill had placed a certain wooden gutter called a trough on the waste of this manor near the mill pond on the east side of the said pond, in a different way than has been accustomed from ancient times, and by reason of the flow of water from the said gutter has greatly damaged the queen's highway there, that is, on the parcel of waste of this manor, to the great damage and annoyance of the liege subjects of our lady the Queen and the neighbours there who hold by inheritance of the lord of this manor. Therefore he is pardoned on payment of 3/4d and must repair and make good the damage aforesaid before the feast of All Saints next, on pain of 20s.

Three years later matters have not improved although Russell has been replaced by John Edington[10] when it is presented that by reason of the flow of water from a wooden gutter by the mill pond at Shottover Mill, the queen's highway there is greatly damaged and made worse to the general annoyance and danger to the liege subjects of our lady the Queen who are passing there, and it is the fault of John Edington, farmer [lessee] of the mill there. Therefore he is pardoned on payment of 12d and he must remove and take back the said trough and fill up the hole which was made by the flow of water aforesaid before the feast of All Saints next, on pain of 20s.

Again in 1587 and 1588[11] John Edington was presented for not moving the trough and filling up the hole and this time he is fined 20s and threatened with a further 20s fine. It would seem that the water from the spring above the ponds flowed in an open course across the road, in theory but obviously not in practice, constrained by a wooden trough. The emergence of the spring near the southern point of the triangle of land behind Arnold's garage can still clearly be seen in wet weather.

In the same year[12] John Edington farmer of Shottover Mill was indicted for making clay on the waste of the Lord in various places, without a licence and was pardoned on a payment of 4d/4s[?].

Perhaps matters were put right as over ten years elapsed before the next miller of Shottover Mill, William White, was indicted in 1601, this time for digging a width called Lorie[?] on the common without licence and was pardoned on a payment of 2d.[13]

The next complaint arose in 1639[14] when it was presented that William Greene and John Greene his brother had lately built a small structure on the waste adjoining their mill called Shottover Mill without the Lord's licence. They were to take it down before the next court on penalty of 6s 8d, viz 3/4d each.

It is then not until fifty years later that Edward Brida (great grandson of Blaise Briday one of the earliest known ironworkers) was in trouble with the manor. The Homage presented in 1689 that Edward Brida did encroach on the waste near Shottover Mill and erect a certain building called in English a Carthouse and extended his pond.[15] In 1691 and again in 1694 the Homage presented that Edward Brida had not thrown out his above encroachment on the waste at Shottover Mill and he was accordingly fined 20s on both occasions.[16]

In 1694, Edward Bredah alias Blaze (a Briday) of the parish of Linchmere, miller, made a will probated in 1696 in the Consistory Court of the Bishop of Chichester. The will shows without a doubt that the mill was a corn mill and also by this date was held freehold. In the will he said, *'I give unto Cousin Gregory Hoade the Younger and his heirs my Messuage or Tenement, Millhous, Corne Mill, mill ponds, waters and watercourses thereunto belonging with appurtenances lying in Linchmore.'*

An inventory of his possessions, dated 20 July 1696, appraised by Charles Breda (his brother), Roger Barden and Gregory Hoade, also survives. Unfortunately, this does not say anything about the mill itself except to state that it contained '3 old chests & lumber in the mill & about the house, worth 10s'. It is however very different from all the other inventories of this date which have been inspected in that under the heading 'wearing apparell & money in his purse & in the house' the sum of £80 is given. Normally cash amounted only to a very small sum indeed. Either Edward had just completed a remunerative business deal or he was a man who preferred to keep his money under the mattress. Most people at this time, even persons of moderate standing, invested or loaned out spare cash at interest. Other Linchmere inventories of this period show that most people were lucky if they had a spare shilling or two to rattle in their pocket. Only the Shotters kept cash about them to the tune of £10 or £20 or more.

Edward was a widower without issue, unlettered, and from his inventory given below, it is obvious that he lived in no style above the ordinary. Just how long he had held the mill is not known except that earlier, in 1664, he appeared in the Surrey Hearth Tax returns as living in a one hearth dwelling in Pitfold and not until 1670 is he listed under the Linchmere returns for a dwelling with two hearths – perhaps the millhouse. In 1675, he was definitely at the mill as he was so described in a 1675 Indenture whereby he also had a malthouse in Haslemere on perpetual lease from James Figg, ropemaker.

Inventory of Edward Breda of Linchmore, Miller, 20 July 1696
Appraised by Charles Breda, Roger Barden & Gregory Hoade:

	Shottover Mill
	£ = s = d.
Imprimis: wearing apparell of the dec'ed & money in his purse & in the house	80=00=00
Three high bedsteds & one trundle bed with matt cords 1 set of Curtains & one feather bed & other beds bedding & furniture thereto belonging	10=00=00
Two chests 3 coufers 1 box 7 joyned stools & 8 chaires & 1 flasket	1=00=00
Nine pair of sheetes 6 pr of pillow covers? 3 table clothes one dossen & a halfe of Napkins 10 towells & other lynnen	5=00=00
Two tables 2 little Cupboards & 1 forme	12=00
Three Iron potts 1 Iron kittle 2 Iron skilletts 3 Iron dripping pans 4 spitts 2 pr of Andirons a pr of [illeg] two fire shovles a pr of tongs 2 pr of grid irons 2 pr of pott hangers 1 iron ovenled & other old Iron	1=08=06
One Iron Jack & chains & 2 Guns	13=00
foweteen pieces of pewter	15=00
Corn of severall sorts about 20 bushells	3=00=00
8 sacks & old clothes & old baggs	10=00
Drink vessells & Brewing vessells & other old tubbs & things in the house	2=17=00
one pr of scales & weights one spitte 2 shovles prongs bills & other working tools	3=00
4 Iron Bars	3=00
1 load of peate 2 cords of wood & fire fewell & lumber without doores	16=00
2 horses	6=00=00
One little Cart & horse harness	3=00=00
One hog & 3 pigs	1=10=00
3 old chests & lumber in the mill & aboute the house	10=00
hay	5=00=00
two brasse kittles 2 brasse skilletts & one warming pan	12=00
Total	**125=10=06**

It is obvious from the next rolls entry that cousin Gregory was working the mill and has started off as he meant to go on as he is immediately presented for an encroachment on the waste near Shottover Mill. In 1699[17] and again in 1712[18] he has encroached and enclosed part of the waste belonging to the manor on the south and west of his water mill called Shottover Mill. He is pardoned on payment of 5s. and is given until Michaelmas to lay open his encroachment under penalty of 10s.

Hoade was followed by John and William Chitty who were presented in 1721 for continuing a certain encroachment on the manor waste on the south and west parts of their water mill called Shottover Mill. It sounds as though whatever Gregory Hoade had been doing on the south and west of the mill had never been amended and the complaint of the Homage had been ignored.[19]

After the Chittys, Shottover Mill was in the possession of Richard Fielder at least from 1723 when he took out an insurance policy on his house and mill for £500[20] until his death in 1778[21] and after that, of his widow or daughter Ann, until the mill was leased from her by William Simmons and eventually bought by James Simmons III (the Diarist of Sickle Mill). This policy refers to Fielder's *new* dwelling house. The history of the mill therefore ends here with a list of the transgressions of Richard Fielder.

In 1725[22] Richard Fielder had continued the above encroachments on the south and west of his water mill called Shottover mill – penalty 10s. In 1747[23] the Court presented Richard Fielder for enclosing part of Linchmere Common lying against Shottermill ponds, and fined him 10s. In 1756 and 1758 he was fined £4 for enclosing part of Linchmere Common lying against Shottermill ponds; and again in 1762 for enclosing part of the Linchmere Common when he was fined £5. In 1766 Richard Fielder of Shotter Mill, miller was fined £10 for enclosing part of Linchmere Common and erecting a carthouse adjoining or near to the pond head or mill pond. He was also fined £5 for taking several thousands of turfs from the Common.[24]

References in Chapter Four

[1] Cockburn, J.S. ed. Calendar of Assize Records for Sussex, HMSO, 1995
[2] Sussex Record Soc. vol. X
[3] PRO. LR2/197, ff 85–7
[4] PRO. SC6 H8 3674
[5] PRO. E.310/25/145
[6] Ibid
[7] PRO. LR2/197 ff85–7
[8] Ibid
[9] WSRO.Cdy 264 No.187
[10] WSRO.Cdy 264 No. 202, 1587

[11] WSRO.Cdy 264 Nos. 210 & 217

[12] WSRO.Cdy 264, No. 219

[13] WSRO.Cdy 264, No.268

[14] WSRO.Cdy 264, f47

[15] WSRO.Cdy 264,1689

[16] WSRO.Cdy 264, 1691, 1694

[17] WSRO.Cdy 264, 1699

[18] WSRO.Cdy 264, f109v,1712

[19] WSRO.Cdy 264, f115v, 1721

[20] Sun Ins. Policy 30285 of 2 November 1723: Guildhall Book No. 11936/16

[21] L'mere Par.Reg. 15.9.1778

[22] WSRO.Cdy 264, 1725

[23] WSRO.Cdy 265, 1747

[24] WSRO.Cdy 265, 1756, 1758, 1762 & 1766

Chapter Five

The Cottages in Linchmere Manor

Appearance of new Cottages – Pelham's (possibly Ramblers), Barden's, Anchor House, the Smithy, the Hammer Cottages, Greene's and Stoneham's Cottages, Pond and Corner Cottages; Others outside the Wey valley.

The Appearance of New Cottages

Documents relating to the Priory and then Linchmere manor holdings in the middle 1500s make hardly any reference at all to the presence of much other than the family farms. A hundred years later, however, there seem to have been a further ten cottages in the manor, their presence demonstrating an increasing population and demand for land. There is nothing, however, to indicate that there was any concentration in any one place. They are located from Fridays Hill on the east side of the manor to Chithurst at the western end. A few legal grants were made in the late 1500s, but many cottages, particularly in the 1600s, start off life as illegal encroachments on the waste, ie untenanted land or rough pasture or woodland.

Such waste lay amongst other places down Linchmere Hill from St. Peter's, and near Shottover Mill, and as it was always on the waste that landless men had to carve out for themselves an unofficial cottage and garden, some of these cottages appear in both these favoured places. It was also on the waste that official grants to build cottages were made. Very often an arrangement was eventually arrived at whereby illicit encroachers were granted the copyhold in return for a rent, though not always.

Why some were treated in one way and some in the other is not obvious from the rolls. This sort of amenable attitude, however, did not apply to those who encroached upon the *common* land where the manor tenants usually vigorously defended their rights. Illegal encroachment was beginning to be a nuisance as can be seen from the 1634 order in the rolls by the Homage that **NO** tenements should be erected upon the commons or waste. Some of the early cottages seem to be connected with the advent of iron workers into the area in the late 1500s. Fig.8 shows the location of some of their properties.

In the Wey valley were:—

Pelham's Cottage *(possibly on or near the site of Ramblers)*

On an official grant of land in 1576, Charles Pelham (possibly a member of a well-known iron industry family) built a cottage on a quarter acre of waste lying near Shottover mill. Pelham, however, did not last long dying in 1578 with his wife and son succeeding him. In 1602 the cottage was leased and after this the family disappear.

It may well be that Pelham's cottage was on or somewhere near the site of the house now called 'Ramblers' as in the first reference to Ramblers (with the same quit rent and description) a few years later, that cottage is already in existence. From 1613 its descent can be traced directly and uninterruptedly to the present Ramblers, and it was the holder, John Bell, who was presented at the Farnham manor Hundred Court circa 1615 for 'stoppinge of a watercourse that belongeth to the fullinge mill in Pitfold belonging to Thomas Paine'.[1]

During the 1600s the cottage passed quite quickly through a number of hands including the Jarlets (another iron worker family) and various non-occupying holders until in 1714 it ended up in the hands of Richard West a husbandman of Farnhurst. His heir, another Richard West, in 1743 took out a mortgage on the cottage for £20.8s from widow Anne Jelly of Isleworth, who was no doubt one of the many ladies in this century and later, joyfully investing their late husband's estate, having control of money (very possibly originally their own) for the first time in their life. By 1752, it had been bought by John Hoad, wheelwright of Linchmere parish, members of which family continued to own this and other properties around the Ponds for the rest of the century.

The Bells, in 1593, were also granted another smaller cottage with a parcel of waste of about a quarter acre 'lying near Shottover myll at the western end of the course of the lane there leading from Shottover myll towards Houndeleys water viz. on the south side of the same lane', but its records ceased in 1647.

Barden's Cottage

A third early grant was that made in 1595 to John Colpis who may have been related to the Colpis/Colpas who was the curate at Lynchmere in 1570.[2] This cottage seemed to be the only one on the top of the hill and is described as lying near the cemetery of St. Peter's church. The cottage eventually passed to another of the iron workers, William Barden a hammerman, after his marriage to the widow Colpis, but unfortunately it burned down and William had to rebuild it. William had also apparently exceeded his rights as, after his death in 1609, widow Margery remarried and his successor was ordered to throw out the fenced encroachment Barden had made on the waste.

In the 1600s it was taken from the Lord's hands by Edward Rapley and it was one of his sons, Stephen, who in 1654 was required to prove his rights to this cottage by presenting his copy of court roll to the next meeting of the homage, which fortunately he was able to do. However, some years later this cottage disappeared from the rolls. It is possible that it became incorporated into Church Farm which the Rapleys held some little while later.

These early cottages (apart from Barden's) which were on the waste all seem to have been on the south side of the road on the small area around the spring which fed Shottermill ponds and which was unsuitable for cultivation. Much of the surrounding land was part of one or another of the farms. Another very small area of waste was immediately around the mill and ponds (which ponds belonged to and were an integral part of the mill) on the north side of the road, but the building of structures on this small area, even those erected by the millers, were seemingly always the subject of complaint by the manor. Another nearby area of waste was that on the west side of Hammer Lane.

Anchor House

Anchor House was almost certainly present at an early date but seems to have been a farm cottage belonging to Springhead, so that it does not have any documentary history in its own right until it was sold off separately from the farm in the late 1700s.

The Smithy

While Stones (the Mill Tavern land) was in the hands of the Bridays, there is a rolls entry in 1590 that Blaise Briday, who was probably one of the original iron workers at Pophole Hammer, had built a workshop [fabrica] on the waste near Shottover mill, and a few years later he made fealty for a cottage and garden lying near the mill which may have been connected with this.

It seems likely that this workshop was the smithy which still existed between Shottover mill and the Wey in the mid 1900s as later entries refer to the surrender of a forge by Blaise's great-grandson Thomas in 1670 and to its subsequent possession by Henry Tribe who in 1687 was granted a licence to pull down (and presumably rebuild) an edifice 'once a smith's [work]shop' there. Nothing more is heard of this smithy until it is shown on the Tythe Map of 1846 as belonging (along with Stones) to the blacksmithing family of Stillwells.

Other Cottages in Linchmere manor

The history of the **Hammer Cottages** (near Pophole), some or all of which are still standing, is discussed in the chapter on the hammer at Pophole.

The remaining cottages were seventeenth century grants and some of them appear to have had fairly short lives as they originated as illegal encroachments.

Robert Greene in 1609 built an unlicensed cottage on the waste near 'Shottover Myll' but was brusquely ordered to demolish it under a (very high) penalty of £5. This he did not do and eventually was given the copyhold for the yearly rent of a cock. The Greenes were a little later millers at Shottover Mill but by 1647 there are no Greenes on the tenant list and the records of this cottage had ended.

John Stoneham in 1639 was also indicted for erecting an unlicensed structure on the end of his cottage on the waste near the mill, but he and his cottage also shortly disappear.

Lastly, in 1633, **Thomas Cover** (probably a younger son of the Covers of Gilhams) was granted a cottage and four acres of waste at Chidhurst, somewhere in the area of Gilhams and Bridge Farms. This cottage was held in the 1720s by the Chittys who became millers at Shottover after which its records end and all traces of it disappear.

These cottages appeared to change hands fairly frequently. However, as properties were holdings by inheritance, it is almost certain that new names very often only indicated married daughters or other kin. It is obvious that the land around the mill and ponds was a favoured destination for people building themselves cottages on the waste in the hope that their encroachments would not be noticed, which is not surprising as this area was near both the highway and the mills on the Wey and presumably most convenient for landless men in need of employment. Many of these cottages had a short life if the records are accurate. It is also very probable that there others which were thrown out without any records at all.

Pond & Corner Cottages

Pond Cottage

Pond and Corner Cottages which lie immediately on the east side of Shottermill Ponds are of a later construction and are listed buildings dated to the 1700s. Pond Cottage was the first to be built although the precise date of the grant is not available as there is an unexplained gap in the rolls between 1702 and 1713. Most probably, however, it was built around the early 1700s as the first rolls entry in 1730 indicates that it was already there, being inherited by John and Elizabeth Baker. Elizabeth was a Moorey holding it from her parents.

John and Elizabeth must have lived on a fairly modest scale as their house was mortgaged for £8 7s 2d. over a period of nearly 30 years first from John Wallis of Frensham, a weaver, and then from John Hoad wheelwright, mentioned above as the purchaser of Ramblers a few years later. In 1758, Elizabeth Baker sold the property to John Tribe, husbandman. It was for his daughter Anne and son-in-law John White also a husbandman, that John Tribe in 1762 built Corner Cottage on the part of his land near the road. They are both of stone with brick decoration.

Many of the new cottages appeared on the waste outside the Wey valley and are not strictly relevant to Shottermill's history. Briefly these were:—

Lynchmere Cottage where Oliver Chittey in 1575 was granted a cottage and parcel of land in 'Aldermarshe near Putfold Hatch' – now Lynchmere Cottage. Aldermarsh was the ancient name of Linchmere Marsh and a hatch was a public right of way between tenanted land and waste or common. This hatch was probably the way from Linchmere over the Ridge to Shottover Mill.

Popmore was an early grant made in 1567 of a parcel of waste down

111

Fridays Hill to William Haywarde on which he built a cottage a few years later. This was only ever a smallholding with a few acres attached to it, held for many years by the Luff family. The later extension to this stone and brick cottage can be clearly seen.

Waterhouse, down Lynchmere Hill from St Peter's was granted in 1622 to Roger Seale who had encroached on about two acres of the waste called Aldermarsh which ran in a broad swathe either side of the present road down the Hill.

Rose Cottage on the bend of Lynchmere Hill was a cottage divided off from the holding now called *Woodmancote* around 1650.

Bridger's Cottage, built illegally by Nicholas Bridger in 1639 on the Aldermarsh waste after an order to demolish it, disappears from the records almost immediately.

Steed's Cottage, now Brookham Cottages, was a legal grant in 1606 to Thomas Steed to build on the waste. By 1670 Steed had also built a malthouse there which was on the south side of the Liphook Road just before the rail bridge. A decayed pond and a field still known as Burnt Malthouse (the malthouse burned down sometime in the middle 1700s) are still discernible.

Some of the above cottages, in particular those around Shottover Mill and the Ponds, seem to have few continuous records. Built without licence, when their occupiers died *not* holding copyholds of inheritance, their houses probably reverted into the Lord's hands and were thereafter held by the manor as leaseholds. There was little profit to the Lord of the Manor from hereditary copyholds from which he received a fee often only once a generation when they changed hands, besides the modest annual rental. He had much more flexibility and profit from leaseholds. There was certainly one such property – later known as Kervell's the wheelers cottage – near the site of the present Arnold's garage.

On Linchmere Hill quite remarkably, apart from the building of the Vicarage, Lynchmere House and one other house (Corner Cottage on Linchmere Hill) in the nineteenth century, nothing much changed over 300 years except that the houses were very often extended and came to be occupied by more than one family. Round the mill and ponds little also changed during this period. The Linchmere Tythe Map of 1846 shows that on the Sussex side around the ponds there were only six houses, plus the millhouse and smithy and the house now the Mill Tavern.

References in Chapter Five

[1] HRO.11M59/E1/148/6
[2] Ponsonby, op.cit. p.164

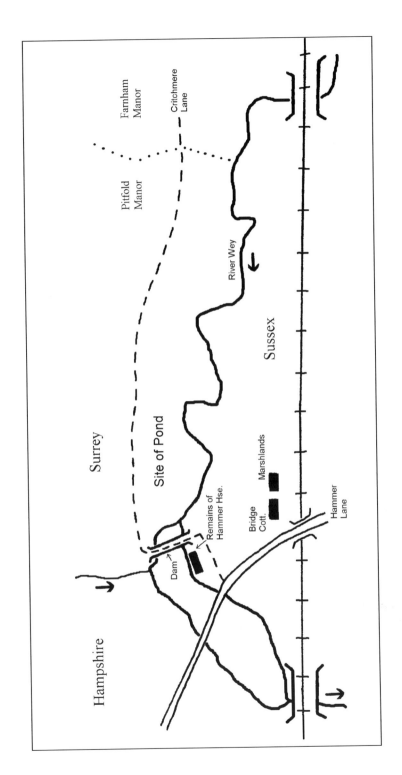

Fig. 7: Pophole Hammer site

Pophole: The Hammer Cottages and the Hammer on the left behind the tree
– Painted by G.W.Rowe of Hammer Lane 1960

Chapter Six

The Hammer at Pophole

Introduction; Origins of the Name 'Pophole'; Background to Ironmaking in the Weald; Technology; Local and Economic Background; History of the Hammer – the Startup Years; Evidence Provided by Some of the Early Ironworkers; Evidence from the Lay Subsidies; the Tythe Dispute 1598; the Workforce; Pophole in the Seventeenth Century – the Formal Surrender to Lord Montague; the Shotter Association with Iron-working; the Hammer Cottages; Seventeenth Century Accounts; Pophole in the Eighteenth Century; John Butler of Bramshott (previously of Stanley Farm); the End of Iron-working at the Hammer.

The remains of Pophole Hammer (SU 87393266) lie on the Wey at the junction of the counties of Surrey, Sussex and Hampshire. On many of the Wealden iron sites of the 16th–18th centuries, little now survives beyond the pond and dam or bay which once formed the pond head and, in the case of Pophole, there only remains the bay, two stone sluices and some stonework immediately downstream of the bay on the south side. A scatter of forge cinder may still be found. The bay has long been breached and the pond is no longer in water.

The bay has at its northern end a 3m. wide stone sluice with a central pillar which is the one usually reproduced in the literature on Pophole and on postcards. At the southern end is a smaller sluice containing a stone channel which was probably one of the wheel pits. Along the southern bank and partly revetting the bay are the remains of a stone building. A footpath leading from Hammer Lane to Critchmere Lane now crosses the bay from which these remains can easily be seen. The whole site is lightly wooded.

The area known as 'Hammer' lying in Sussex and extending roughly from Hammer Lane to the roundabout at Shottermill Ponds takes its name from these ironworks. On the Surrey side (historically in the parish of Frensham) lay the manor of Pitfold and on the Sussex side the manor of Linchmere, both of which were owned by the Montagues of Cowdray from the sixteenth to the nineteenth centuries. On the Sussex side in the manor of Linchmere at this point lay Watts Farm (Linchmeres Wattmans & Elliotts) held according to the Linchmere Rolls from 1533 by the Theyre and then the Person families.

On the Surrey side lay an area immediately near the hammer about which little is known at that early date but from later field names such as 'rough' or 'moor' seems to have constituted poor quality land. The hammer land occupied both sides of the Wey.

Fig.6 shows the relation of Pophole Hammer to Watts Farm and its situation in the Wey valley.

Few of the early iron sites are distinguished by the survival of detailed records but, as part of a very large estate held continuously over a long period by the same family, it might have been expected that Pophole and other Montague iron works would have proved an exception. In 1793, however, the last direct male Montague heir was drowned in a boating accident on the Rhine and in the same year, Cowdray House, the principal seat of the Montagues was destroyed by fire, and in the circumstances little or no effort seems to have been made to preserve much of the paper work which survived the fire.

William Cobbett who visited Cowdray on one of his 'Rural Rides' was depressed by the sight of the neglected house, and more than fifty years after the fire, heaps of papers, mouldering and rendered illegible through damp, were still to be seen in corners of the ruined building. Such records as existed relating to Pophole hammer may well, therefore, have been lost at this time. Only two fragments of seventeenth century accounts and some late eighteenth century leases survive in the Cowdray Archive.

In fact very little detailed information about the Montagues' connexion with the iron industry, which was considerable, remains. A Montague will of 1592 merely refers unhelpfully to 'All leases concerninge any my yron—workes and all wooddes underwooddes cole myne and stockes by me alreadye bought provided or appoynted'. Fortunately, the three great bound volumes of the Linchmere manor rolls did survive and these contain a few entries which throw a little light on Pophole hammer in its early years.

Also for the six years 1826–32, when James Simmons III (paper-maker at Sickle Mill) was on the Pitfold Manor Homage, he seems to have kept the Pitfold manor records. These were found amongst his papers[1], contained in a small hand-sewn paper notebook, very much after the style of the home-made volumes of his own Diary, but very much unlike the large bound volumes of Linchmere manorial rolls. It is possible that the original Pitfold rolls being gone by then, this notebook replaced them for a time.

There are, therefore, many questions which cannot be answered, so that 'The Iron Industry of the Weald', by H. Cleere and D. Crossley and containing contributions by members of the Wealden Iron Research Group,[2] was extensively consulted to provide a background against which the sparse and in many cases uncertain information available on Pophole hammer could be placed. This book – the result of many years of fieldwork, excavation and documentary research – should be consulted by anyone wishing to know more about the complex technology and development of the Wealden iron industry. A copy of the second edition, 1995, can be seen in the Haslemere Museum Library.

The character of the entire area of the Linchmere and Pitfold manors from earliest times to the late 1800s was predominantly agricultural. In the middle 1600s, Montague's manor of Linchmere contained 20 farms and 10 cottages. The land on the Surrey side – up to Hindhead – contained half that number of farms and only a few cottages, some near the river and in the area of 'Shottermill Street', a few at Critchmore and on Lion Green and one or two distributed about the remainder of the area. The population was accordingly small.

In the mid 1600s, the number of adult males in Linchmere Manor was only 64, giving a total population of the order perhaps of about 180. The 1664 Hearth Tax returns for Pitfold (selected as far as possible from the combined returns of the Tything of Pitfold and Churt) show there to have been a population of somewhere around 150, although calculations of population based on these sources are generally recognised to be extremely crude. However, the presence of the infant Wey, eminently suitable as a source of water power, resulted in the construction of the various mills in the area and provided over a long period a key focus for additional employment, but at no time until the 1800s did any of them (with perhaps the exception of Sickle Mill) employ a large number of people.

Origins of the name 'Pophole'

The name 'Pophole' originally Poppehalle or Popehale (and var) – nothing to do with holes – is generally considered to derive from its association with the Pope family which, from early times, held land and mills in the area. Today and in hammer times, the name Pophole is specifically attached to the site of the hammer. In mediaeval times, however, it may well have been attached to a much wider area when members of the Pope family held land on the Surrey side of the Wey and also on the Sussex side. The possibility that the old Pophalle corn mill present in late Saxon times may not have been on precisely the same site as the later hammer has been discussed in Chapter 1 so that before the construction of the hammer at Pophole in the late 1500s there may have been for at least two centuries, if not more, little activity in this area beyond that normally associated with farming and heath and woodland occupations.

The name Pophole lingered on after the departure of the Pope family from the area and has given rise to erroneous associations in some of the prior literature. Initially only the odd page of the early Linchmere manor rolls appeared to have survived, but the first complete volume covering the period 1545–1727 coming to light in the 1950s, makes it clear that as far as the manor was concerned, the land parcel known as Pophole signified the land of the later Hammer Farm which lay to the west of the hammer. Allusions in the rolls, therefore, to Pophole refer always to Hammer Farm and not to the ironworks, unless the ironworks are specifically mentioned.

This confusion was reinforced by the unfortunate coincidence that the copyhold tenants of Pophole Hammer Farm were Quennells, other better known Quennells being iron-masters of the furnace at Imbhams in the parish of Chiddingfold. The Chiddingfold and Pophole Hammer Farm Quennells were almost certainly at some point related but were not the same. Thomas Quennell of Pophole Farm was reported in the Linchmere rolls as being dead by October 1570, leaving the farm to his son Roger, a minor. Thomas Quennell of Imbhams did not make his will until April 1571, leaving his property to his brother Robert, and dying later that year.

All references to the hammer in the records of the Linchmere manor courts are to be found amongst the entries relating to the land parcel known as Linchmeres Wattmans and Elliotts, colloquially Watts or Watses Farm. Watts Farm lay immediately to the east of Hammer Lane and extended from the Wey south over the Liphook road. Its farmhouse is now known as 'Watchers' and owned by Dexam International.

New Watts Farmhouse today – now Watchers [Dexam]

Amongst earlier comments on the hammer are those made in 1901 by Canon W.W. Capes in his *'Scenes of Rural Life in Hampshire'*.[3] On p.94 he says that the 'Manors of Bramshott and Dureford met … at the river bed between Hammer and Lynchmere, and the boundary was a matter of dispute, as recorded in a Court Roll [of Bramshott] of 1605'. This mutual boundary and ownership of land near the hammer by the Abbey of Dureford (near Rogate) has long been regarded as odd. If, however, for Dureford we read Dutford, which the manuscript supports according to Laurence Giles of the Bramshott & Liphook Preservation Society, meaning the manor of Dutford/Durtford/Dertford, sense is easily made of this 1605 rolls entry and also one of 1609.

From 1373 to the Dissolution of the Monasteries in 1535, the manor of Pitfold was held by the Priory of Dartford in Kent, and is sometimes referred to in later years as the manor of Dutford or Dertford. The 'running water' which has been taken to describe the river boundary between the manors of Bramshott and 'Dureford' was not the Wey but the small stream flowing from the north through the Trout Farm and which is the present Surrey/Hampshire border. This interpretation also makes sense of references to encroachments on Bramshott Common by Richard Bettesworth who is simultaneously described both as a tenant of Dutford manor and a tenant of Lord Montague. The Montagues held Pitfold/Dartford Manor from 1566 when it was bought from John White in exchange for Tongham Grange. It is possible to speculate that Montague, in addition to the generally known fact that he was at this time concentrating some of his scattered possessions may, when purchasing Pitfold manor, have had in mind that possession of both sides of the Wey could be useful.

Over time it is obvious that the area became better known as 'Hammer' and the name 'Pophole' to have been used less often. When the Victoria County History for Surrey was published in 1905,[4] the editors seemed to be uncertain about the whereabouts of Pophole.

Background to Ironmaking in the Weald

Not until the 6th or 5th century BC did iron come into use on any scale in this country, and its production became common in the first century BC.[5] Caesar after his brief incursions in 55 and 54BC recorded a small output. The Romans themselves during their stay in Britain characteristically developed the iron of the Weald on an industrial scale, but this was in the eastern Weald only, and they made no fundamental changes to the production method. Little or nothing is known about the subsequent Saxon period but there is some evidence during the mediaeval period, of trade in Wealden iron although this is insufficient to enable any detailed picture of its organisation or size to be drawn.

Technology

All iron products up to the end of the Middle Ages (c1500) would have resulted from a technology which basically had not changed since its inception. This was the bloomery process. Here, small bowl-like kilns of the order of two feet in diameter were set into hollows in the ground, and mixed layers of iron ore and charcoal placed within and fired, the temperature being raised to about 1,000°C by means of hand bellows. A small escape was left at the top for waste gases although ore and charcoal could also be top fed into the bloomery during the smelt when the escape would have been somewhat larger. This temperature was not high enough to melt the iron but enabled some of the combustion products to escape as gases and others to form a liquid slag.

The metal product of the bloomery was known as sponge iron from its appearance, its interstices still containing molten slag which needed to be removed. This was done by repeated heating and hammering with sledges (sledge hammers) until a small quantity – a bloom – of surprisingly pure iron resulted containing virtually no carbon and for that reason being highly ductile and subsequently easily fashioned in smiths' forges. This iron product, the result of much working, was known as wrought iron. Essentially this was a simple and discontinuous[†] process requiring only ore and wood for charcoal, both plentiful in the Weald. Remains of bloomeries (undated) can be seen around the Punchbowl, Bramshott Chase and in Combeswell.

In the late 1400s, however, a new technology was introduced into the Weald involving the harnessing of water power. The use of water power was in itself not new and may have been applied to some bloomeries before this date, but the paucity of informative remains of this period means that the early development of water power in this country is not as yet fully understood. Nonetheless, between about 1490 and 1540 there was a perceptible change from the bloomery to the water powered blast furnace, with the immigration of French Huguenot iron-workers being largely instrumental.

In the blast furnace, a water powered wheel drove a pair of very large bellows which supplied a powerful and continuous draught to the base of the furnace enabling higher temperatures to be achieved. The furnace itself was a high shaft structure top-fed with ore and charcoal, the molten iron being tapped off at the base.

This new technology brought about a number of important changes. First, the amount of iron produced was greatly increased. Secondly, the iron tapped at the base was molten, making casting possible, in particular the profitable casting of ordnance. Lastly and very important, the properties and character of the iron produced were different from those of wrought or bloomery iron. In the blast furnace, the ore was exposed to carbon-rich charcoal for a long period as it slowly descended the shaft and this resulted in the molten or cast iron having a high carbon content (between 2 and 4%) which made it hard and brittle and virtually impossible to be subsequently worked by smiths.

This was not just a local problem nor was it a matter of minor importance. Much of the Wealden wrought iron had always gone to the London wholesale market. Where guns were cast, the molten iron was run directly from the base of the furnace into gunpit moulds, and the Wealden iron industry, where the techniques of gun casting eventually surpassed those of the Continent, supplied much of the demand for ordnance until well into the eighteenth century.

[†] The process could be started up or closed down at will, unlike the process at a furnace which would be in continuous operation.

However, with the immense range of domestic, agricultural and industrial artefacts, not to mention those at specialized sites such as shipyards, produced from wrought iron which could be fashioned by smiths, a huge demand for it remained. A method, therefore, was necessary to reconvert much of the molten or cast iron back into wrought iron by lowering the carbon content, and this was done by harnessing water power to the old bloomery process where the water-powered wheel drove both bellows for the hearths and also the hammers. This was the process carried out at hammers such as Pophole. Where the molten or cast iron from a furnace was destined for further processing at a hammer, it was run off into shallow moulds, often a large one with smaller ones alongside. This reminded the early iron workers of a sow with piglets, and 'pig iron' was the term given by them to these castings.

It was in the form of pigs or sows that a hammer was supplied with iron for processing. The uses of wrought iron were many but its very softness limited its use for weapons and edge tools. For this, steel was required and further reference will be made under the account of Sickle Mill which was producing edge tools.

The hammer at Pophole would have had at least two hearths; some forges had three – two finery hearths and a chafery hearth. In the finery hearth, the cast iron was gradually re-melted in a blast of air which removed the carbon as CO_2 from the iron. It was then hammered to consolidate the iron which had accumulated in a mass at the bottom of the hearth. In the chafery hearth the iron was simply reheated to forging temperature and fashioned into bar form in which shape it was usually marketed. No change in the chemistry occurred in the chafery hearth.

In the finery forge or hammer, the bellows for the hearths, and also the hammers were water-power driven. A scatter of forge cinder can still be seen at Pophole although, according to a local resident, quantities of this were removed within living memory for road-making purposes, a use with a long tradition. The surface of the land on the south bank has been raised since the hammer operated, but the remains of stonework immediately downstream of the dam or bay probably indicate the position of a building. There is reference in the 1598 Tythe Dispute to the 'hous' but it is not clear whether this term indicated the building housing the hammer, a worker's dwelling or possibly the presence of an 'iron house' which was a wholesale warehouse adjoining a forge where local smiths could purchase bar iron. A portion of a bar can be seen in Haslemere Museum.

The materials used to construct the pond dam or bay were usually those most easily available, eg clay, cinder etc. Pophole has never been excavated so that the original materials used in the construction of the bay – or for its later strengthening perhaps – cannot be commented on. Of the two sluices in the pond bay, the southernmost still has a stone channel indicating the position of a wheel. The northernmost sluice would have acted as a means of controlling the level of the water in the pond and a picture of it, taken from the east is shown below. A third watercourse would have allowed for a storm overflow.

The Northern sluice at Pophole

A number of methods were used to operate the action of the hammers but again nothing remains at Pophole to indicate the precise mechanism employed there. There were no pen (water storage) ponds upstream.

On the opposite page is a drawing of a typical hammer showing the wheel and the hammer which was raised and lowered by a cam shaft. Here, only one hammer and hearth is depicted but at Pophole, according to the eighteenth century Pitfold rate books, the description is always of hammers in the plural. If these entries were a statement of fact, they would have had implications for the layout of the forge building and its watercourses.

Local and Economic Background

The ore, or myne, in the Weald was recovered for the most part from near the top of the Weald clay, locally from the ferruginous greensand. During the water-powered period in the High Weald it came from the Hastings Beds and in particular, the Wadhurst clay. The ore was dug from pits about 2m. plus in diameter, usually dug close together. Filled in after extraction, the remains of these minepits are still visible locally especially after rain as shallow saucer-shaped, water-filled depressions.

The influx of French immigrant iron-workers in the early 1500s was initially into the eastern Weald, the new technology not reaching the western Weald until around the 1570s. Encouraged by the apparent profitability, many of the great landholders are found to be participating in the industry either by renting out to an independent entrepreneur a valley in which the stream could be dammed to form a pond, or by themselves building an ironworks and leasing out its management. Amongst these estate holders were the Montagues of Cowdray.

History of Pophole Hammer

The Start Up Years

The first mention of Pophole in connexion with iron working comes in the 1574 List. This list (of which there are other later ones) was an attempt by Elizabeth's Privy Council to exert some measure of control over the production and, more importantly, export to the (largely hostile) Continent of the ordnance being produced in the Wealden iron works. The Privy Council required owners and farmers of iron works to enter into bonds not to cast ordnance without special licence and then not to sell to foreigners without adhering to expressly defined conditions. There was a later list of 1588 but this only survives for Kent. For Surrey, it exists only in its preliminary form, is cursory and is probably a copy of the 1574 list. The Sussex list has not survived at all.

Sketch of Forge Hammer [taken from Straker]

Although in 1574 the appearance in the Channel of the Spanish Armada was fourteen years into the future, the threat from Spain was very real and war was being waged, albeit unofficially, between England and Spain, to wit Elizabeth's support for the rebellion in the Spanish Netherlands and for piratical expeditions in the Spanish Americas. In 1572, therefore, a Royal Proclamation was issued which attempted, as described above, to impose control over the production of ordnance.

The 1574 List included in the Introduction: 'a new Furnace sett up in Haselmere by my lord Montague which as yet hath never wrought and whether they shall blowe sowes for iron or ordinnance I knowe not'.

Later, in a list of iron works under Sussex appears: 'The Lord Montague 1 forge 1 furnace in Hasellmoore and thereaboutes, also a furnace called Pophall'

There are, therefore, questions relating to the hammer at Pophole: Was this the furnace which was not at that date operating? Was it ever a furnace? At what date did it start operating as a hammer which shortly after 1574 it was undoubtedly doing?

There are in all about twenty documents bearing in some way on Pophole, six of these relating to its early period. In none of these (except the List entry) is there the slightest hint that Pophole was ever anything but a hammer. Nonetheless, the important question remains that essentially a hammer was built to process iron from a furnace and there is no firm evidence to suggest where such a furnace might have been.

It is possible that the Montague furnace referred to in the 1574 List was at Imbhams or even Northpark. Straker suggested that Imbhams was built about 1570, and there is a letter from Anthony Viscount Montague to Mr More of Loseley in 1570 referring to the existence of Montague's clerk of the works who superintended his ironworks,[6] but Cleere & Crossley are of the opinion that the early Imbhams information is insufficiently certain to make it other than a probable, and the first definite evidence for the existence of Northpark does not appear until 1614.

The entry in the 1574 List indicates that somewhere Montague was building a new iron works, and there is in the Linchmere rolls an entry which seems to indicate that he might already have been planning or building a local iron works of some kind as early as 1567 (see below). There are other local ironworks such as Inholmes and Verdley but nothing is known about these, not even whether they had a Montague connexion. Evidence from the Lay Subsidy returns of this period which itemised alien iron-workers and which are discussed in more detail below, makes little contribution.

At Pophole Hammer an examination on the ground by Mr Jeremy Hodgkinson, Chairman of the Wealden Iron Research Group and Mrs Carla Barnes, author of a paper on the furnace at Northpark, Fernhurst,[7] revealed no traces of the typical detritus produced at a furnace – slag – which is clearly distinguishable from the cinder and hammer scale produced at a hammer.

It is quite possible that this return for Pophole in the 1574 List was an error. The returns for this area must have been carried out between 1572, the date of the Proclamation, and 1574 the official date of the returns. It is possible that if at that time work had only just begun on the construction of the pond and bay at Pophole, its ultimate use was not obvious. It is also possible, as Montague (Anthony Browne the first Viscount) according to Mrs Barnes, never appeared before the Privy Council to take his bond, that the returns for his iron works were never checked and an erroneous statement persisted. However, the ironworks were visited in February 1574 by Richard Pedley, the Privy Council messenger, so that the 1574 information should have been pretty well up to date and accurate.

According to Mr Jeremy Hodgkinson, who kindly ran his eye over the ironworks chapters, it can be safely concluded that an ironworks of some sort at Pophole was in existence at that date but the Jury is still out with regard to

124

the identity of the furnace.

Evidence regarding the date and function of Pophole in various early documents comes from the local parish registers, the rolls of Linchmere and Farnham manors, returns for the Lay Subsidies and the depositions given in a Tythe Dispute of 1598. These are as follows:

First, there is in the Linchmere manor rolls of 1610[8] an entry possibly referring to a Montague iron works prior to 1574 although, as is so often the case, the entry is not absolutely clear and no indication is given of the ironworks' whereabouts. In 1610, William Boxall had obviously carried out a wholesale tree-felling exercise on his copyhold of Stanley Farm without Lord Montague's permission. (The Boxalls held Stanley before it passed to the Butler family). Evidence was given in 1610 by Robert Luffe, keeper of the little North parke *'touching the wronge committed by William Boxall in woodes upon his Coppyhold land called Stanley...that in the time of Anthony late Viscount Montague grandfather of the now lord of this Mannor [someone – word omitted] did fell and Coale for his Iron works – divers Birches and Alders in the land called Stanley and that all the Alders and Birches were felled which did growe upon the land which was soe done about xliii yeeres sithence [since] and divers tymes sithence'*.

Robert Luffe gave his age as precisely 93 years and the date of this felling as precisely 43 years previously which would date it at 1567. Birches and alders were favoured woods for the production of charcoal and, if at the age of 93 years Luffe's evidence can be depended upon, it would suggest that on this scale charcoal was being produced for use at a furnace or forge which must have been not too far from Stanley as the distance charcoal was able to be transported without suffering degradation was fairly small – about 5–6 kms. Imbhams was six miles away as the crow flies, Pophole close and Northpark very close. It is, however, quite possible that the wood felled at Stanley was carried as cords of wood and coaled (charcoaled) on site.

Other entries in the Linchmere rolls show with certainty that ten years after the entry in the List, ie in 1584, the bay or dam at Pophole had been constructed and the pond had filled. In 1584, Thomas Payne who was probably the most important of Montague's tenants in Pitfold Manor received a reply from the Linchmere Manor Homage to his complaint about the maintenance of the pond. Thomas Payne somewhere about this time held the lease of Shottover Corn Mill[9] and also the copyhold of Pitfold Mill and the adjacent Lower Pitfold Farm and therefore would have had a strong interest in the use of the Wey upstream of Pophole, although Pitfold Mill was on small tributary of the Wey and Shottover Mill was supplied from a spring (Springhead) feeding the pond(s) from the south. The entry says:[10]

'It is ordered [by the Homage] here in [the Linchmere Manor] court at the request of Thomas Payne of Frensham [parish], that two impartial people, and two similar people chosen by the Lord of this manor should adequately repair the boundary covered by the water of Pophole Pond

between this manor and the manor of Farnham and Pytfold because the said boundary is not only the boundary between the holdings of the said manors, but also the border between the Counties of Sussex and Surrey. This is to be done whenever the pond should happen to be emptied.'

This entry does not specify the use of the pond. However, four years later, in 1588, a further entry in these rolls confirms that Pophole was working as a hammer. Thomas Person, the copyholder of Wattmans & Elliotts (Watts Farm) on which land the hammer stood, had presumably complained to the Linchmere Homage that he was unable to fulfil the obligations of his manorial tenancy in regard to the maintenance of his boundary hedge, which from descriptions elsewhere, ran immediately along the north bank of the Wey. The Homage replied (in English) that:[11]

'Whereas Thomas Peerson and his ancestors owners of his customary lands of this manor have been used in times past to keep the Sheere[Shire] Hedg that did divide Surrey & Sussex in the place where it is now overflowen by the hammer pond of Pophole by reason whereof he cannot mayntayne the Hedge aforeseyd as it hath been used Therfore it is orderyed heare in Shul[bred] Court that the seyd Thomas Person and his heyres shall mayntayne so much Hedge agaynest the uttermost parte and brymme of the water upon his owne Land as before was done and used in the place accustomed...'

In other words, he was to do the best he could where he could.

Evidence Provided by Some of the Early Iron-workers

Two additional approaches were made to obtain any pointers which might exist as to the start date of the hammer. These are first, the dates at which known iron-workers, particularly fyners or hammermen, were to be found in the area, and secondly, the dates at which members of iron-working families were found to be buying local properties, this information again from the early rolls of the manors of Linchmere and of Farnham, from the local parish registers and the Lay Subsidy returns.

The Denization Returns of the 1540s (the registration of aliens by Central Government) listed many individual iron workers in the eastern Weald and sometimes described the precise nature of their occupations. A comparison of these names with those appearing later locally have enabled some of the early iron workers to be identified.[12] A search was also made through early wills, ie those dating to the late 1500s, but it seems that the early iron workers either were not in the habit of making wills, or that they have not survived.

At this time information on 'the rural poor' is almost impossible to come by. Manor rolls which provide information on manorial tenants of land and property rarely concerned themselves with the occupiers of that land or property, so that only three iron-worker names appear in this context and of those only one is directly connected with Pophole hammer. However, the early dates at which they appear is of interest, as is also their subsequent history which shows that they settled in the area and in some cases continued to have a long association with the iron industry.

Fig.8 is a map of the farms and cottages which are associated with the local ironworkers who are mentioned below.

Prior to 1570, the only names which can be associated locally with iron-workers of alien extraction are Perigo and Larbie, with Pelhams, Bridays, Bardens, Jarletts/Garretts, Doogynes and Turkes and others appearing from 1570 on. Also there appears in 1577 in Linchmere the burial of one Thomas Pavye. In 1580 in the Sussex Coroners Inquests[13] there is an account of a fracas at Plaistow involving a number of iron workers, the result of which was that Charles Pavye, a fyner late of Northchapel, suffered a broken head and died shortly after from 'le styche' in his left side. Also present was another Pavye, a fyner known as Adrian Pavye alias Foye. Later members of this family, a John Pavey or Pavie alias Forie a blacksmith of Thursley parish (probably the Shottermill end) left a will in 1697, and another, by then Stephen Forey but still a Thursley parish blacksmith, purchased two small houses above the *Staff of Life* in Shottermill in 1835.

One of the first references in the Linchmere rolls was in 1571 when Charles Pelham was given the lease of 'Washers' for 7 years.[14] Washers was the small farm lying immediately to the east of Watts Farm and Pophole, where in the late 18th century New (paper) Mill was built. Its land ran south from the Wey across the Liphook Road and its farmhouse was on the site of the present Rats Castle. This arrangement seems not to have lasted for very long or may never have come to anything as in the following year, 1572, a new undertenant there was named. Charles Pelham had apparently built himself a cottage on the waste near Shottover Mill and in 1576 he was given the copyhold of this cottage and half an acre.[15] This cottage may have been the predecessor of or at any rate on or near the site of 'Ramblers'.

Charles Pelham died in 1580[16] and the above cottage passed according to the custom of the manor to his son and heir Blaise Pelham. Blaise being a minor, his mother Margaret was admitted to the property on his behalf and given a licence to sublet it for 7 years.[17] In 1602 Blaise sublet the cottage for a further period[18] and the Pelham family thereafter disappears from the records. Members of the Pelham family were well-known iron masters in East Sussex from the middle 1500s, but the significance of the presence of Charles in Shottermill is not known.

The new undertenant at Washers in 1572 was James Barden who is described in the rolls entry as a hammerman.[19] Bardens were connected with the iron industry in East Sussex from the early 1500s, at times working for the Pelhams. In 1551 and 1552 a Bardyn was at the Dunsfold Burningfold forge and it is probable that they had a long history as hammermen.
The Bardens are the only family with a member mentioned directly as working at Pophole at this early date, see the Tythe Dispute of 1598 below.

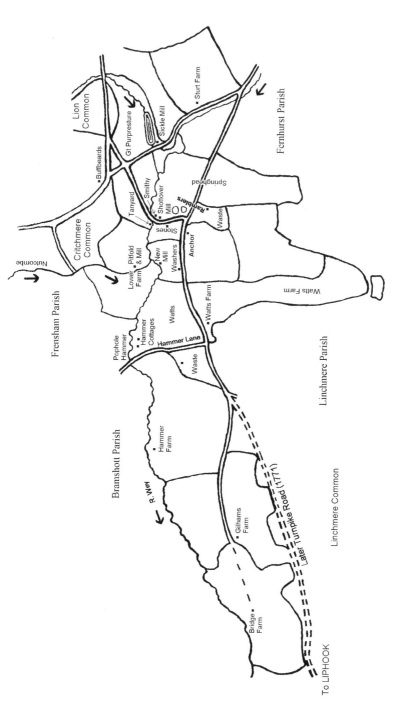

Fig.8: Properties near Shottermill associated with the Iron Industry

Ironworker families: at Bridge, Covers & Shotters; at Hammer Farm, Quennells; on Waste, Bridays Hatch Cottage; at Watts, Persons & Shotters; at Washers, Pelhams & Bardens; at Lower Pitfold Farm, Paynes, Bardens, Shotters; at

This was Charles Barden who is first heard of in 1586 in the Linchmere parish register when he married Alic Bettsworth. In 1599 he is shown in the manor of Farnham Rolls as having bought the smaller part of Rose Cottage (opposite Shottover Mill) which for much of its history was regarded as two cottages each with a separate descent of ownership.[20] Charles Barden died in 1632 but his widow Agnes [sic. see Alic above] held the property until 1640 when she also died and her son John sold it to Robert Heyward who was a bellows maker.[21] Robert Heyward was possibly of alien extraction.

Another Barden mentioned was William, also a hammerman, who in 1600 was widowed and in the same year re-married in Linchmere the widow Margery Colpas. With Margery Colpas, William the hammerman acquired a cottage lately erected on the waste near the cemetery of Linchmere Church, rent 2 fat capons.[22] He was dead by 1609 but not before he had had to rebuild his cottage which had been destroyed by fire, a not uncommon occurrence. It is possible he had come to Linchmere from Northchapel (see below).

The Bardens were one of the families who obviously prospered within the local iron industry. In connexion with property deals concerning Wakeners and Courts Hill, Roger Barden born 1597, son of the above Charles, is described in 1624 and 1630 respectively as Iron Founder of Linchmore (parish) and as yeoman of Pitfold.[23] In 1631 he purchased Pitfold Mill and Pitfold Farm (ie Lower Pitfold Farm adjacent the Mill) on a £424 mortgage, and held them for ten years.[24] The 1624 description of him as a founder suggests that he may have been concerned primarily at that date with the furnace at Northpark. The move to Pitfold, plus the record of the death of a Samuel Barden at Sturt Hammer (later Sickle Mill) in 1624[25] suggests he may have had an interest there also.

The last two references to members of the Barden family – also in the Pitfold area – shows some of them at least to have turned farmer. In 1629 Phillipp Barden the Elder was in possession of what is now Cherrimans (a house and ten acres) and by 1655 had purchased Sturt Farm (the precise date is unknown owing to a gap in the manor of Farnham records during the Civil War and Interregnum) when he is described as yeoman.[26] He was also Churchwarden of Linchmere Parish in 1631. Bought on a mortgage, the purchase of Sturt Farm seems to have represented the peak of the Bardens' fortunes. His son, Phillipp the Younger, was obviously not able to keep up the payments on this mortgage and forfeited Sturt Farm. After this, no more of relevance is heard of this family in the area.

The third family of interest is the Brydays. Blaise Bryday, a known fyner (he was a fyner at Worth in the 1560s) is found in the Linchmere registers baptizing children from 1570 on. No direct connexion can be made between Blaise himself and Pophole, but it is strongly suggested that there was one. In 1573, Blaise Bryday was admitted to a farm in Northchapel called Jakfyshers (now Fisherstreet Farm) in the parish of Petworth. It came to him by the surrender of Elizabeth Launder who was sister and heir of Thomas

Holloway.[27]   Bryday immediately sold this farm to one of the Mellershe family.[28] As, according to the custom of the manor (and this farm was an outlier of the manor of Linchmere and Shulbrede) copyholds descended to kin, it is tempting to speculate that Blaise Bryday had lived previously in the Northchapel area where there were other iron works before moving to Linchmere and had, perhaps, married a Northchapel lady. Unfortunately, the Northchapel parish records are so mutilated at this early date as to make confirmation of this impossible.

In 1584 Blaise Bryday purchased the messuage and 8 acres called Stanes which is opposite Shottover Mill and is now occupied by the Mill Tavern.[29] This house and land the Brydays held until 1648, first Blaise himself, then his son John and finally John's son Charles. Again Blaise applied for licences to sublet during much of the period of his ownership, ie until his death in 1610,[30] and there is also evidence to suggest he may have built the smithy between Shottover Mill and the river.[31] In the Farnham rolls there is record of a further purchase. Sometime around 1580 he appears to have bought the land known as Buffbeards Farm (the records here are not entirely clear) but he is seen to have a licence to sublet it for 10 years in 1594[32] and to have sold it in 1598.[33] The Buffbeards farmhouse is near Holy Cross Hospital.

His death is recorded in the Linchmere parish register in 1610. Like the Bardens, if not more so, the Brydays were a family the members of which under several variations such as Blaze and Breda are to be found in neighbouring parish registers for the next 250 years or so, often connected with some aspect of the iron industry. One of Blaise's sons and a grandson are found in Chichester in 1652, both blacksmiths, transferring from Briday the Elder to the Younger a ¼ acre outside the East Gate,[34] and in the Rev. T.S. Cooper's 'History of Chiddingfold' there is mention of two Brydays blacksmithing there in the 1800s. Blaise's grandson, Charles, (referred to above) in the middle 1670s seems to have had a possible connexion with the hammer at Sickle when he paid rents to the Tamplins for land near Sickle Mill,[35] and his will of 1703 describes him as a hammerman.[36]

Blaise's son Samuel, born 1573, was almost certainly a worker at Pophole hammer. Having married Elizabeth Farnden in 1600[37] and presumably wishing to set up a home of his own, he encroached on two small pieces of land, one on the waste near the hammer. In 1600 he was granted the copyhold which included a cottage he had built there, this property being described as 'near Le Hammer Lane'.[38] This track which was obviously an ancient right of way through Pophole Hatch which connected three counties and manors, thus received at this early date the name by which it is still known today. Samuel's rent was 2 fat capons to be paid at Cowdray. The waste in Hammer Lane was on its western side so this cottage might well have been on the site of the present cottage known as Old [Pophole] Hatch Cottage.

After Samuel's death, the copyhold passed to his son Thomas who held it for the term of his life. After this second entry in 1648[39] nothing more is heard of this cottage until it reappears in the early 1800s as a Montague leasehold, the most probable explanation for this being that Montague took it back into his own hands and used it as one of the houses set aside for the workers at the hammer (see further below). In 1670 when Thomas is buried, he is described as living in Pitfold.

A last family of interest is that of Turke alias Tamplin, originally two separate alien families. It is not known what connexion, if any, that they had with Pophole, but they appear in the Linchmere parish register from 1608 to 1659 and also in the early Bramshott registers, and it is possible that they were working at the hammer at Sickle Mill from the middle 1660s when they move to Pitfold and encroach on and then purchase various plots of land close to Sickle Mill. Certainly one of them – John Tourke – had been working at Brookland Furnace at Wadhurst in 1534.

The purchase of local properties by members of the ironworker families as against merely becoming occupiers suggests that the fyners and hammermen at least, the skilled core, were by this date men with some money behind them and certainly more than casual labourers. They would certainly have needed access to land and its produce, but not necessarily as owners.

For some time at least until their skills became disseminated amongst the local inhabitants, there is evidence to suggest that their wages were considerably higher than those paid to the ordinary labourer. In the middle 1500s labourers' wages – around 6d to 8d a day – were about half those paid to skilled iron workers.[40] It also suggests that the three cottages at the hammer were in fact where the core workforce lived.

They seemed initially to marry within their own community but some at least prospered more than most. Thomas Jarlett who inherited but immediately sold 'Ramblers' in 1663, (if the same) married in 1667 Jane the heir of Edward Fauchin a wealthy Farnham man, and with her came into a good deal of property.[41] An earlier Jarrett had been a noted iron founder and at one time had been member of a partnership running a furnace in the Battle area.[42]

In 1640, when the Oath of Protestation was taken, the returns for the parish of Linchmere seem to show that the percentage of those with iron-worker names who were literate and could sign their names was greater than the average, although this standard did not appear to be maintained.

Whilst in many cases it is not possible to associate these various iron-workers firmly with any specific works, it is suggested that – at least until the end of the 1600s – members of the Briday, Hoad and Barden families were all closely associated with the hammers at Pophole and Sickle Mill. All three, and also the Tamplins, had intermarried, in particular the Bridays and (sickle-maker) Hoads. Briday (Breda) wills of 1696 and 1703 refer to a host of Hoad-married sisters, cousins and nephews. The Bridays in particular (var. Breda and Blaze) are to be found in practically all the neighbouring parishes where, if not directly involved at hammers, they are associated with the iron industry as white- or blacksmiths.

In the 1660s in the Hearth Tax returns for Pitfold and Linchmere, there are entries for members of the Briday, Hoad, Jarlett and Larby families, the Bridays having four houses of 1 or 2 hearths and Robert Larby one of 1 hearth. The Hoads were of course at Sickle Mill House. The Garletts (Jarletts) who are referred to as working at 'ye hammer' in the 1630s have at this date three entries in Linchmere for houses with 4, 3 and 2 hearths respectively.

Evidence from the Lay Subsidies

Another source of information relating to these early iron workers are the returns of the middle/late Elizabethan lay subsidies – a tax on the laity levied by the Crown at irregular intervals usually in response to some specific financial requirement. In these returns at this early date the French workers were usually identified as 'aliens'.

The Surrey returns contain no names relevant to Pophole, although one of the Larbie clan – Orbery [Aubrey?] – is to be found at Abinger in 1571 possibly working at the early hammer there, and another, or possibly the same heavily disguised as 'Wooberie alias Larbie' is found in 1593 at Cranleigh where the Vachery forge had been operating.

The Sussex returns were equally disappointing in relation to Linchmere and Fernhurst, only one document for 1570/71 providing any information. Of the other two, for the years 1600 and 1610, in the one case apart from the heading and one name the rest of the document was missing, and in the other the Linchmere entries had faded into oblivion. In the returns for 1570/71[43] only one alien is shown in Linchmere parish 'Blasse an alyen – iiiid'. No aliens at all were listed under Fernhurst. For Northchapel in a list headed by Thomas Blackwell (an iron industry family) two aliens were listed – Charles Payve and Nicholas Mores. Under Dydlesfold William Barden (see above) paid viiid for himself and a female, presumably his wife. Diddlesfold was not a parish and the assumption has been made that Barden also should be associated with Northchapel. In 1600, the single name shown under Lynchmere inevitably was that of 'Blaise Bridaie alien for land...'. There were no aliens listed in Fernhurst in either 1600 or 1610. Other local families such as the Lamberts, Jellys and Harmans may find their antecedents among the early iron-workers.

The Tythe Dispute 1598

The last document relating to the early years of the ironworks at Pophole is the Tythe Dispute of June 1598.[44] This dispute which was ex parte Stephen Terry (farmer of the Linchmere Tythes) versus Roger Shotter and Edward Tanner, concerned the tythes payable by the iron works, and also by Shelbrede [Priory] Farm which was occupied by Roger Shotter but which had never paid tythes, being ecclesiastical property prior to the Dissolution.

132

The evidence was concerned to show, amongst other things, in which parish or parishes the ironworks lay, what tythes it had paid to Linchmere parish, how long it had been there and who had been the occupiers. The deponents were four local men of standing, Roger Quennell of Pophole Farm, Nicholas Cover of Bridge Farm, Thomas Ireland of Watts Farm and John Bennett who had had the cure of Linchmere parish for ten years.

On looking at the depositions which vary in quality and detail, it is immediately obvious that nowhere is there the slightest hint that the 'yron worke' at Pophole had ever been other than a hammer. Asked to state how long it was since the hammer had been built, Roger Quennell and Nicholas Cover both said about twenty years. On the other hand, John Bennett, who as the incumbent of Linchmere parish must have had a close interest in the outcome of the dispute, deposed that it had been set up about 26 years ago. Thomas Ireland, who was the then under-tenant of Watts Farm, ie the actual worker of the land on which the hammer had been built and was operating, said that he had dwelled in Linchmere for 25 years and occupied land there, and gave a start date of about thirty years ago. Depending on whether these dates referred to the start of construction at Pophole or to the start of operations, the conclusion is that there was some activity there in the 1570s. Ireland also gave evidence that he knew iron had been wrought and forged there but had no knowledge of amounts or value.

Fig.7 shows details of the site of the hammer, pond and the Hammer Cottages – now Bridge Cottage and Marshlands.

The location of the hammer pond was given as being half in Sussex and half in Surrey, in the parishes of Linchmere and Frensham respectively. It was, of course, the fact that Montague owned the land on both sides of the Wey at this point that governed its location. Ireland deposed that the 'part of the pond ... put to the use of the same hammer which do ly within the parishe of Lynchmere [is] comonly ... taken to conteyn ii acres & a half'. Bennett said that the area 'broght into the pond with some other land thereto adioyning & being as yt were hindered by the waters & helpful to the yron work & lying within the parishe of Lynchmere ... conteyns in all iiii acres' with other land put into the pond being within the parish of Frensham.

The only maps showing the area of the works in any detail is the considerably later Tythe Map and also the map drawn by Mellersh immediately prior to the building of the railway line in the 1850s by which time, however, the bay had been breached and the pond dry for many years so that information regarding the pond's original extent is non existent.[45] At a rough guess the pond, which cannot have extended upstream beyond the boundary of Pitfold manor (at the western end of what is now the Shottermill Sunvale cemetery, about 350 yards upstream of the works) probably covered about two acres, certainly not more. Compared with the extent of some other hammer and furnace ponds, it was very small. Ireland related that a 'bound' was placed at the pond head to show – in the absence of the shire hedge now destroyed by the waters of the pond – the boundary of Surrey and Sussex.

Both Cover and Ireland refer to the 'hous' at the ironworks but not making clear what this was. Ruined stone walling can still be seen immediately downstream of the bay on the south side but the present level of the ground at this point has been raised above its original level. Bennett deposed that the main part of the works was on the Linchmere side and that the hammer block stood 'in the place of the very dividing [of] the parishe of Lynchmere & the parishe of Frynsham'. Since this date the boundaries have been altered so that the site of the actual hammer now lies within the County of Hampshire. Bennett also usefully included the information that there were two fyners at Pophole which, as Mr Jeremy Hodgkinson commented, suggests that there may indeed have been two finery hearths there.

Fortunately, there is general agreement between the deponents about some of the past occupiers and the dates of their occupancy of the hammer. Unfortunately, their information does not include the period before 1586. It is agreed that the present occupier (1598) is Edward Tanner who is the receiver of the profits of the hammer and who, according to Bennett, dwells in the parish of Tillington near Petworth.

Up to twelve months previously Tanner had had a partner, one Thomas Amy, but Tanner had lost his partner a year ago and now held the hammer on his own. Tanner and Amy had been partners for five years. Ireland then deposed that eight years ago, for a period of four years before that, the previous occupiers had been Old and Young Fawkener and that Charles Barden (referred to above) had been hammerman to one of these. Cover deposed that Edward Tanner who had the iron work of the late Lord Montague (Anthony, Visc. Montague, died 1592) had been joined therein by one of Lurgashall whose name, unfortunately, he could not remember. Whether he meant Amy or someone else entirely is not known. Members of an Amy family are found in the Lay Subsidies to be paying taxes at Shere and Abinger 1622–42 when Abinger Forge was active.

The remaining information contained in the Tythe Dispute concerns the amount of tythe payable by the hammer. All the deponents were in agreement that this annual sum was 40s, agreed between the farmer of the tythes and Lord Montague's officers for as long as Lord Montague's ironworks should stand there. Payment of tythes was universally detested and disputes were fierce and frequent throughout the long life of this system. It is therefore not surprising to find, according to Bennett, that Charles Barden had offered on one occasion to pay only 10s. and even less surprising to find that this offer had been refused. Of more interest is Bennett's statement that in 1595 Edward Tanner had denied payment of the 40s. altogether. Without further information it is difficult to interpret this denial unless at this date Tanner was finding his profits from the hammer less than he had anticipated.

There is no information about what the arrangement with Lord Montague had been, of what quality or experience these occupiers were, nor who had supplied the original capital finance. Some members of a Fawkener family are connected earlier with the iron industry at Maresfield and Worth both areas connected with the names of Barden and Bryday, and between 1622–42 there is a Fawkener family paying taxes in Cranleigh although there is no evidence that the ironworks at Vachery were operating during this period.

If the depositions that Tanner took the profits from the hammer are correct, the implication is that he held a lease from Montague, himself taking the financial risks. Also, it may be that Tanner was connected in the early 1600s with the building of the nearby Wheeler's hammer (see further under Sickle Mill). There is nothing in Cleere & Crossley to connect any Tanner with the iron industry and, unfortunately, the name of Tanner is quite common locally. All that is known about Edward Tanner is that he dwelled in Tillington.

The Workforce

The above Tythe Dispute has indicated that there were two fyners and a hammerman at Pophole. These workers would have constituted the normal core of the skilled craftsmen there, but there would have been others, probably unskilled, to cope with the maintenance and mechanical and handling requirements. The pond for example, as was common, would have required de-silting at regular and fairly frequent intervals. (In the mid 19th century James Simmons needed nine men and boys over two days to de-mud New Mill pond which was very small). The wheel and bellows would have required maintenance and possibly the bay strengthening from time to time. The regular labour force would not have been very large, certainly not as large as that at a furnace where the number of operations was greater and more diverse, although if the peripheral workforce concerned with the supplies and carriage of the necessary raw materials and product is taken into account, this would of course be greatly increased.

There would also have been apprentices. There exists a John Perigo will of 1584.[46] Perigo was briefly an early local iron-worker name, but this will emanates from a site near Horsham where Perigo was a hammerman working at Nuthurst for Steven Frenche. He left to his prentiss Thomas Frances 20s over and above the wages afore bargaynd if he serve out his tyme, and to his prentiss Peter 10s at the end of his yeres. Unfortunately, no idea of their basic wage is given. John Perigo also left £30 to his daughters, and a cow, sword and bow and arrows to his siblings.

There would probably have been along the south side of the hammer a number of shacks and hovels, one at least for storage and possibly sorting of the charcoal, soggy or over-dusty charcoal being of little use to anyone. There might also have been hovels for the casual workmen.

The owner of Marshlands, one of the workers' cottages to the immediate south of the hammer, had occasion in early 1997 to dig down a few feet on the south bank of the stream and came across what appeared to be a reinforced surface. Bearing in mind that along this stretch of the bank there would have been heavy traffic with waggons bringing and taking away iron and charcoal etc, this is not surprising. The problems associated with carriage and transport on the Wealden clay are too well known to require further comment. Further remarks on the organisation of the carriage of supplies for the hammer can be found below with the comments on the 1683 accounts

Various operations at and relating to the hammer were seasonal. Wood cutting was carried out during the winter and early spring and charcoal burning seems to have continued throughout the year, whilst the ore was mined during the summer when the land was drier. Carriage was also a summer activity for the same reason. Work at a forge, essentially discontinuous, probably took place as and when convenient according to weather and demand and mostly during the winter, leaving appropriate parts of the year for work on the land which was always necessary.

Fortunately for Pophole, fed as it was by water which percolated gradually from the surrounding greensand, although itself on the clay, the supply of water power – even in the absence of additional pen ponds – may not have been too much of a problem. Any sort of mill required above all a flow of water which was constant without too much seasonal variation.

Pophole in the Seventeenth Century

The Formal Surrender to Lord Montague

After the above 1598 evidence, nothing further is heard of the hammer until 1610, although in 1609 Thomas Person of Watts Farm was reprimanded by the manor for 'lopping' his trees (probably for charcoaling).[47] In 1610 there are three entries in the Linchmere manor rolls concerning the Person family holding of Linchmeres Wattmans & Elliots (Watts Farm) on which the hammer stood.[48] Summarized here, these entries are given in full below. In the first entry it is presented that – out of court – Thomas Person had surrendered his customary land of Linchmeres Wattmans & Elliotts to the Lord of the Manor with the intention that this should be regranted to Roger Shotter senior of Shulbrede. This has been done and Roger Shotter admitted but, unusually, without him being required to pay the fees normal for such a transaction.

The second entry describes Roger Shotter's formal surrender of Linchmeres Wattmans & Elliotts to his sons William and Roger but states explicitly that this property transfer excluded all the land on which 'the house and all the iron mill (in English, the Iron Hammer Worke) commonly called Pophole Hammer now stands, and excepting 3 cottages parcel of the said virgate of land where the workmen of the said iron mill ... live, and lastly excepting certain lands now covered with the waters of a pond of the said iron works ... containing by estimation 6 a[cres]'. Again the fees are pardoned.

The last entry covers the surrender by Roger Shotter of Shulbrede to Montague himself, of the above described Iron Hammer Work, the pond, the houses and the 6 acres 'so that he [Montague] can do whatsoever he wishes with it, at his own will'. In return for this, Montague granted for himself and his heirs to Roger Shotter and his heirs in perpetuity a yearly payment of £3 13s 4d.

In the first two entries it is recorded that Montague pardoned the fees because he was 'extra specially moved' for this occasion. This expression (not met with elsewhere in the rolls) and the three consecutive entries, suggests that this was the formal record of an arrangement which may have been in process of negotiation for some time previously. No financial details are given other than the annuity.

1610 Court Entries in full

Presented that Thomas Person surrendered to the Lord of the Manor out of court, since the last court, by the acceptance of Thomas Cover and William Person, two of the customary tenants of the manor, a messuage and virgate of land in Linchmere called Linchmeres Wattmans and Elliotts with appurtenances, with this intention, that the Lord should regrant the property with appurtenances to Roger Shotter of Shulbrede and the heirs of the said Roger. As a result of which the Lord is owed a heriot as appears afterwards with a fine. And now the said Roger comes to this court and asks to be admitted to the property aforesaid with appurtenances. The Lord, through his seneschal grants him the property to have and to hold to the said Roger and his heirs at the Lord's will according to the custom of the manor aforesaid for an annual rent of 10s. suit of court, and other services owed for it and by the usual rights. And he gave to the Lord nothing, either fine or herriot for this transaction because the Lord, being extra specially moved for this occasion pardoned the fine and the herriot. He was therefore admitted tenant and was given seisin by the rod and did fealty to the Lord.

To this court came Roger Shotter and surrendered into the hands of the Lord of the Manor a messuage and virgate of land in Linchmere called Linchmere Wattmans and Elliotts; excepting the house and all the land on which the iron house (in English, the Iron Hammer Worke) commonly called Pophole Hammer now stands, and excepting 3 cottages parcel of the said virgate of land where the workmen of the said iron house, (in English called the Iron Hammer Worke) live, and lastly excepting certain lands now covered with the water of a pond of the said iron house, (in English called the Iron Hammer Worke) containing by estimation 6 a[cres] land, previously surrendered at this court by the said Roger Shotter to the use of the Lord of the Manor and his heirs, which were all part of the said messuage and virgate of land. The surrender was with the intention that the Lord through his seneschal should regrant the property, except as excepted above, to William and Roger Shotter sons of the said Roger, and to the heirs of Roger the son, to hold at the Lord's will according to the custom of the Manor. The Lord, through his seneschal, granted him the property to have and to hold the said property (except as excepted) to the said William and Roger and the heirs of the said Roger the son for an annual rent of 10s. and other services previously owed, and by the usual rights [repeats pardon of herriot and fine]. They were therefore admitted tenants and had seisin by the rod and the said William did fealty to the Lord.

To this court came Roger Shotter and surrendered into the hands of the Lord of the Manor the house and all that land on which the house aforesaid (called in English the Iron Hammer Worke) now stands and three cottages and certain land now covered with the water of a pond for the said house (called in English the Iron Hammer Worke) containing by estimation 6 ac. land all of which premises were part of a messuage and virgate of land formerly Thomas Persons; to the only and proper use of the said Lord of the Manor and his heirs and assigns, so that he can doe whatsoever he wishes with it, at his own will. In consideration of this, the Lord of the Manor grants for himself and his heirs to the said Roger Shotter and his heirs and assigns a yearly payment of £3. 13s. 4d. to the said Roger Shotter and his heirs and assigns as tenants living on the said virgate of land. The money is to be paid in equal portion, at two times in the year, viz. at Michaelmas and the Annunciation viz; 36s.8d. at each of these feasts yearly.

Whatever the previous relationship had been between Montague and the early occupiers of the hammer, the 1610 entries suggest a new arrangement, and one explanation is that it had a connexion with the building of the furnace at Northpark, whereby Montague would have had an integrated unit of furnace and forge under common management. The furnace at Northpark was built on the Linchmere manor land of Hatch Hill which, with the adjacent lands of Parrys & Hurlands, was held by another branch of the Shotters – the William/Robert Shotters of Highbuilding.

The entry in the Linchmere rolls relating to Northpark does not appear until four years later, in 1614,[49] but it can be read to indicate that Montague and Sir Thomas Gray, (Montague's sister Mary had married the late Lord John Gray), had already completed the building of the furnace there. A similar compensatory agreement was drawn up or formalised with the Northpark Shotters in 1626 whereby they received 6d for every load of myne (ore) dug there, together with an assurance that the myne pits would be filled in and as little damage done to the surrounding land as possible.[50] The siting of furnaces and forges were rarely close or on the same stream owing to water requirements.

One of the problems associated with the start up of Pophole and the first forty years of its operation is, of course, that the source of the iron it processed is unknown and by 1614, the furnace at Imbhams, whatever any

138

earlier Montague connexion, seems to have reverted into the hands of the Quennell family some time previously. In the Haslemere parish register in 1607 is a reference to the baptism of a child at Mr Robert Quynnel's furnace in Chiddingfold [parish] and also in 1609 record of the burial of John [Blank] at Mr Quennells furnace. On the other hand, there is evidence in Cleere & Crossley that pig iron could come from quite a distance.

The Shotter Association with Iron-Working

The known association of the Shotters with iron-working sites has led to the suggestion that they were iron masters. This term has in effect two meanings, first, those who supplied the necessary finance (and this could be considerable) and, second, the day to day managers – but the Shotters do not fit easily into either of these categories.

Certainly in 1574 they had no connexion with Pophole and in 1614 their connexion with the ironworks at Northpark is clearly only that of the manorial tenant of the land utilised. The landlord/tenant arrangement whereby people were able to live off their rents had by this date long become an established system and this seems to have been main source of Shotter income. Certainly as far as the copyholds held by the Pitfold Shotters are concerned, for example Watts Farm, Pitfold Mill, Pitfold Farm and other properties in the manor of Farnham, it is quite clear that the local holdings at least were rented out for the whole period of the Shotter manorial tenancy up to 1781.

There is no real evidence for any connexion of the Shotters with the iron industry other than their participation, along with most other local yeomen, in such casual commercial opportunities as the industry presented. Roger Shotter of Pitfold who was manorial tenant of Watts Farm is, for example, referred to in the 1659 and 1683 accounts discussed below as taking supplies of cords of wood for delivery to William Yalden lessee of Lurgashall park, and as carrying iron from Pophole.

The Hammer Cottages

Entries in the Linchmere rolls in 1610, and when William Shotter died in 1620[51] refer to the three cottages on the hammer land which were where the workers at the hammer lived. In 1988 Audrey Sutton of the Petersfield Area Historical Society's Building Study Group surveyed the two listed cottages which now remain. A summary of her report is given below.

'Bridge Cottage' and 'Marshlands': 'Both these listed cottages are of 16th century origin. Their basic structures are that of a Tudor frame house to which additions have been made over the centuries. It is possible that Bridge Cottage (the most westerly) was a high quality open hall house of the 15th or 16th century, with three bays. The use of fairly substantial close studding indicates a quite high quality building. The many internal beams had been utilised prior to the cottages' construction and it is suggested that the timbers

are from a previously demolished building. Both cottages have unusual curved inglenook fireplaces, suggesting construction by the same builder. Extensions have been added to both cottages, possibly during the 18th century. In 1980, having become dilapidated, they were extensively renovated and modernised and, although these cottages were never a pair, a funnel-like chimney which joined them was removed.'

The above report has promoted the thought that 'Bridge Cottage' may in fact have been the original messuage or farmhouse of Watts Farm. According to the Linchmere rolls and the 1536 Ministers Account, there was at least one building there in 1533.[52] With the surrender of this area for hammer use, Watts Farm might well have been deprived of its original farmhouse, necessitating the building of a new one. The later Watts farmhouse (now Dexam International, with its name changed to Watchers) just south of the Liphook road has in its cellar a beam inscribed with an early 1600s date and might be this replacement, although in view of the strict requirements prescribed by the manor that all structural timber should be re-used wherever possible, this dated beam is, of course, not proof of anything.

Hammer Cottages in 1876

Better proof is found in the fact that 'Watchers' is one of the very few farmhouses which was not described as decayed or falling down in the period from the late 1500s to the middle 1600s, indicating that it may have been built later than most. Certainly, although it is not known whether it was ever lived in by the Shotters before they built the so-called manor house at Pitfold, Watchers is of a superior quality similar to other Shotter houses in the local area. Although the three cottages at the hammer are not referred to until 1610, it is probable that they housed the hammer workmen from the startup of Pophole. For the later history of these cottages, see further below.

Cleere & Crossley show that both furnaces and forges had lives varying considerably in length and fortune. They should, in effect, be regarded in the light of small businesses and subject to all the usual pressures such as fluctuations in supply and demand in times of war and peace, accidents, lack of available skill, bankruptcies, foreign competition and rises in the cost of raw materials. It would seem, however, that Pophole may have been working for much of the 1600s, although possibly not continuously. References to the working of Northpark furnace in the parish registers can be found only between 1631 and 1637, and it is described as ruined in 1664.[53]

Pophole appears on most of the seventeenth century maps, for example:

1595   Norden's Surrey as 'Pophall' and his Sussex as 'Pophole'.

1610   Speed's Surrey as 'Pophole' and his Sussex as 'Pophall'.

1646   Joan Jannsson's Sussex as 'Pophall'.

1648   Johann Blaeu shows Pophole.

There are also a number of entries in the Linchmere parish registers to people from 'ye hammer'. It is, unfortunately, not always clear as to which hammer was being referred to in some of the following entries. Wheeler's Hammer (later Sturt Hammer and then Sickle Mill) was also operating during the early 1600s. Some entries, however, are specific to Pophole:

1626   bur. William Alwinn a vagrant who died at Pophole Hammer.

1633   bap Ann dau. of Thomas Hoare at Pophall Hammer.

1662   bap Margret and Jane daus of John Kilsham of Pophole Hammer.

Other Linchmere parish register entries refer only to 'ye hammer':

1599   bur. Alce Osmande the dau of a pore traviller wch was drownde at the brok at the Hammer.

1631   bap. and bur. Elizabeth dau of Thomas Hoad at ye hammer.

1631   bur. Joahne wife of William Jarlott at ye Hammer.

1632   bap. Thos son of Thomas Jarlott at ye Hammer.

1636   bap. William son of Thomas Jarlott at ye Hammer.

1637   bap. Thomas son of Thomas Hoade at ye Hammer.

1637   bur. George Richardson at ye Hammer.

There are also references to known iron-worker names without any reference to their place of work such as:

1604   bur. Nicholas Olde als Marian (previously of Maresfield Forge in 1576) that was slayn. He was stabbed to death by William Coggyn, glazier of Kirdford, who was hanged.[54]

Thomas Hoade the Elder (1637 above) described as a Lynchmore fyner in 1640[55] was probably the brother of John Hoad the Elder who bought Sturt Hammer in 1649, but the Hoad connexion at this date could have been with either hammer. Thomas Hoad's will of 1645 in which he describes himself as a fyner shows him to have been a man of only modest means, but contains no information as to his place of work. He leaves 40s apiece to each of his two daughters along with a cubbord, table, chair and chest valued in all at 26s; to his son Thomas 40s and his wearing apparel valued at 21/6d and the remainder of his estate to his wife Rose who, unusually, was literate.[56]

In connexion with the suggestion that in the early 1600s Northpark furnace and Pophole Hammer were run under one management, the comparatively short working life of Northpark furnace (to 1664 at latest) seems curious. It may be, however, since the Montague estates were sequestrated and occupied by the Parliamentary forces for much of the Civil War and Interregnum, that the furnace was dismantled at this time, as was Imbhams furnace.

Seventeenth Century Accounts

One of the only two surviving scraps of accounts which mentions Pophole is dated 1659.[57] This acknowledges receipt in full from William Yalden Esquire in March 1659 *'of his halfe yeares Rent for the Iron Works; the wood; popholl pond, Breday's house & land, the some off fortie pounds'* [£40].

Breday's or Bryday's house and land may well have been that referred to above as being in Hammer Lane and which is now included as an extra house chargeable to the hammer works, the three cottages actually on the site being included in the overall rent. William Yalden the Elder, of Blackdown (1578–1659) was steward to Viscount Montague and had the lease of Northpark and probably also the furnace there.

In 1653 and 1664 there are two further Lists, in both of which Pophole is recorded as a working forge.

The seventeenth century was politically disturbed to say the least. Although James I made peace with Spain in 1604, mercantile war continued in Africa and the East Indies with the Portuguese and later the Dutch, and finally with France. After Marlborough's victories, peace was made at the Treaty of Utrecht in 1713 and a period of relative stability was ushered in. Also, of course, there was the Civil War in England itself in the 1640s, but the local area did not see very much in the way of military activity. It is not surprising therefore that the production of ordnance versus pig iron fluctuated.

In general, however, prior to the end of the second Dutch War in 1667 forges and furnaces had been closely connected under common management and there had always been an active market in pig iron. After the middle 1600s there was a shift to the production at furnaces of moulded objects (for example firebacks), and forges faced increased competition from foreign bar and also bar from the English Midlands. The number of forges and their output decreased. Pophole, however, seems to have survived. In 1675, Aubrey in his 'Natural History and Antiquities of the County of Surrey' simply says without any further detail that Viscount Montague had a Hammer at Pope's Hole in Frensham, meaning the parish.

In 1683 a second Cowdray account[58] survives entitled: 'A booke of what Moneys is Disburst uppon Carage to the Hammor at Pophole in the yeare 1683 & 1684' (includes to 1686).

These accounts contain a number of points of interest. Many names are quoted of the local yeomen who were involved in the carriage of iron to Pophole, some of this iron being sows and some 'old iron'. Many of the local furnaces have no information to show that they were still working. Northpark was described as ruined in 1664, although the names of many of the carriers referred to in these accounts are those of landholders in the area of Northpark. From the entries in these accounts alluding to carriage of iron by water along the south coast, eg from Portsmouth to Littlehampton and by water to Stopham, it would seem that Pophole was having to get at least some of its pig iron from some distance away.

The payment to Mr Roker of £1.10s. for carriage of 3 tons of *old* iron from Guildford to the hammer is also of interest. Ponsonby says that 'In the claybed of the brick fields close by [Pophole] cannon balls have been dug up and part of a heavy cannon'. It was not unknown at this time for waste iron as well as pig, if of an inferior quality, to be converted at forges into bar iron so that it is possible that the items referred to above might constitute such waste iron never utilised. Loads of coale (charcoal) are also itemised as being carried to the hammer.

Most of the carriers named are local yeomen and one of these was Roger Shotter of Pitfold. In his will of 1689[59] he leaves to a younger son, William, 'all my iron at Pophole'. (William and John, the two younger sons were left land in the Tything of Frensham. This iron bequest was a minor matter).[60] It is probable that if he made a regular practice of ferrying goods to and from Pophole, it was this sort of iron to which he was referring. Some of the tonnages referred to were extremely large, for example Henry Cooper was paid £24 for the carriage of 43 tons of sows, and Henry Mansfield over £30 for the carriage of 68 tons of sows. At 1 ton load per waggon, this hints perhaps at contracts for carriage of iron over a season with payment annually. This arrangement suited both sides of the operation. It saved the hammer from having to maintain its own transport waggons and animals and utilised those of the local yeomen farmers when not required for their own purposes. There is nothing in Shotter's will to show that his connexion with the iron industry related to anything other than carriage. If he had had a lease to operate the hammer at Pophole, the will would have mentioned it as was normal practice.

The accounts also contain an item: 'Tho Elliatt for faching Jo Shippards goods from tinsley forge £2:15:00'. It would seem that on requiring a new hammerman (Sheppard describes himself as a hammerman in his will of 1717) and no suitable craftsman being available locally, it had been necessary to seek one from some distance away. Tinsley forge was near Crawley. It may well have been this John Sheppard who was responsible for the digging of the ponds near the hammer in Bramshott parish now part of the Trout Farm. In 1711, a John Sheppard is indicted in the Bramshott Rolls for illegally digging two ponds on Bramshott lands near Pophole. As these ponds (possibly the ones to the north of the hammer) flow today into the Wey slightly downstream of the hammer it is more likely that this was a bit of private enterprise rather than anything to do with the hammer water supply.

In the same year, 1711, John Shepherd purchased Lees Cottage in Shottermill, went to live there and died there. His modest will of 1717 on which he made his mark and in which he described himself as a hammerman is, for the most part, nothing out of the ordinary and he leaves Lees Cottage to a kinsman in Midhurst. He also, however, leaves to his servant, Joan

Berry, £20 which is to be paid to her after the £100 which is owed to him by Lady Montague (the fifth Viscount had just died in 1717) had been received. This amount is described as being due to him under Lady Montague's hand. Lees Cottage was no concern of the manor of Linchmere and the Montagues and the conclusion must be that this debt was related in some way to his sojourn at Pophole.[61]

Before the subject of the Shotters is left, one additional point of interest arises. Referring back to the 1610 arrangement whereby Montague paid the Shotters the annual compensatory amount of £3.13.4d. for the part of Watts Farm on which the hammer stood, it transpires later that a further sum of £5 per annum had been paid to the copyholder of the land on the Surrey side of the hammer. The evidence for this payment comes in 1781 when the then Roger Shotter of Pitfold auctioned all his land in Pitfold, Farnham, Bramshott and Linchmere manors.[62] For one farm, easily identifiable in the Auction Notice as Lower Pitfold Farm, the prospective buyer is informed that he is due to 'a Yearly Sum of Five Pounds, payable by the Lord of the Manor of Linchmere and Shulbred, to the Owner of this Estate, for the flowing of Water over part thereof near Pophole Hammer'.

On an Estate Map dated 1772 we see that Roger Shotter had purchased High Pitfold Farm. The map shows that, attached to High Pitfold's land but at some distance from it at the end of a track marked 'road to Pophole hamer' were two fields – the Hammer Coppice of nearly 5 acres and the 3 acre Hammer Meadow. These two fields were almost certainly the land near Pophole described above as warranting the £5 annuity.[63] In 1781, when Shotter sold High Pitfold Farm, these two fields and the £5 annuity had become attached – as seemed more logical – to Lower Pitfold Farm.

If, as seems likely, the £5 award for the land on the Surrey side was made in 1610, as was the award for the Sussex side, the holders of both Lower and High Pitfold Farms at that date were members of the Payne family. One of the Thomas Paynes, Elder or Younger, is a likely candidate as there was some sort of iron industry association. In 1622 Thomas Payne of Pitfold is found as joint Lord of the Manor of Frydinghurste (otherwise Ashurst) with Peter Quennell of Imbhams. Frydinghurste was close to Imbhams. Payne and Quennell had purchased this manor in 1622 from Thomas Burdett of East Worldham and John Mydleton of Horsham[64] who previously in 1610 had bought it from the Blackwell family (Thomas Burdett being then described as of Abinger).[65]

All these names are associated with the iron industry, and in 1610/11, Burdett had been granted a six year lease of his mill and watercourse and certain lands (in Chiddingfold) at £25 p.a. plus a £60 payment, by Robert Quennell.[66] Whether, however, this denoted actual participation in the iron industry on the part of Thomas Payne or whether he was making a purely financial contribution, it is not possible to tell. The Thomas Paynes, Elder and Younger, were yeomen of means, had a finger in many local financial pies and had held land in Pitfold from the middle 1500s. By 1625 the manor of Frydinghurste was held by Henry Hooke of Bramshott.

Pophole in the Eighteenth Century

When Northpark furnace re-started sometime in the 1730s after an unknown period of inactivity, there is evidence that the necessary skilled labour was no longer available locally. In 1717, John Fuller, who was active in the production of ordnance in the 18th century at Heathfield, obtained a list of iron works which contained reference to an unnamed forge of Lord Montague's making 50 tons. Almost certainly this was Pophole.[67]

With the Treaty of Utrecht in 1713 and the consequent decline in the demand for ordnance, this was not in general a good time for the iron industry which had in any case been in decline for some time. Shortly after 1712 the hammer at Sickle Mill ceased operating, although this may have had as much to do with the death of John Hoad the Younger, the sicklemaker, without male issue, as with prevailing conditions. Pophole continued to appear on 18th century maps; in particular it is shown as a forge in 1724 on Budgen's map of Sussex. It also appears on Taylor's map of Hampshire in 1759, and on Rocque's map of Surrey in 1768. It would seem, therefore, that production at Pophole had probably continued.

There are, unfortunately, in the local parish registers during the 1700s few entries which also specify occupation, so that none of the workers at the hammer are definitely known. One exception might have been Israel Hussey of Linchmere who, when acting as witness at his sister's marriage in 1714, describes himself as a hammerman. There is, however, no way of associating him with any particular hammer, and he has other strong associations with Rogate. Secondly the Haslemere Register contains the baptism of the son of John Colyer 'at ye hammer' in 1732 when the only local hammer operating would have been Pophole.

John Butler of Bramshott (previously of Stanley Farm)

During most of the middle years of the 1700s, the forge at Pophole and the furnace at Northpark were run under the common management of John Butler of Bramshott. The sources for this are a Butler Family Memorandum written in 1815 by John's grandson, and a series of Cowdray leases. According to the Memorandum, the first member of the Butler family, Walter, fled from Ireland for political reasons and he is found in the Linchmere Rolls as purchasing Stanley Farm in Fernhurst from the Boxalls in 1634 where he and two succeeding generations pursued lives appropriate to respectable and prosperous yeomen.

Straker in his book 'Wealden Iron' described John Butler (1697–1775) as a farmer with no previous experience of the iron industry. However, it appears that in 1738 Butler had sought to buy guns from Heathfield furnace and Cleere & Crossley suggest that prior to reviving the furnace at Northpark, he may have been an arms dealer.[68] In effect, however, a letter from John Fuller to John Butler (9th September 1738) shows Fuller had declined to supply him with the guns he wanted. If, also, the 1732 reference above to the existence of a local hammer worker (Colyer) related to Pophole, it may be that Butler took over the working of the hammer at an earlier date than is generally supposed. Although after the Treaty of Utrecht there had been more or less 20 years of peace, this was again interrupted by quarrels with France in India and North America and finally by the Seven Years War 1756–63, providing once again demand for ordnance.

Butler's operation was not without difficulty. The Memorandum says that 'Workmen were scarce, he could meet with no persons who understood the employment, and was obliged to hire workmen from the north at a high price' – after which apparently he trained his own workmen and dismissed the northerners. This statement almost certainly refers to the lack of skill *a propos* of the furnace and indicates that Northpark had continued in abeyance for some time after its last firm date for operating in 1664. A number of Hollist papers 1708–12 refer to Montague's rights to take ore at Northpark, but these were later copies of the original Montague/Shotter agreement of 1626 in the Linchmere manor rolls which was included in every subsequent alienation by descent of the Shotters' copyholds of Hatch Hill and Parrys & Hurlands.

The Memorandum continues: 'He [John Butler] had reached the middle of life before he engaged in business' and 'during first the American and afterwards the Spanish War … he rented and established a cannon foundry and a hammer at Farnhurst'. (The pond at Northpark was in Fernhurst parish and the furnace in Linchmere). Butler sold Stanley Farm in 1755 but earlier he had moved to Bramshott where he had in 1732 built Shorts – now Bramshott Vale House. The Memorandum also refers to the contribution made to the running of his business by his faithful clerk George Denyer who died in 1779 and who is buried in Bramshott. It is possible that the 'Blank' Denyer mentioned in the Shotter Auction Notice of 1781 as having been the occupier of Watts Farmhouse was the same George. Watts would have been suitably centrally placed with regard to furnace, hammer and Bramshott Vale House. It is also probable that the 18th century alterations to the hammer workers' cottages immediately to the south of the hammer, referred to in Audrey Sutton's description, took place during Butler's tenancy of the ironworks.

There is no lease made between Montague and John Butler which survives. The information regarding Butler is obtained from a lease made out to his successors in 1769[69] where Northpark and possibly Pophole are described as having been 'formerly in the occupation of John Butler'. It was not absolutely certain from the wording whether Butler occupied the hammer as well as the furnace. This lease was made out to Joseph Wright and Thomas Prickett, Southwark gunfounders, for a term of 21 years. A further lease of 1774[70] gave James Goodyear, ironfounder of Guildford, the tenancy but he went bankrupt in 1777. The probable final reference appeared in 1777 in the 13th & 20th January issues of the Sussex Weekly Advertiser where an 'Iron Foundry' was advertised for sale.[71]

Fortunately, confirmation of Butler's connexion with Pophole appears in the (intermittent) Rate Books for Frensham Parish where he is found to be paying the rate in Pitfold 'for the hammers' from 1750, the start date of the rating records, to 1761, after which there is a gap so that the precise year when Butler ceased activity is not known. The rate set for the years 1772–4 shows Prickett to have been paying and the last relevant entry is for the year 1777–1778 when James Goodyere's name is entered. After this entries for the Hammers from 1782 to 1788 have no name alongside and thereafter the Hammers are no longer listed.[72]

There is no Rate Book for the parish of Linchmere covering this period. Sometime, therefore, around the middle 1770s local iron-making ceased. In 1793, William Shotter of Parrys & Hurlands (High Building) sold his estate on which Northpark furnace lay to Anthony Capron the Younger of Moor in the parish of Easeborne.[73]

The End of Iron-Working at Pophole Hammer and After

A late light is thrown upon activities at Pophole in a proposal in 1767 to move the Toll Gate situated on the north side of Godalming on the Turnpike Road between Guildford and Liphook. The opening of the Wey Navigation had enabled payment of tolls to be evaded by transferring goods from the turnpike road to water south of this Godalming gate. Particular complaint was made about use of the road but subsequent avoidance of payment of the toll in the above manner on the materials carried to and from the Iron Works at Thursley and Pophole.

There is one final amusing footnote to the history of Pophole. In 1781, the last of the Pitfold Shotters (who had not resided in Pitfold for some considerable time, being an Attorney at Law of Guildford) put all of his considerable Pitfold and Linchmere lands up for auction. Although not named, the farms are easily identifiable as Watts, Lower Pitfold, High Pitfold and Lane End & Buffbeards. With the exception of High Pitfold, these were bought by the up-and-coming Simmons family of paper-makers of Sickle Mill, and reference is made on the Auction Notice to the £3.13.4d. and £5 annuities, payable in perpetuity by the manor of Linchmere to the tenants of Watts and Lower Pitfold Farms.

It is not, however, until 1825 – some fifty years after the demise of Pophole and the end of any profits – that someone, almost certainly the Manor, remembered that it was still paying out these annuities on an ironworks from which it was no longer getting any return and on which it was also still paying the Land Tax. The result was that the copyhold of the six acres or thereabouts lately containing the hammer and pond was awarded

147

to James Simmons III in exchange for his agreement to relinquish the annuity which went with Watts Farm.[74]

Presumably also, some similar arrangement was made with regard to the annuity on the Pitfold side, but there is no record of this. The three cottages on the Hammer lands described in 1825 as 'now altered into two' were not included in this deal, having been sold in 1822, with James Etherington and John Madgwick as occupiers, to John Neale of Bohunt. Quite what was meant by 'now altered into two' is not absolutely clear. One cottage may have disappeared entirely, or one of the remaining two, not a pair, may have originally been used to house two families. According to the leases of 1769 and 1774, there were still three cottages on the site, but this may easily have been a formal repetition of the original description. The Linchmere Tythe Map of 1846 shows the two remaining cottages and their gardens to have been owned by the Revd Frederick Ford of Hewshott, but Ford only appears by virtue of his being the husband of Mary Ann Neale, John Neale's daughter and heir, and he receives no mention in the Rolls.

The last activity near Pophole was, of course, the building of the railway line by the Portsmouth Railway Company. This passed almost immediately behind the Hammer Cottages which, with their gardens, were bought by the Railway Co. although not in effect touched by the line.[75] The first engine went up the line on 1st January, 1859, and was watched by members of the Simmons family.

The Simmons did not hold the Hammer Lands for long, selling them in 1835 to the Rev. Richard Henry Baker of Linchmere for £110, along with much of their other land. On Baker's death, the land passed to his heirs, the Parson family and then to John Edward Ward of Pimlico, an estate agent. Watts Farm passed briefly into the hands of the Oliver family of Shotter Mill. The cottages seem to have gradually deteriorated and in 1871 one of them is described as uninhabited and occupied by squatters.

Some of the twentieth century owner/occupiers are known, such as the Denmans, Larbys, Glovers, Denyers and Youngs. In 1980, by then derelict, the cottages were the subject of extensive restoration.

The demise of the Wealden iron industry was essentially due to the discovery of a cheaper way of smelting iron using coke instead of charcoal, after which the industry moved to the coalfields of the Midlands and North. It is also probable that the sources of ore in the Weald were becoming depleted. In her account of Northpark furnace, Mrs Barnes relates how in 1738, in a letter to her son, Lady Mary Caryll of Harting described how Mr Butler was beginning to dig for ore on Lord Montague's land but was finding little, and hoped that he would find more on her son, John Caryll's land, in Harting Combe.

The destruction of the woods on which the supply of charcoal was based has also been put forward in some early literature as a contributory factor to the demise of the industry, but it is today considered that, far from being the case, careful management and coppicing was for the most part, if not always, normal practice. The consumption of wood for a furnace and forge would have required areas in the region 2,500 and 1,500 acres respectively[76] and the necessity for managed regeneration of the woodland was as obvious to the iron masters then as it would be today. Examples of the specific requirement to leave 'living roots' can be seen in felling agreements in the Linchmere manor rolls. However, the most potent cause of the decline of the Wealden industry was the high cost of charcoal and the relative inefficiency of the small 'winter' furnaces there. Set against the coal-based industry in the Midlands and North with its lower costs and improved technology, they were no competition.

References in Chapter Six

[1] Has.Mus.LD. 5.231
[2] Cleere, H & Crossley, D:The Iron Industry of the Weald, with contributions by members of the Wealden Iron Research Group, Merton Priory Press, 1995
[3] Canon W.W. Capes: Scenes of Rural Life in Hampshire, MacMillan 1901
[4] Victoria County History for Surrey, 1905, vol.2 p.272
[5] Cunliffe, B: Iron Age Communities in Britain, London 1975
[6] VCH Sy. Vol I, p.369 quotes Loseley Ms Feb. 20, 1570 x 28
[7] Barnes, C. Bull. Wealden Iron Res. Group 2nd ser. 11, 1991, 11–23
[8] WSRO.Cdy 264 Jac.8,1610
[9] PRO. LR2/197 f.87
[10] WSRO Cdy 264.f.11v 13 Sept, 27 Eliz. 1584
[11] WSRO Cdy 264, No.223,1588
[12] Awty, B.G. Bull.Wealden Iron Res. Group, 2nd ser. 4, 1984
[13] Hunniset, R.F. ed. Sussex Coroners Inquests, PRO 1996,
[14] WSRO.Cdy 264, No.136
[15] Ibid No.163
[16] L'mere Par.Reg
[17] WSRO.Cdy 264, Nos.172 & 173
[18] WSRO.Cdy 264, No. 272
[19] WSRO.Cdy 264, No.142
[20] HRO.11M59/E1/114/6
[21] HRO.11M59/E1/ 120/9
[22] WSRO.Cdy 264, No.271
[23] Has.Mus.L.D.6.221
[24] HRO.11M59/E1/120/7
[25] L'mere par.reg.
[26] HRO.11M59/E1/151/5 & Ibid 125/2 & 125 /6
[27] WSRO.Cdy 264, No. 146
[28] Ibid No.147
[29] WSRO. Cdy 264, No.190
[30] WSRO.Cdy 264, Nos.206, 250, 256
[31] WSRO.Cdy 264, No.225
[32] HRO.11M59/E1/113/5

[33] Ibid 114/3.

[34] WSRO Add. Ms H834

[35] HRO.11M59/E2/158142 & 158144, 1674–5

[36] WSRO.Consistory Court of the Bishop of Chichester 30 f.618 1703

[37] Bramshott Par.Reg

[38] WSRO.Cdy 264, No.267

[39] WSRO.Cdy 264, 1648

[40] Cleere & Crossley, op.cit.p.140–1

[41] HRO.11M59/E1/ 126/3 & 126/5

[42] Cleere & Crossley, op.cit.p.152

[43] PRO. E.179 190/283

[44] WSRO. EPI/11/8

[45] WSRO.Cdy 266, p.118

[46] WSRO. Mf. 174.

[47] WSRO.Cdy 264, Jac. 7, 1609

[48] WSRO.Cdy 264, ff19v–20r, 23 April, Jac 8. 1610

[49] WSRO.Cdy 264, Jac.12, 1614

[50] WSRO.Cdy 264, 2 Car.I, 1626

[51] WSRO.Cdy. 264, Jac 18, 1620

[52] WSRO.Cdy 264, No. 42 & PRO.SC6/H8/3674

[53] Barnes, C. op.cit

[54] Cockburn, J.S. ed.Calendar of Assize Records, HMSO.1975

[55] Has.Mus. LD. 6.242

[56] WSRO. Mf.187

[57] WSRO.Cdy 5149 f.18

[58] WSRO.Cdy Ms 96

[59] PCC prob. 1694

[60] HRO.11M59/E1/130/4

[61] Archdeaconry Court Surrey, 1717/103

[62] Has.Mus.LD.5.371

[63] Has Mus. LD.5.240

[64] PRO C.54/2512 m.15

[65] PRO.Close Roll 7 Jac.I, m.45

[66] PRO.CP.25/2/359 Jac. 8 Easter Term

[67] Cleere & Crossley op.cit. p350

[68] Cleere & Crossley, op.cit. p331

[69] WSRO.Cdy 1443–4

[70] WSRO.Cdy 1445

[71] Barnes, C. op.cit.

[72] GMRPSH.FREN./8/1

[73] WSRO.Cdy.265,1793

[74] WSRO.Cdy.265,1825

[75] WSRO.Cdy.266,1860

[76] Cleere & Crossley, op.cit. p.135

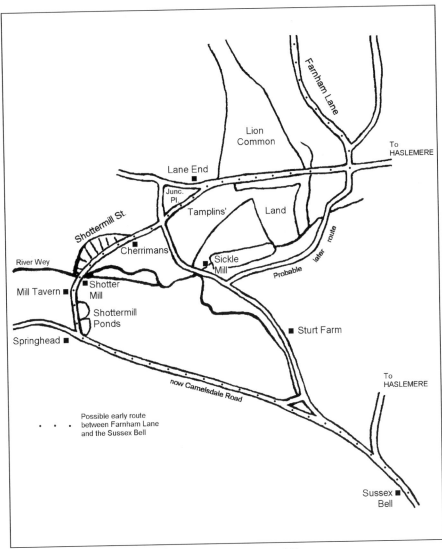

Fig.9: The Shottermill Road System

Chapter Seven

The Shottermill Road System

Before turning to an account of the Surrey side up to the advent of the Simmons family in the 1730s, a few comments should be made about the local road system.

Haslemere was not advantageously placed as far as the early main road system was concerned. The 'great and ancient' road from London to Portsmouth (A3) passed it to the west. Of the two main roads from London to Chichester, one branched off the Portsmouth Road near Milford and proceeded to Chichester via Chiddingfold, and the other left the Portsmouth Road near Gibbet Hill, ran down Farnham Lane and went on to Midhurst and Chichester via Sturt and the Sussex Bell at the end of Fernhurst Lane. This route via Farnham Lane – an ancient trackway – was turnpiked in 1749.[1]

Neither of these routes, however, touched Haslemere directly and accordingly, in 1763, members of the Haslemere Borough applied successfully for an act to turnpike roads leading from Milford into Haslemere and out of it on the south side to Midhurst and Chichester, with a continuation from the Sussex Bell west to Liphook on the Portsmouth Road.[2] The old roads north from Haslemere until then had branched off east and west at the north end of the High Street, the upper road going via Weydown joining the Portsmouth-London road some way above the entrance to Farnham Lane, and the lower road proceeding via Clammer Hill and Witley to join the London road at Mousehill near Milford.

The object of establishing a road leading directly through Haslemere was twofold; first to provide a direct way from London to Chichester passing through Haslemere; and secondly to provide a route whereby travellers on the Portsmouth Road might also leave it at Milford and, again having passed through Haslemere, by means of a newly turnpiked road starting at the Sussex Bell and running westward, could rejoin the Portsmouth Road between Liphook and Rake. Thus, the notoriously difficult and much disliked section of the Portsmouth Road over Hindhead which, according to the Haslemere burgesses included 'deep sand, precipices and frequent tempests' could be avoided. In both cases, Haslemere would have benefited from an increase in carriage trade.

As far as the direct route to Midhurst and Chichester through Haslemere was concerned this was a huge success – so much so that the old route down Farnham Lane was no longer used to any degree, and it was 'disturnpiked' in 1770.[3] As far as the second objective was concerned, however, whatever the difficulties and discomforts of the Hindhead section of the Portsmouth Road, most people continued to use it and to ignore the new route west along the (later) Camelsdale road from the Sussex Bell. Before describing the life of this road, however, a few comments will be made about the early roads in Shottermill.

According to Rocque's map of 1768, after descending Farnham Lane to Clay Hill (Wey Hill), the road to Midhurst and Chichester appears to go along the south side of Sickle Mill pond (now the King's Road) turning south to run past Sturt Farm to the Sussex Bell, and this route may have been later used by coaches as being an easier route, avoiding crossing the stream at the bottom of Wey Hill, although still having to cross the main stream flowing from Haslemere via Foster's Bridge and the King's Road into the eastern end of Sickle Mill pond.

The map[4] on page 6 – drawn by John Andrews and Andrew Drury, published 1777 – shows the road through Haslemere to Midhurst and the road down Farnham Lane to Midhurst and also toward Liphook to have numbered milestones, although this map in many places is wildly inaccurate. Also, whereas Rocque's map of 1768 indicates that the main Weystream was forded, Andrews' map seems to indicate that there was a bridge.

There is, however, earlier evidence to suggest that the 'king's highway' originally passed down 'Shottermill Street'. The lane along the south side of Sickle Mill pond may not have existed before the hammer pond was dug out circa the early 1600s, when the land on both sides was the jointly-farmed land of Sturts and the Great Purpresture, and the northern boundary of Sturt Farm proper was the stream around which the pond was dug. The lane along the south side of the pond was later described merely as an occupation or farm lane. Similarly, the land of Sturt Farm was bounded on the west side by the stream behind the houses in Sturt road, not by Sturt road itself which was also probably just a farm lane. Shottermill Street was the name by which, later on, the road from Junction Place to Shotter Mill and containing the Post Office, Cherrimans and Brookbank, was known – now the Liphook road.

Tamplin's land which comprised the area now occupied and fronted by Kingsdale and the parade of shops in Junction Place extending via the church traffic lights down toward Sickle Mill was always described in the 1600s and early 1700s as abutting on the north the kings highway from Haslemere to Midhurst.[5] In 1625, Cherrimans is described as lying on the king's highway with only a lane to Sturt Farm on its eastern side[6] and in 1641 Thomas Combes living at Lane End Farm is described in the Haslemere parish register as living by the same highway. When the Combes held the above Tamplin land in the 1700s, it is described as having the kings highway to Midhurst on its west side. See Fig.9. It is possible therefore that in the early

153

days at least, the principal highway went past Shotter Mill and also the Shotter Mill Inn opposite.

There are early references to the 'kings highway from Haslemore to Shotover mill' which bisected the Lion Common into Upper and Lower Commons along the line of the present road. (The road leading up the centre of the Lion Common was until the early 20th century only a rough track and would have wandered over the ages). From Shottover Mill the king's highway continued round the south side of the Shottermill Ponds, where the Shottover millers were in trouble with the manor between 1584 and 1588 for allowing the water led from the spring – at Springhead – to the mill pond to damage the then queen's highway.[7] This road went on east to the Sussex Bell. There is nothing to indicate that this traffic had any visible effect on Shottermill other, possibly, than the above-mentioned presence of the Shotter Mill Inn (now the Mill Tavern) in the 1650s, which may have catered for travellers.

It was also from Shottover mill that the early road to Liphook ran west. In the garden behind Rose Cottage opposite Shottover mill, the old road surface of Critchmere Lane can be seen and this continued along a track, probably only a footpath, on the north bank of the Wey leading to Pophole. From Pophole onward the road to Liphook continued along the south side of the river through the farms of Hammer and Gilhams to Bridge. This 'old road to Liphook' and the proposed turnpike along the line of the present Liphook road are shown on a Cowdray estate map of 1771.[8]

A lane from the Ponds also ran west past the farmhouses of Springhead, Washers/Rats Castle and Watts/Dexham, being joined by the way from Hindhead passing through Pophole and up Hammer Lane. Hammer Lane was in existence and so-called in 1600.[9] At the top of Hammer Hill there was a turning off south to Linchmere, and the 'old road to Liphook' also turned off at this point proceeding via Gilhams Farm. The new turnpike road ignored the old Liphook road winding through the farms and went directly towards Liphook across the common – see Fig.8.

North of Shottermill a track – but no more than a track – seems to have led up to what is now Hindhead Cross Roads, ie the present A287, being joined by another leading from the top of Lion Common up Polecat Hill. On either side of the A287 was the Polecat Valley lane and a track up the Nutcombe valley. There was nothing of importance about a route to what is now Hindhead Cross Roads for the simple reason that in the 1500s certainly and probably in the 1600s and long after, it would have led to nowhere in particular, and certainly not to an important junction.

A document of 1582 describing the Pitfold manor boundaries refers only to the presence in the Hindhead area of 'divers auncyent decayed hollowe wayes'.[10] As late as 1839 the Frensham Tythe Map shows the track (now the A287) to pass though a meadow in the middle of Critchmere Farm (No. 1085) but nonetheless it must have been a public right of way at an early date

154

as from it other lanes lead off to Critchmere Common and Woolmer and to Nutcombe and High Pitfold Farm. The story of the forging of a useable route from Junction Place to the Hindhead Cross Roads is dealt with in the later appreciation of James Simmons IV (the last paper-maker of Sickle Mill) whose work it largely was.

To return to the Turnpike Road from the Sussex Bell to Liphook (the Black Fox on the old A3), on the 1771 Cowdray estate map it is shown as a dotted line only, and may at that date still have been unfinished. Swanton noted that it suffered obstruction from John Butler, who had the lease of Northpark furnace and Pophole Hammer, as the projected route passed through some of his land near Liphook. Swanton also noted that in 1805 some parcels of Dene Farm on the Midhurst Road were described as lying on either side of the turnpike road to Petersfield.

That the turnpike operated for some time is indicated by the description in the 1851 Linchmere Census of Rats Castle as the 'Old [toll]Gatehouse'. However, the life of this turnpike road is obscure and it seems to have been of relatively short duration. In 1806 there was a petition from the Innkeepers of Haslemere.[11] They protested against the necessity of receiving and billeting soldiers on the march to Portsmouth, stating that this practice had originated during the existence of a turnpike road through Haslemere to Portsmouth. When Haslemere had had the benefit of the carriage trade the turnpike brought, the cost of billeting was sustainable. However, as this road was no longer a turnpike, this was no longer the case. They also commented sourly that the Anchor Alehouse at Shotter Mill escaped receiving soldiers altogether. It would seem, therefore, that already by 1806, the turnpike along the present Camelsdale road to Liphook and beyond to Portsmouth no longer functioned as such.

References in Chapter Seven

[1] Act 22 Geo II c 35
[2] Act 4 Geo III c 63
[3] Act 10 Geo III c 82
[4] WSRO PM11
[5] HRO.11M59/E1/132/3 & 133/4
[6] HRO.11M59/E1/119/3
[7] WSRO.LM rolls 1584 No.187;1587 Nos.202 & 210 & 1588 No.217
[8] WSRO.Cdy MS 1660
[9] WSRO.Cdy 264 No.267
[10] Has.Mus.LD. 5.234
[11] PRO.WO.40/3

SECTION 3

Shottermill from the 1500s to the 1700s

The Surrey Side

-ooo0ooo-

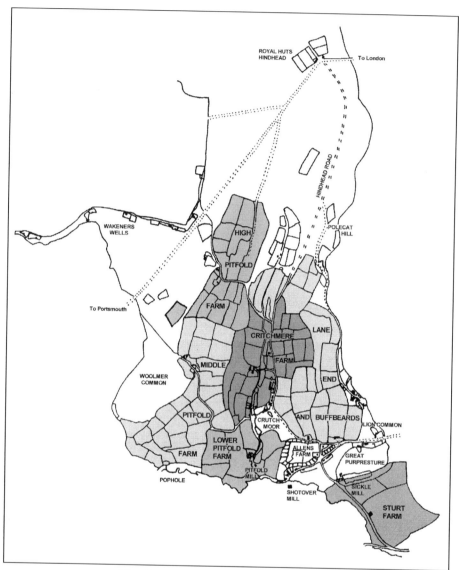

Fig.10: Farmlands in Pitfold Tything

Chapter Eight

Introduction to Pitfold

Pitfold manor through the Montague, Poyntz, Pritchard and Baker families; suggestions why the name of Shottermill superseded the old name of Pitfold for the Surrey side; Shottermill in the 1600s; the Social Scene, Attitudes, Population.

The manor of Farnham lands which occupied the south eastern part of Pitfold tything were not affected by the Dissolution, but the Pitfold manor lands of the Priory of Dartford in Kent were and seemed to remain in the hands of the Crown for some time, a number of Ministers Accounts existing in the 1540s in which its annual value was reported to the Crown by Commissioners. Not until 1562 did Elizabeth I grant the Lordship to John White and Thomas Kerton, when it was described as the manor of 'Pytfold Dertford otherwise Highe Pitfolde'. John White, later Sir John, who was alderman, citizen and grocer of London and brother of the Bishop of Winchester, had spent the previous twenty years taking the opportunity to accumulate vast amounts of church property. His associate was Thomas Kerton a merchant of the staple of Calais.[1] Both these characters were typical of the new men.

In 1566 John White exchanged Pitfold manor with Viscount Montague for the Grange at Tongham and a payment by Montague of £177 10 6d. Pitfold manor remained in Cowdray hands until it was sold by Stephen Poyntz to Richard Preston Pritchard in November 1831 for £330.[2] Pritchard died in 1836. He was an absentee landlord living in London.

Richard Preston Pritchard junior who succeeded his father in the lordship of Pitfold lived at Milland Place and sometime in the 1840s sold Pitfold manor either to Edward James Baker (brother of the Rev. Richard Henry rector of Linchmere) or more likely to his son James Baker. Edward James was already holder of much of the land of both Pitfold manor and also Farnham manor in Shottermill. James Baker, his son, held Pitfold manor until 1881 when he was adjudged bankrupt – the result it is thought of a penchant for gambling – when the manor ceased to exist. Its lands were sold off and much of it was subsequently built upon in late Victorian and Edwardian times. The manorial system was ended by Act of Parliament in

159

1922.[†]

As mentioned previously, the Pitfold manor rolls are lost with the exception of a short run from 1826–32. That these survived is probably due to the fact that they had been in the possession of James Simmons III paper maker of Sickle Mill who was on the Pitfold Homage and whose papers were collected by John Wornham Penfold jnr., surveyor and antiquary of Haslemere.

If the rolls had survived the earlier Cowdray fire, then it is likely that they disappeared at the time of James Baker's bankruptcy and the selling off of his estate in the 1880s and after. E.H. Malden who edited the Surrey volume of the Victoria County History was seeking them a hundred years ago and wrote to Penfold in 1904 to ask if he knew their whereabouts.[3] Penfold suggested he try Baker's solicitors but to this day nothing has been heard of them. There is, however, in the Haslemere Museum a collection of deeds of the 17th to 19th centuries which allows something to be said about some of the tenants.

The bounds of Pitfold Manor, very roughly, split the Tything of Pitfold into two by a line beginning on the Wey immediately to the west of the Shottermill cemetery at Sunvale and after going round the top of Critchmore Common – now Deepedene – made its way in a northeasterly direction towards Hindhead. This manor boundary is important to remarks made elsewhere about the very early corn mill on the Wey and can be seen on Fig.5 although as it approached Hindhead there were always queries as to its precise location. The first thing carried out by any new Lord of the Manor was to walk and confirm his territorial bounds but nowhere does a description survive which does not leave queries behind. Arguments and disagreements on this head abound in Simmons' Diary and are discussed in greater detail below.

Why is Modern Shottermill So-called?

The following are suggestions as to why the name Shottermill superseded that of Pitfold, the historical name for the Surrey side of the Wey up to Hindhead. The evidence points to Shottermill being derived from the corruption of Shottover Mill although the mill itself was in Sussex. The suggestion that it took its name from the Shotter family is less likely as the term is first found in use some considerable time before the Shotters bought Pitfold Mill and Lower Pitfold Farm in the 1640s and settled in Pitfold and

---

[†] No definite date for the sale of Pitfold manor by Pritchard to the Bakers has been found, but from an account of the treading of the manor bounds on 18th July 1848 in James III's Diary, it is evident by implication that James Baker junior was Lord of the manor by then. There is also reference to a deed of release of some unidentified property between Pritchard and James Baker dated 11th October 1845 in Has Mus. LD.5.636.

built their house in the 1660s, unless of course, the name of the mill derived from its association with this family which itself is uncertain. No connexion between the Shotters and the mill was seen after the Linchmere records began in the mid 1500s. In 1563, many years before the Shotter presence in Pitfold the phrase 'near Shottover mill' appears in the Farnham rolls to describe the location of a house on the Surrey side in Pitfall,[4] and in 1568 the Baldwyns who were indicted for selling leather illegally were described as of the hamlet of Shottover myll although again they lived on the Surrey side.[5]

The Linchmere rolls always refer to the mill by its formal name of Shottover although there are a couple of slips (to Shotter) in the early 1600s which suggest that in local speak Shottover had been conveniently shortened to Shotter. Around 1650 the present Mill Tavern was referred to as the Shotter Mill Inn in the Linchmere rolls. The early Haslemere and Linchmere parish registers, when alluding to people on the Surrey side not of their own parish had always referred to these, where appropriate, as 'of Frensham' (parish) or 'of Pitfold'. From about 1600, however, 'Shottermill' begins to appear denoting the hamlet, as in the Haslemere register in 1606 when three children 'of Shottermill' are baptized. In 1602 in the will of Alice Michell she describes herself as 'widow of Shottermill in the parish of Frensham'.[6]

Seventeenth and eighteenth century maps contain only variations of 'Pitfall' usually signifying High and Lower Pitfold farms on the Surrey side. They do not refer to Shottermill anywhere. By the middle 1600s, references to the hamlet as 'Shotter Mill' become increasingly common as in the will of 1647 of Sarah Launder (of Sturt Farm on the Surrey side in the parish of Haslemere)[7] and as in the entry in 1643 in the Linchmere register for Mary Elridg 'of Shottermill'. Lastly, in 1697 in the Linchmere rolls there is an entry reflecting the prevailing difficulty in knowing quite what to call the area which refers to 'a hamlet called Pitfold and Shottover Mill'.

During the 1700s and after, the use of 'Shotter Mill' both for the mill and community generally rather than Shottover Mill becomes common, and also 'Shottermill' although less so. As late as the middle 1800s, James Simmons III of Sickle Mill, was only able to write the word Shottermill in his Diary, meaning the hamlet, with difficulty. For most of the earlier years he wrote Shotter Mill, and when eventually he was able to bring himself to express it as a single word he was still unable to write it without putting a capital M in the middle. As late as 1898 Thomas Wright in his *Hindhead, or the English Switzerland*, called the hamlet Shotter Mill.[8] Nonetheless, when in the 1840s James Simmons III initiated the founding of St. Stephen's church, he had no difficulty in writing about it as the church for the hamlet of Shottermill or in locating it on the Surrey side in the centre of the increasing population and dwellings there. In an appeal for funds for the church in 1848 it was referred to as 'The Shotter-Mill District Chapel'. There seems to be little doubt that Shottermill derived, if gradually and painfully, from Shottover the mill rather than from the Shotter family.

The reasons for Shottermill eventually superseding Pitfold are probably that first, whereas Pitfold tything historically covered the whole area between the Wey and Hindhead, Shotter Mill was a specific and extremely well known location quoted many times in deeds and rolls as a means of identifying, relative to it, the situation of other lands and houses. A second reason is that Shotter Mill lay on the original king's highway from Haslemere to Liphook and beyond and on the road from Hindhead to Chichester via Farnham Lane. Pitfold Mill and Lower Pitfold Farm, lying as they did along the Critchmere Lane which went nowhere of any great significance, became something of a backwater, the area around Shottover Mill and 'Shottermill Street', becoming the favoured location for houses. The remaining part of Pitfold up to Hindhead until the late 1800s had neither important roads nor industries nor on the whole occupiers other than squatters and broom-makers to render it an area of any particular significance.

What would Shottermill have looked like in the 1600s?

To the modern eye accustomed to metalled roads edged with kerbstones and neatly cut verges, close mown greens and in selected places ornamental trees, the earlier reality would have been unkempt and unappetizing. As late as the end of the nineteenth century, as the picture of Clay/Wey Hill on the opposite page shows, the overall impression is unbeautiful.

By the Victorians the Tudor Age was romanticized and usually contained visions of buxom maidens and ruddy-cheeked yeomen (no doubt resulting from a diet consisting entirely of roast beef) emerging from thatched cottages with roses round the door to practice archery on the green. If roses there were round the door, they were more likely to have been briars springing unbidden from the nearby dungheap or the aptly named 'boghouse' as all the farms were working farms and, as described above in regard to Linchmere, up to 1650 or thereabouts were nearly all in a decayed state. The same certainly applied to the Surrey side. As the 1600s progressed, however, much improvement took place and some houses like Bridge Farm, Watts Farm and the new house built by the Shotters near Pitfold Mill – the so-called manor house – clearly became quality residences.

The Lion Common might well have been unkempt, close grazed in patches and rooted up in others, used for charcoal burning, being littered with assorted refuse including night soil and stacks of fuel, and traversed by a number of tracks. The roads in general – the neglected responsibility of the parish – would have been rutted and muddy and probably little improved by the routine failure of the tenants to clear their ditches. By 'roads' is meant nothing like modern roads – as late as the early twentieth century Lion Lane running up the Green was a rough track only. Pitfold during this period was well furnished with timber which was probably due to its regeneration during the stagnant period after the Black Death. In the 1600s and 1700s there are many rolls entries for permission sought and granted for the felling and sale (always of a specific number of trees) of mature timber. For example in 1626 William Tribe paid a fine to fell and sell 40 trees[9] and in 1724 Mary Sadler of Buffbeards paid a fee to the manor of £3.4s. for the felling of 67 oaks.[10]

Of all the photographs in the Haslemere Museum Collection, this view of Wey Hill looking eastwards from the valley bottom c.1888 gives the most dreary and desolate impression of the local landscape. The shop on the right is now the Public Library.

Of smell and noise there would have been an ample sufficiency. The hammer at Pophole was working and from some time around the early 1600s also the one at Sickle Mill. Hammering would also have come from the smithy between Shotter Mill and the Wey. The stench of rotting flesh on the hides awaiting treatment at the tanyard opposite Shotter Mill must have permeated the entire neighbourhood and combined disagreeably with the acrid stench of charcoal burning on the Lower Lion Common, where colliers were burning as late as the middle 1800s.[11] Sometime around the early 1600s men would have been digging out the hammer pond at Sickle Mill and carting the spoil to raise the dam. The surrounding woodlands would have resounded to the noise of the saw and axe as the many agreements for felling and [char]coaling show. They would have been also busy at the saw pit just above Sickle Mill House fashioning the timber for the hammer wheel, and possibly sometime in the early 1700s brickmaking was already going on on

Clay/Wey Hill.

During recent building work at Sturt Farm, a tile was found there inscribed with the names of two of the Billinghurst girls from Haslemere and also the name of Sary Hull, probably a servant of theirs, with a date of 1733. This must have been done whilst the tile was drying before firing, a tile which may have been made at the works on Clay Hill where William Berry was residing. Sturt Farm may well have been undergoing repairs at this time, John Combes and his wife who were living there being newly married in 1729. The Berry family had moved out of Frensham into Thursley parish (Clay Hill where the brickworks were situated) by the early 1700s. From 1717 the William Berrys are described as of Thursley parish in the Haslemere registers and in 1758 William Berry's wife was living on Lion Green. The Berrys were certainly on Clay Hill a hundred years later, brick burning.[12]

Carts or pack animals carrying hides, corn, iron and charcoal to and from the mills would have been seen and on the ponds, commons and waste, grazing animals and fowls, some animals being driven to Haslemere on the Tuesday market days and, as was still happening in the late 1800s, sheep being washed in the mill stream along the Wey at appropriate times of the year.[13]

The first picture of Shottermill as a whole containing dependable information about the size of the population, about the occupiers of the land and houses as well as the owners, their occupations and wealth, does not appear until the mid-18th century and after, principally in the form of the Frensham Rate Books (1750 on), the Land Tax returns (1780–1830), the Frensham parish Tythe Map of 1839 and the Census Returns from 1841. In the earlier period dealt with here, particularly as the returns for Pitfold have to be selected (with difficulty) from returns for larger administrative units, an insight into the way the area developed can be gained only by following the history of the farms and houses – when and where they first appeared and what sort of people owned, built and lived in them.

Overall in the 1600s and early 1700s on the Surrey side there did not seem to be much change; some of the farms increased in size and some of the smaller land parcels became consolidated into larger units, but the sites of the principal farms remained unchanged. As far as the cottages are concerned, besides an early small cluster around Shottover Mill present in the 1500s, the Farnham rolls show further development in the 1600s/1700s of dwellings on the Surrey side in Shottermill Street; of a couple of houses near the road from Haslemere to Shottover Mill on the Lion Common, and a small group on the waste at the Common's apex. Farmland which abutted Lion Common on both sides prevented more houses being built around its edges.

A Pitfold manor record shows there to have been a small group of cottages round the top of Critchmere Common (now Critchmere Hill) and including Kiln Cottage near the *Royal Oak* and two or three others on the slip road to the Hindhead Road, where it would have been easier to encroach on unused land. There were also a couple of cottages in the Nutcombe valley and one on Woolmer; and there is the first appearance of a cottage on land called Helders near High Pitfold Farm. These cottages appear in a 1727 Pitfold Manor Rental[14] but they were almost certainly there in the 1600s. Rocque's map of 1768 confirms this picture.

Below is a facsimile of the start and the end of the 1727 Rental —

Part of a Rent Roll of 1727 of the Quittrents of the Copyhold Tenants for Pitfold Manor. It will be noted that the value of the manor has only increased by a very small amount since the valuation in 1549.

The Social Scene

Many of the local holders of the farms remained in the area for three or four generations or about 100 years, and some even longer. There is evidence of some social polarization but because cottages and farms were passed on by inheritance according to the custom of the manors, or if sold went to neighbours or friends, the property market probably did not much affect the social scene as in nearly all cases such properties passed to persons of a similar social standing.

Elsewhere after the Dissolution new owners interfered with the rights of copyholders and deprived them of their lands. In Pitfold, however, the process of customary holding and inheritance continued undisturbed, the only known exception being the acquisition by the Montagues of the Hammer lands, some of which were on the Surrey side, and this was obviously done by agreement and with financial compensation. In an area of mixed farming and, north of the Wey of poor land, there was no great incentive to dispossess copyholders by the Lords of the manor. The accumulation of smaller parcels of land into larger units was mostly the work of the copyholders themselves but expansion was limited as there was by this time little cultivatable waste land left untenanted.

In the main the people who served as jurors at the Hundred Court, who acted as Tythingmen and Constable (albeit often unwillingly and often failing to carry out their duties) were without exception the yeomen manorial tenants. The cottagers do not appear in this context. Information about people's occupations from parish registers is spasmodic and infrequent. Often people are described as labourers but this was a lump term which could mean many things. Many would have been agricultural labourers but others must have been workers in the woods, performing work on the land and in the woods according to the seasons. Small tradesmen and craftsmen such as tailors, chandlers, mercers, carpenters etc were identified as such much more frequently. Also many of the yeomen landholders were engaged in trade and these are as often identified by their craft or trade as by their yeomen status.

It seems, however, that these craftsmen did not all possess the same status. There lived in the various cottages carpenters, glovers, wheelwrights and cordwainers, etc who were most likely craftsmen in a small way. However, many holders of land also identify themselves first as craftsmen. Some of these latter obviously started off advantaged, perhaps as younger sons of small landed families for whom an apprenticeship had been purchased, on whom a small sum of money had been settled and who were able to marry into other small land holding families. They were essentially no different in kind merely being members of families who had got their foot on the ladder at an earlier date.

Such a one was Francis Jackman – one of the Jackmans of Thursley End in Haslemere – who is described as a carpenter when buying Brookbank and the Great Purpresture in 1730s[15] but having also inherited Kitts Farm near Churt from his father in 1687.[16] The Jackmans of Thursley End (so called because the house was at the eastern end of Thursley parish which included an arc of land running along the ridge to the south of Haslemere) appear early on as property owners and extensive dispensers of loans.

Others were the William Sadlers of Chiddingfold who when acquiring Sturt farm in 1660[17] and Buffbeards Farm in the 1680s are described as blacksmiths.[18] The Uptons of Haslemere who are usually described as mercers, glovers and maltsters in the first half of the 18th century had long held the lands in Linchmere manor and Fernhurst which were eventually acquired by the Simmons. Others such as the Hoads of Sickle Mill and the paper-maker Simmons after them were tradesmen or craftsmen first and only land holders later. In addition to the small plots around Sickle Mill bought by the Hoads after operating the hammer from 1649 or earlier, they also purchased Lower Farm in Fernhurst in 1691 on a £200 mortgage, which became the marriage settlement on Dorothy Combes nee Hoad and sold after her death, in 1755.[19] The Simmons, as will be seen in a subsequent chapter, essentially used the profits from their paper-making enterprise to accumulate a large local estate, but only after they had been there long enough to make money, and like most, they started off with mortgages. Members of the Combe family of Pitfold, although primarily important yeomen farmers for many generations, are described sometimes in the 1600s/1700s as tanners and tailors.

Many of these latter must be seen as owners or managing directors of small businesses rather than persons engaged directly in manual labour. The occasional 'gentleman' whether or no they ran businesses or were engaged in trade, in the 1600s at least seemed to derive their status from the possession of land, and the possession of land can increasingly be seen as a mark of social superiority although as late as the middle 1700s the social divide seemed to be easily crossed. By this date the Benifold family had held Middle Pitfold Farm for a hundred years as well as other land in Bramshott manor, and they make one of the largest contributions to the Voluntary Subscription towards the debts of Charles II in 1661. In 1765, however, from a family document[20] it appears that one of their daughters had married a gardener, not on the face of it a match of high status.

The Surrey Hearth Tax for the joint Tythings of Pitfold and Churt in 1664 shows, of those selected as far as possible for Pitfold, that only Roger Shotter's house had 6 hearths, the rest all having between 1 and 3. The returns for Linchmere parish in 1670 show also that of the 34 dwellings listed, only 5 had 4–6 hearths, the rest again having only between 1 and 3. There seemed to be no enormous disparity as far as housing was concerned, most of it – even the farms – being modest. The inventories of possessions (including their crops) for which there are hardly any for the Surrey side but a good number for Linchmere parish show, between about 1600 and 1700 that for yeomen, their value fell into the range of £100 to £300, a typical bracket suggested by other studies as being occupied by the majority of yeomen.[21] The smaller husbandmen left less, up to about £50. There was on the whole not a vast disparity in wealth.

In an age when a man had either to make or sell something to survive, the purchase of an apprenticeship was a useful start. A man with only his labour to sell was at the bottom of the heap and likely to remain so. Some labourers were fortunate enough to become farm servants which meant that they were found living room and food at the farms themselves in return for doing whatever was required. Others, however, were casual labourers on the land for whom winters must have been hard.

Apprenticeships of course cost money and were not an option open to all. Many pauper children were compulsorily apprenticed by the parish to avoid their being a charge on the rate payers and in spite of the lurid tales of ill-treatment many of which were undoubtedly true, they may well eventually have been counted as among the fortunate in having a trade. There are no early records concerning treatment of the poor or the size of the problem on either side of the Wey at this date.

There is until the middle 1700s no description of anyone as a broom-maker, although logic says some were about. The records of apprentice-ships[22] have been published for the first half of the 18th century and there are a number of entries for Haslemere, but the only one for Shottermill is the apprenticeship in 1744 of John Chalcraft to Israel Hussey of Frensham, who was a carpenter living at this time near Shotter Mill.[23]

Attitudes

Before going on to discuss the cottages and farms and their holders, something needs to be said about what the locals knew and thought during this period – lasting from the Tudors to the Hanoverian Georges – which saw the Civil War and immense religious, social and economic changes.

Nobody locally until James Simmons in the middle 1800s left a diary and few records deal with attitudes. In the 1500s and 1600s much of the inform-ation about what was going on in the outside world would probably have come to the ordinary man via the markets and also the church. Nothing, however, has been seen about the attitudes of the Frensham incumbents. It is not even certain that the connexion between Pitfold and Frensham was particularly close. At the end of this period, between 1751 and 1754 the first James Simmons of Sickle Mill was a Frensham parish churchwarden[24] but it is noticeable that even so, all his children were baptized and he himself buried in Haslemere, as were later Simmons before St. Stephen's was built.

It is likely that visits by the Frensham incumbents to the Shottermill end of their parish were not all that frequent. In the parish of Frensham, there were no recusants[†] in 1592. Toward the end of this period in the Visitation of the Bishop of Winchester in 1725, the returns for the entire parish of Frensham show that there was no chapel, no papist, no Dissenters Meeting House, only three Dissenters and no school (nor any in Haslemere) all this pointing to a conformist population.[25]

It is not even known what the immediate local attitude was during the Civil War on the part of the local yeomen and their inferiors. Very generally in the south east the landed gentry were for the Parliament, for example the Yaldens of Blackdown, but there were also the Montagues to the south and the Quennells of Lythe Hill who were for the King, and the towns of Guildford and Farnham were Royalist strongholds. When Charles I raised his standard in 1642, Peter Quennell[26] (suggesting he was not alone in his allegiance) raised a company of 74 men to protect the Imbhams iron works and the guns it was producing for the Royalist cause, but this was easily and quickly dealt with. In 1662 Roger Shotter of Pitfold married a Yalden daughter which suggests that their respective fathers may have seen eye to eye politically, and in 1664 an unknown Shotter of Fernhurst was presented by the churchwardens as being a schismatick,[27] but opinions in 1640 and 1660 were not necessarily the same.

After a decade and more of Parliamentary rule, direct taxation to support the controlling armed forces had risen to a level previously unexperienced or imagined. In the 1650s the armed forces cost £2½ million as against £200,000 for the remaining expenses of the state and there is nothing like heavy taxation to have a dampening affect on enthusiasm.[28] An early levy of £565 in support of the Royalist Cause had been levied on the Tything of Churt, and documents surviving which relate to the taxes collected in the parish of Elstead 1644–54 by the Parliament show that many of the villages in the northern part of Farnham manor were 'full of soldiers' quartered there and constituting a financial burden, whilst other places were expected to provide hay and oats for the cavalry mounts.[29]

Amongst these records are references in 1644 to James Payne as Assessor and Collector of taxes in Elstead. Almost certainly this James Payne was a younger son of Thomas Payne of Pitfold (of whom more below) who in the late 1630s had sold his Pitfold properties and returned to Elstead. James Payne was also an Elstead churchwarden so whether he engaged in this unpopular activity with enthusiasm for the Cause or whether, as is possible, he was 'volunteered' by virtue of his office, it is not possible to say.

In Linchmere manor, if Linchmere village itself did not suffer quartering, it was certainly feared as an entry in the 1651 Rolls relating to Springhead Farm shows, when such a financial burden was specifically excluded as an excuse for the non-repayment of a mortgage. In Linchmere parish also, the

---

[†] A person who refused to attend Church of England services – they could be Roman Catholics or Dissenters.

tax collectors were the churchwardens. Probably most of the Pitfold and Linchmere yeomen just gritted their teeth and endured; there is no evidence of any strong tradition of religious Dissent and, although there did not seem to be more than the odd Roman Catholic, the influence of the Montagues whose tenants many of them were, must have had some bearing on their attitudes.

A few things are certain. Most people – even those of the most modest means – knew about money, how to raise it and how to invest it and, closely associated as many were with the iron, tanning and later paper industries, this middle stratum must have been familiar with the London market and the country's external as well as internal affairs.

On the edge of the Weald with a plentiful supply of tannin from oaks, tanning was an important industry in both Haslemere and Shottermill. In the Haslemere Museum is a document showing that as early as 1547 Peperhams, according to the will of John Scrugge (unknown), was to be sold by the Mystery [Guild] of Leathersellers of London to Sir Edmund Walsingham, uncle of Sir Francis Walsingham, the Elizabethan statesman.[30] Sir Edmund was M.P. for Surrey in 1544. In the first half of the 18th century, of the total of 24 apprenticeships being taken up with Haslemere craftsmen, ten were with cordwainers, surely indicative of a market extending beyond the immediate locality, although the only records surviving for this industry are for the London Guild. (Personal communication from Guildhall Library).

There was a postal service which Charles I in 1635 converted into a public service, and in 1674 the first reference appears to the use of this in Hasle-mere.[31] Recourse to the law was undertaken readily and several local names appear in civil cases concerning disputed inheritance viz Baldwyn, Breda (Briday), Launder, Maunt, Rapley, Tamplin, Hall and Gammon.[32] Many wills and certainly all property deeds were drawn up in due form by attorneys. The schools which were to become the Midhurst Grammar and the Guildford Grammar School were established around the middle 1600s and there is a perceptible increase in the number of documents signed rather than being inscribed with a cross, this, however, showing a marked difference between social strata. Recent research[33] on the pace and extent of the rise in literacy, shows that in the mid 1500s perhaps 20 per cent of men and 5 per cent of women could sign their names although these would have been predominantly gentry; by 1760, these figures had risen to 60 per cent and 40 per cent respectively. The returns for the Linchmere Oath of Protestation in 1641 show – for adult males only – a 24 % literacy.

The sons of yeomen start to go to university as did Roger Shotter of Pitfold. In 1712, John Hoad the Younger of Sickle Mill left his widow instructions for the maintenance and education of his daughters. Just what was meant by this he does not say, education at this time being generally regarded as superfluous for women. Women had always played an important part in the economic management of small businesses and particularly of farms but could usually survive without a knowledge of Latin or quadratic equations. Throughout the seventeenth century the three 'r's were 'reading', 'riting' and 'religion' (rather than 'rithmetic'), the first two being essentially taught for a fuller appreciation of the third, so that probably this was the sort of instruction the Hoad daughters received. John Hoad of Sickle Mill was literate.

For witchcraft, a reality probably to many in the 1600s and 1700s, no local prosecutions have been seen, the decline in its belief probably reflecting the influence – at least among the educated classes – of the scientific revolution and the adoption of a more rational approach.

Regarding popular pastimes, apart from the welcome feastdays which were an excuse for letting off steam, it is generally agreed by historians that then as now (until perhaps the advent of television) the most common recreation was going to the pub. By the middle of the sixteenth century the alehouse was an established part of life and although no mention has been found of the Shottermill 'local' at this date, nothing is more certain than that there was one or probably several. Not until the 1800s do references to the *Red Lion* and the *Staff of Life* appear as inns or beer houses, but the *Blue Anchor* had probably been an inn since the late 1700s and the *Royal Oak* an ale house at an even earlier date. The popular *Royal Oak* was certainly the place to which James Simmons III in 1850 unhesitatingly headed in his self-appointed campaign to curb the beer-swilling habits of the local youth on the Sabbath.[34]

Population – Its Increase and Effects

With regard to the population trend from the 1500s, over the whole country, this rose until the middle 1600s and then after a period of stagnation continued to rise again, so much so that between 1750 and 1850 the population of England as a whole almost tripled, although most of this occurred in towns. Shottermill seems to have reflected the pressure occasioned by this trend to some small degree but not as much as in other parts of Farnham manor where in the 1600s there was an increase in applications for small grants of purpresture land of between 2 and 6 acres. There was only one small local encroachment on the Lower Lion Common (see further below) but this is not surprising as in the local Farnham manor lands there was little land suitable for cultivation remaining untenanted.

What went on in the Pitfold manor lands is not known but it was in the second half of the eighteenth century that there seemed to be a perceptible drift into Pitfold of families who were later recognizable as broom-makers.

A very crude estimate based on the returns of the Lay Subsidy for the tything of Churt in 1628[35] and the 1664 Hearth Tax[36] suggest that the population on the Surrey side may have been something of the order of 130 to 150 persons. In the returns of the Bishop's Visitation of 1725 for the entire parish of Frensham a figure of 'near 600 souls' is given. Although this latter figure agrees with earlier estimates (the Pitfold population was usually about a quarter to a third of the Frensham parish total) the returns do not promote a feeling of total confidence, the population of Godalming, for example, being quoted as somewhere between 2[000] and 3,000 – a close calculation which cannot have given the incumbent many sleepless nights!

The manor rolls and in particular the presentments to the Farnham Hundred Court show that one of the main complaints was the illegal use of and encroachment on both the waste and commons indicating that there certainly was land hunger on the part of landless men but also, as many of these complaints concerned over-grazing by people already holding land and rights of common, they show that men who held such rights wanted more.

The commons, of course, were only open to use by the manor copyhold tenants but their rights theoretically were limited to a fair share. The local commons which were the property of the Lords of the manor of Farnham and Pitfold on the Surrey side occupied some of the area on the south side of Hindhead, probably including much of upper Nutcombe, Woolmer Common and the projection down to Wakeners Wells, and the Lion and Critchmere commons – see later discussion of Boundaries and the Broom-makers.

If a comparison is made between the names appearing in neighbouring parish registers such as Haslemere and Linchmere where people are designated as being of Frensham parish or of Pitfold or of Shotter Mill, as well as those in the Frensham register itself, and the names appearing in the rolls as property holders, on the Surrey side such a comparison shows only a few names which remain unfamiliar. Lands and houses seemed to revolve endlessly through familiar names, apparent change of ownership only indicating kin.

In effect much of the population at least until the middle 1700s showed an unexpected degree of stability in spite of other evidence showing that a part of it was more mobile than hitherto assumed. There seemed to be a number of stable families holding land and cottages but also a distinctly transient section of the population. On the whole more Pitfold people seemed to migrate to Haslemere town where the employment opportunities would have been greater, than Haslemere people to Pitfold looking for opportunities to invest in land. This latter was more a feature of the subsequent period in the middle 1800s.

Intermarriage between the local families was constant, the local peasantry marrying for the most part other local peasants, although by no means always the girl next door. If the bicycle was supposed to mark the end of the village idiot, there is plenty of evidence at this earlier date to support the idea that the radius achievable by horse or foot led to partners being selected as often from neighbouring parishes as one's own. Quite often brides coming from more distant places reflected their father's occupational associations. The higher up the social scale one was, the greater was the distance from which partners came. Two of the families researched in some detail – the Hoads and the

172

Bridays – show that by the late 1600s, a century after they had first appeared, the Pitfold lines had close kin in Woking, Worplesden, Farnham, Kirdford, Chiddingfold, Northchapel, Selborne and Chichester as well as in the more immediately neighbouring parishes, pursuing their various livelihoods. Dispersion was increasing.

Particularly difficult to detail are the people increasingly described as 'farmers' rather than yeomen or husbandmen – ie the leaseholders. These were the men who worked other people's land and who, when a lease ended, often moved on to look for something better elsewhere. They had probably been present locally for long periods without any distinguishing records.

One such was the Bennett family. Present in Pitfold in 1597[37] they were still farming leased land almost to the end of the 1700s. In his 1732 will Robert Bennett[38] left the remainder of his leases of Lane End Farm (held by the Combes) and Stoatley Farm to his sons Robert and John but by 1772 one of these had left for new and presumably better pastures in Kirdford. Hannah, Robert's wife, ended her life in a cottage on Lion Green and, on her death in 1736 was described as the local midwife. From an inventory accompanying the will, it is obvious that leasehold farming could be a good way of earning a living. The inventory which included Bennett's household furnishings, crops and animals for both farms, showed him to have been worth £916 which included £454 owed to him out on bond.

Another was the Luff family which in 1839 was shown to be Baker's undertenants for Lane End and Buffbeards, and prior to this undertenants of the Simmons family, farming there until about 1870. Other members of the Luff clan, long established land holders in their own right elsewhere, may have had a longer connexion with Buffbeards as there was a dispute in 1739/40 with Mary Sadler the holder.[39]

The Randalls may have been another. Many of them are seen in the area around Witley, but they may also have been local undertenants – they were certainly at Buffbeards in the early 1700s[40] – and it is obvious when James Simmons III engaged Randall as a paper maker in 1842 that the family was well known to him. Randall's father, James said, had worked for him for many years.[41]

A last family whose members farmed in the area for a very long time but who rarely appeared in the records, as they were not on the whole land-holders but long-time under tenants were the Madgwicks.

Because the amount and character of the information arising out of the records of Farnham manor and Pitfold manor are so different, before using this to describe the farms, the boundaries separating the two manors will be discussed in the following chapter.

References in Chapter Eight

[1] PRO.Pat 4 Eliz.pt 4 m 51
[2] Has.Mus.LD.5.259
[3] Has.Mus.LD.5.636
[4] HRO/11M59/E1/110/3
[5] PRO.Exch.K.R.Mem.R.East.10 Eliz 234 & Mich 266
[6] HRO.1602B 31/1
[7] PCC 25/5/1648,
[8] Wright, Thomas: 'Hindhead, or the English Switzerland', Marshall & Co. 1898
[9] HRO.11M59/E1/119/6
[10] HRO.11M59/E2/153007
[11] Simmons Diary 27 Oct 1847
[12] Ibid 6 Nov 1839
[13] Fenn, A.M: The Century Magazine, 1885, pp709–723
[14] Has.Mus.LD. 5.258
[15] HRO.11M59/E2/153020 & 153022
[16] HRO.11M59/E1/129/6
[17] Ibid 125/2
[18] Ibid 128/10
[19] WSRO. Lucas & Albery papers
[20] Has.Mus. LD. 5.247
[21] Sharpe, J.A: Early Modern England, Arnold, 1997, p.207
[22] W.Sy.Fam. Hist.Soc. Rec.Ser. No. 6 and Ssx.Rec.Soc. vol. XXVIII
[23] WSFHS No.6, No.4268
[24] GMR PSH Fren/8/1
[25] Ward,W.R: Parson and Parish in Eighteenth-Century Surrey, Surrey Record Society vol.XXXIV, 1994.
[26] Rolston, G.R.op.cit. p.55
[27] Ssx.Rec.Soc.vol.XLIX
[28] Sharpe, J.A: Early Modern England, Arnold 1997, p.106
[29] Hunot, E: Farnham & District Museum Society Newsletter, vol 5, p.176
[30] Has.Mus.LD.8.1006
[31] Moorey, Peter: The Post of Haslemere, 1998
[32] W.Sy.Fam.Hist.Soc.Cases in the Court of the Exchequer 1561–1835; vol. XIX. Rec.Ser.19,1994
[33] Sharpe, op.cit. p.277
[34] Simmons Dy. 21 Apr 1850
[35] W Sy Fam. Hist. Soc.Rec.Ser. No.4
[36] W Sy Fam. Hist. Soc. Ms. 7
[37] Haslemere Par.Reg.
[38] PCC.Prob. 22.2.1733
[39] HRO.11M59/E2/153022
[40] Ibid 153024
[41] Simmons Dy. 29 Oct 1842 & 11 Jan 1835.

Chapter Nine

The Farnham and Pitfold Manor Boundaries

When John Wornham Penfold, antiquarian and collector of many local deeds and documents, engaged in correspondence about Pitfold with H.E. Malden who around 1900 was editing the Surrey part of the Victoria County History, he took the opportunity to remind Malden that the Tything of Pitfold and the Manor of Pitfold did not have the same boundaries.[1] Penfold did not go on to define the manor boundaries as it is very likely that by that date he could not precisely remember them. As a consequence of the extensive allotments of common and waste of both the manor of Farnham and of his own manor of Pitfold awarded to James Baker in the 1850s enclosures, Baker had gained much of the land hitherto in dispute, but by 1904 Pitfold manor no longer existed and the matter had become academic.

Circa 1285 the manor of Pitfold had been carved out of the Bishop's manor of Farnham which then comprised the entire tything of Pitfold, ie all the land between Hindhead and the Wey. Only some of this area – the western and south-western parts – came to constitute Pitfold manor, the rest of the tything – essentially the part on the south and east around and extending northwards from Lion Common and Junction Place, and an area of commons or waste in the extreme north of the tything – remaining in the hands of the Bishop. It is obvious, however, from various surveys and the treading of bounds, that the northern edge of Pitfold manor was always the subject of doubt and disagreement and had probably over time been the subject of creeping extension.

There was no argument that some of the land on the south side of Hindhead and the Portsmouth Road constituted the Bishop's commons and waste, and in 1549 the inhabitants of Pitfold paid the Bishop 2d for its use. The argument was how much and where. Fig.5 shows the lands and bounds of the two manors.

Briefly, the Pitfold manor boundary ran from the top of Critchmere Common which was the Bishop's land down Critchmere Hill past the *Royal Oak* and up Woolmer Hill about as far as Lower Hanger Road/the Hatchetts. From there (the western boundary of Lower Pitfold Farm) it ran south to the Wey which it joined at the western end of the later cemetery at Sunvale and went along the river to the bridge at Pophole. Going north from there it followed the county boundary, taking in Woolmer Common and branching off the Portsmouth Road to include the arm of land known as Wakeners Wells as far as the present ponds and, returning to the Portsmouth Road and possibly taking in a small portion of Kingswood, it then struck east along the north side of High Pitfold Farm.

It was at this point that the arguments always began. At what point did the boundary cross the Portsmouth Road after emerging from Wakeners Wells; how much of Upper Nutcombe did it include; at what point did the boundary strike the present A287 Hindhead Road and where did it go from there? It is significant that in the 1831 document transferring Pitfold manor from Poyntz to Pritchard although many terms are included to describe the physical features over which the lord of the manor had rights, nowhere is there a single sentence describing the boundaries.[2]

The eventual settlement of this matter did not come about until the enclosures of the commons and waste in the middle 1850s when the Commissioner, acknowledging that the position was unclear, laid down the boundary by decree.[3] Before this, nowhere does any early account survive which does not raise more questions than it answers.

One of the first activities of any new Lord of the Manor was to tread his bounds and confirm his territory. The first survey seen, dated August 1582, was entitled 'Survey of the Manor of Pitfold' and was made for the Montagues.[4] It has unfortunately only survived in part and even that is not wholly legible.[†] The document starts at the 'hyghe way to Chase Banks' (presumably the Portsmouth Road) and describes the diversion along the watery valley containing a well spring called Wakeners Well. Back on the highway the boundary goes eastwards through High Pitfold wood where there are marked trees dividing Pitfold from the Bishop's land. From this point on, the boundary lurches from tree to tree (including a birch called the 'ward tree') which stood upon the heath amongst divers ancient hollow ways until it descends into the Nutcombe valley and to the Nutcombe well spring which lies near a marked beech with a great multitude of stones lying about it. After 400 years reference to marked trees, especially marked birch trees, is of little value.

From the Nutcombe valley the boundary climbs eastward again to a hill called myllridge which runs north-south and has on its narrow top a greenway leading from 'hyndhed to Shottover myll'. Eastwards from the top of this hill the boundary descends to a valley called Chertenwude, presumably Polecat, and there the document ends.

The second survey comprises two pages only from a small notebook, and from the ages of the tenants mentioned as participating, dates to 1834/35.[5] It was probably the boundary survey carried out for Pritchard after he had

---

[†] Advice taken indicated that the date of this document which was unclear was, from the writing style, more likely to be 1582 than 1682.

purchased the manor from Stephen Poyntz. It covers only a fragment of the boundary, starting at Hammer Bridge and ending a little way up the road, but it includes an interesting description of the bridge at Pophole.

'And first beginning in the South at Gyldhall Bridge or Pophole Bridge which Bridge is on the West part of the Forge or Hammer ... and is a Common way for Passage between Linchmere and Hyndhead, and so from thence extending North by the middle of the highway lying in the Valley called Wyke Dean, between the Hill belonging to the Manor of Bramshott on the West, and the Hill belonging to the Manor of Pitfold on the East leaving the little Lake called Wollmore Lake on the Right...'

The name 'Gyldhall Bridge' applied to Pophole bridge has been met with at no other time and its origins and significance is unknown.

Later information comes from James III's Diary. He was one of a party treading the bounds in 1834, and again in 1848[6] for James Baker along with George Parson the Pitfold manor steward and Stephen Harding for Mr Butler's manor of Bramshott. In 1851[7] there was a further treading of the bounds on which occasion the party included Mr Wetherley the Land Commissioner as the enclosure process was imminent. James III was singularly lacking in the capacity to describe clearly where he was and where he was going to. At one point he walks for some (crucial) way parallel to a fixed point!

What is (partially) clear from his Diary is that there were three areas of continuing dispute. First, at what point did the boundary cross the Portsmouth road and go east from Wakeners Wells. Some of the party on one occasion went 'round by Laurences', possibly the Huts or an enclosure belonging to one of the Lawrences a little way to the SW of the Huts, but James did not agree with this. He proceeded east on a line some way to the south. There seem to have been boundary stones everywhere but some of these, according to James, were the relics of earlier incorrect surveys.

The second area of dispute was the Nutcombe Valley. As described in 1582, the boundary touched the well spring at Nutcombe but in the 1549 Ministers Account there is no reference to any habitation in the Nutcombe valley. Observations in Nutcombe over a considerable period in the hope of identifying the well spring have shown that, according to the weather, water lies in the valley in various amounts and places but none above the pool lying near the point where the Nutcombe Lane turns sharply up the hill (by the Coachhouse) toward High Pitfold Farm. After 400 years, however, it is quite likely that the water table has altered.

For what it is worth, Rocque's map of 1768 shows the stream to begin at this point as also does the Frensham tythe map of 1839. If this was the well spring it is quite possible that the boundary was later pushed further north up the valley into the Bishop's land. According to the 1727 Pitfold Manor Rental there were two dwellings in the valley near the assumed site of the well spring. James refers in 1848[8] to uncertainty about whether Stephen

Combes' hut was in Pitfold manor or not. This is now Combe Cottage at the top end of the cleared land in the Nutcombe valley (Frensham tythe map No. 1129). Combes had encroached on some land there but had eventually made his peace with Pitfold manor. By James's time at any rate this extension seems to have been accepted as being Pitfold land.

The third debateable area was the land running immediately south from the present Hindhead Cross Roads. It had always seemed odd that the part of Farnham manor lying in the south and east part of the tything of Pitfold should have been totally disconnected from its lands to the north. Most parties treading the Pitfold manor bounds went over the top end of the Hindhead Road (Myllridge) into Sandy Lane (now Polecat Valley) – the boundary of the Farnham Manor and Hundred, and of Frensham parish – and down to Lion Green.

James III always strenuously disagreed with this, maintaining that they should have proceeded some way along Down End (the top part of the A287) before turning off down Polecat Hill. His father, he said, had told him 50 or 60 years ago that the land between the Hindhead Road and Sandy Lane (Polecat Valley) was the Bishop's land.[9] James had had in the 1830s[10] two annoyed letters from Pritchard accusing him of putting some new enclosures in this area (and possibly also in Nutcombe) into the wrong manor, although by the much later date when this matter was raised (a meeting at *The Huts* on 10th July 1851) James did not have the faintest recollection of it. In the event, when the boundaries were officially laid down, he was proved to be correct. The land between the A287 Hindhead Road and Polecat Valley was designated the Bishop's land.

Probably at a very early date the precise dividing line between the two manors in the northern part of Pitfold tything was of no great moment. As the land rose toward Hindhead it became poorer and steeper and less well watered. There were few habitations and the relatively small number of copyholders who had rights of grazing and turbary etc on the commons probably shared it without too much friction. In any case there were no real barriers between this area and the vast amount of heathland waste continuing on the northern side of the Portsmouth Road.

As time progressed, however, and the population and illicit encroachments increased, boundaries assumed a greater importance. Action against encroachments was partly a matter of rent money but by no means the whole nor even the more important part. No Lord of the Manor ever made much out of his copyhold tenants from whom he was due a fee on inheritance or sale which very often occurred only once a generation, whilst the annual quit rents paid to him remained nominal. Rents from encroachments of a quarter or half acre or a squatter's cottage would only have been shillings. In a late Pitfold manor rent agreement made in 1858 between James Baker and Henry White, broom-maker of Wakeners Bottom, White paid an annual rent of only 10s for a cottage and half acre, whilst Baker paid the rates and taxes and maintained the fences. Baker, however, retained all rights of shooting, trapping and sporting which were increasingly becoming a valuable social asset.[11] Action against encroachers seemed to be as much as anything a matter – in which the Lord and his copyholders were usually united – of retaining control and defending their actual and legal rights.

Illegal squatters and landless men could not easily be called to account if they were suspected of trespass, illegal use of the commons and its products, poaching and being responsible for missing animals, nor were they easily ejected if they were allowed to settle and build. Also, encroachers made detrimental use of the commons by stripping the turf for fuel, some of it in great quantity used to burn lime and to provide ashes for arable land. Last but not least, as the long-awaited enclosure of the commons came ever closer, when allotments of land were made to copyholders in proportion to the value of the holdings they already possessed, manor and even smaller boundaries became significant.

Later chapters show how this process developed in Pitfold manor amid the destruction of illegal dwellings, actions for trespass, the odd shooting and bouts of arson and threats of legal prosecution of squatters. If the small men had been allowed to build and stay on the local common land and waste, its story, whereby much of it became National Trust land, would have been very different.

References in Chapter Nine

[1] Has.Mus. LD.5.636
[2] Has.Mus. LD.5.259
[3] WHC. P.57/8/3
[4] Has.Mus.LD.5.234
[5] Has.Mus.LD.5.251
[6] Simmons Dy. 18 Jul 1848
[7] Ibid 25 Jan 1851.
[8] Ibid 18 Jul 1848
[9] Ibid 10 Jul 1851
[10] Ibid 6 Jan 1835
[11] WHC.Zs 183/1

Chapter Ten

The Landholding Families (1)

The Combes family of Critchmere Farm; Lane End Farm; Allens Farm and Lees Cottage; Sturt Farm; parts of the Great Purpresture and (briefly) Brookbank.

Many of the mediaeval landholders whose names appear in the Ministers Account for Pitfold manor in 1549[1] and in the early Farnham manor rolls, such as the Baldwyns, Hardings, Persons, Popes, Stevens, Warners and Wakefords etc disappear in the later 1500s, but others of them continue. From mediaeval times until the early 1800s the Combes continue to play a leading role in Shottermill, and the Payne and the Wheeler families before disappearing in the mid 1600s, consolidate and even extend their holdings. From the early 1600s the Benifolds of Bramshott inherit some of the Paynes' Pitfold holdings and purchase others, and new families of standing appear such as the Shotters who continue to extend their holdings until the late 1700s. Lesser names appear such as the Hoads and Nappers, Cherrimans and Tamplins, and with the building of new cottages the names of small cottagers become visible for the first time.

Whilst most of the farms were held during this period by families who lived on their holdings, there were a few interventions on the part of non-local families. Sturt Farm and the Great Purpresture were held by the Rapleys of Linchmere, and part of the Great Purpresture by the Wests of Roundhurst in Lurgashall, but only for a brief period. Buffbeards Farm was the main exception amongst the farms, being held between 1630 and 1744 by the Tribe family only some of whom were local, and then by their heirs the Sadlers of Chiddingfold who were not.

For most of the 17th and 18th centuries, however, the Pitfold copyholders either lived on their lands or maintained their local connexions. The families and the history of their fortunes and holdings have been taken in turn, first those who held the Surrey side farms and mills, after which, in a subsequent chapter, the history of the cottages is given.

These families – the Tudor and Stuart yeomen – illustrate the emergence of a peasant aristocracy in the period after the Black Death, the Paynes and Wheelers in particular being recorded as holding Farnham manor land from the Bishops of Winchester on long leases, a practice obtaining in the period after the Black Death.

Fig.10 and Fig.13 show the location of the farms and cottages on the Surrey side.

The Combes Family

The Combes family held land on the Surrey side in both the manors of Farnham and Pitfold for at least 300 years and very probably longer. For the whole of that time they lived and farmed locally and, although the Pitfold manor rolls are lost, the Ministers Account of 1549 to the Crown which held Pitfold manor until 1562, a Pitfold manor rental of 1727[2] and various deeds and wills in the Haslemere Museum archive enable some idea to be gained about what was happening in Pitfold, a good deal of which concerned the Combes. They held Critchmere, Lane End & Allens and Sturt Farms, parts of the Great Purpresture, and Brookbank.

When the lands of the dissolved Priory of Dartford passed into the private ownership of Kerton and White in 1562, the manor was described as 'Pytfold Dertford otherwise Highe Pitfold'. Whether this implied that the manor was administered from High Pitfold Farm or whether it was merely describing the Pitfold manor area which was mostly high land, is not clear, but as in the 1549 minister's account the manor court is described as being held 'at the house of John a Combe, once in every two or three years', it probably was not referring to High Pitfold Farm. John a Combe's house was almost certainly on the site later known as Critchmere Farm and now Frensham Hall (and at times Frensham Hall Farm), and the Combes family had at no time any discoverable connexion with High Pitfold Farm.

For a small unremunerative manor such as Pitfold, holding its courts relatively infrequently, there may well not ever have been a manor house. Probably a bailiff would have sufficed and perhaps this office had been filled by members of the Combe family. Their farm was obviously the main farm in the manor and in the 1500s was also the largest. It may also have been, as seen in the first chapter, that the manor rents were paid at an earlier date to a representative of the Bishop of Winchester and that there had not been any close connexion between the Priory of Dartford in Kent, the owner of the manor, and the tenants.

The Early Combes Holdings

From the 1727 Manor of Pitfold Rental it can be seen that the Combes' holding on the west of the A287 Hindhead Road (Critchmere Farm) had absorbed the land originally of Richard Person on the east of the road. A surviving Pitfold manor roll of 1829 shows Critchmere Farm to have been bought by Edward James Baker, and an estate map of Critchmere Farm[3] undated but somewhere in the 1820s drawn up for Baker shows its lands to have included Person's holdings. Also by 1727 the Combes had acquired additional *lands* known as Helders & Downes. Downes extended northwards in the direction of Hindhead.

According to James III's Diary[4] the hill descending from Hindhead to Shottermill was then known as 'Longdown or Down End'. 'Helders', the *cottage* only, by 1727 had passed into the hands of William Deacon and was near High Pitfold Farm. The Combes in 1727 still held the cottage (location unknown) called Develyns. All these holdings – Helders & Downes and Develyns – are described as 'parcel of Combes' and it looks as though in the 1600s the Combes' lands had comprised much of the central part of Pitfold. Sometime, however, during the 1600s these holdings became divided and reapportioned – probably between two Combes sons – and two Combes Farms appear thereafter, one in Pitfold manor and the other in Farnham manor.

In 1615 Thomas Combes had acquired Lane End Farm (manorial name Curtis) in the manor of Farnham through marriage to Alice, the Harding heir[†]. In the 1727 Pitfold manor rental there is simultaneous reference to Thomas Combes of Combes (the original Critchmere farm and land) and to Thomas Combes of Lane End, the latter having added the Helders and Downes *lands* and Develyns to his part.

In 1646 Thomas Combes of Lane End purchased Allens Farm (details below) and from this date held a farm extending from behind Shottermill Street up the east side of the Hindhead Road to an undetermined point toward Hindhead. The main farmhouse remained at Lane End (at Junction Place, but now gone) and in 1641 Thomas Combes is described in the Haslemere parish register as 'living by the highway from Haslemere to Shotover Mill'.

The lands of the Combes of 'Combes' or Critchmore Farm did not appear to alter much, although one line of the Combes, probably this one, had accumulated two small parcels in the west of the manor – Portbrewers and a few acres on Woolmer Heath – and John Combes sold these to the Benifolds

---

[†] The Hardings, although they disappear from Shottermill in the 1600s, reappear in the early 1800s. In 1561, the Hardings at Frensham were well-known clothiers. From a very early date they were referred to as Gentlemen and throughout the whole period of the rolls are centered on Frensham, having settled at Spreakley and Dockenfield in the 1500s. In 1562–3 they and other members of cloth makers, among them Chittys and Hookes, are accused of making kerseys at Pitfold, Headley and Linchmere. Bartholomew Harding of Pitfold [see West Sy.Fam.Hist.Soc. Early Surrey wills, MW2] was descended from this family and it was his daughter Alice who married Thomas Combes in 1615 and brought with her Lane End Farm. Bartholomew Harding had also held in 1549 a small tenement called Brownes (possibly now Brownescombe) and by 1727 a John Harding owned a cottage at Critchmere. Never far away, in the 1800s they reappear in Shottermill and are intimately connected with the paper industry and, later, another branch with the building industry and the post office.

in 1668.[5]

The Combes of Lane End, however, seem to have been more active in enlarging their holding. In 1665 John Combes of Lane End purchased Sturt Farm[6] which was held until sold to the Simmons family in 1752;[7] in 1712 Thomas Combes of Lane End purchased parts of the Great Purpresture[8] and lastly in 1734/5 Thomas of Lane End bought Brookbank.[9]

The last early Combes holding was that of Nicholas Combes which in 1549 he had from his father John a Combe. This was situated near High Pitfold Farm and always (very confusingly) also called High Pitfold although only comprising a barn and 3 closes of 4 acres. It is referred to here, for clarity's sake as 'Little High Pitfold'. By 1727 this property had also passed into the hands of William Deacon who also held another nearby but not previously mentioned property called Parke Combe, a close of land with half a draught well (in Well Field near High Pitfold Farm which can be seen on the Frensham Tythe Map No. 1010).

Subsequently this small group of holdings near High Pitfold Farm and including Helders, the cottage, pursued an independent course. Deacon, who was a Frensham parish yeoman (he had other land in Bramshott)[10] left a will in 1740[11] in which these properties were left to his daughter and son in law Ann and Thomas Heckford. Also, from his will of 1732[12] John Berry seems to have had some sort of connexion, probably being an occupier. By Tythe Map time, 1839, all these properties – Helders cottage, Park Combe and 'Little High Pitfold' – had passed into the hands of the Cleasbys of Regents Park London about whom nothing is known.

The Combes family is a difficult one to sort out. The naming of an eldest son for his father was a long-established custom but the Combes elevated this custom to an art form and for a long period all the Combes inheriting land in the line of direct descent were without exception called Thomas. It has not therefore been possible to decide whether the two holdings of 'Combes' (Critchmere Farm) and 'Curtis' (Lane End Farm) were ever combined or were always separate. Had there been two strands of the Combes clan or did all these holdings divide and recombine according to one family's fortunes?

The Combes did appear at times to run into inheritance problems. On occasions sons died before their fathers leaving a grandson still a minor to inherit, and on other occasions properties went sideways to younger brothers (always Johns). Quite often the Combes wives (sometimes second wives) outlived their husbands so that they continued to hold the properties for their bench, as a result of which the date of the conveyance of the properties did not necessarily correspond with their husband's date of death. In the early 1700s there existed simultaneously a Thomas of Combes and a Thomas of Curtis[13] and in 1757 Thomas Combes yeoman, specifically of Critchmore, was buried. Mostly the Combes are referred to as 'of Frensham parish' which unhelpfully covered both holdings. On the whole the evidence points by the 1600s to a division of the Combes family holding into two separate farms. It was certainly the case by the early 1700s.

Of all the Pitfold families, the Combes were amongst those who continued longest both to live and work farms in the area and they do not disappear as important Shottermill landholders until the 1820s. They continued, in fact, to hold land in Linchmere manor until 1864 after Bridge Farm came to them in 1773 from the last John Shotter there who was uncle to Thomas Combes of Frensham parish. Previously they had held various other properties in Linchmere manor (mostly acquired through marriage) during the 1700s which seemed to be the high point of their relative wealth and importance. The Linchmere holdings were part of Church Farm, Woodmancote, the Mill Tavern land (Stones) and Clouds Hill Cottage.

The enrolled Combes wills did not always greatly assist in sorting out the various family members, but an extract from the 1696 will of Thomas Combes of Lane End[14] (see later) illustrates typical provision for widows and second sons. Quite often wills were not made until the last moment. In light of the primitive medical care then available, a person falling ill assumed that most likely he would die, but with an eye to the possibility of a sudden demise without notice, it became normal upon inheriting land and property to surrender these 'to the use of one's will' which was recorded in the rolls. This meant that the terms of any will overrode the custom of the manor whereby manorial property went automatically to the eldest son.

With increasing prosperity people often wished to divide their property between several sons. This obviously upset the manor authorities and the Linchmere Rolls in 1699 rather irritably reminded the copyhold tenants that they should adhere to the custom of inheritance whereby 'the Eldest child ought to inherit as heir and all widows ought by ye like custom to enjoy the Copyhold Lands & tenements for their chaste widowhood for their Bench paying to ye Lord one peny fine only'. There was, however, no indication subsequent to this that anyone took the slightest notice if it did not suit them.

If a tenant was happy to adhere to the normal custom of inheritance, then his manorial lands would not need to be detailed in a will, only his money and personal effects. Even paupers made wills as they had at least the clothes they stood up in. Daughters on the whole seemed to have been, locally at least, generously catered for. Married daughters were usually awarded a small sum as a kindly gesture, but not too large a one as they were now, thankfully, some one else's responsibility. Single daughters were left a considerably larger amount to act as a dowry or, if they continued to live single and blessed (or were considered to be past praying for), to enable them to achieve some degree of independence although they were expected to continue to live with their mother or eldest brother. In his will of 1638 Thomas Payne the Elder of Pitfold, left his married daughters 1s each and a single daughter £100.

The sale of manorial land as opposed to freehold land, was always the subject of some nervousness as essentially it was in part governed by feudal law and was therefore held conditionally to some degree. It is the reason why such sales are on occasion knee deep in documentation whereby the seller repeatedly agrees that he is selling land which is free from claims of dower or distant kin and any other conceivable claim arising out of manorial custom. These take the form of quitclaims, sometimes including reference to cousins removed to the nth degree, and the signing of bonds whereby the seller agrees to repay twice the purchase sum involved in the conveyance if this does not prove to be satisfactory.

Critchmere Farm (Pitfold manor)

The history of Critchmere Farm is fairly simple. The Combes held it at least from the 1500s until 1826 when it was sold to Edward James Baker, and an account of its fortunes will be continued later. The Bakers during the later nineteenth century were the Lords of Pitfold manor.

Lane End Farm (Farnham manor)

Lane End Farm in 1877

Lane End Farm was obviously seen as one of the Combes family's main holdings from the naming of several Combes as 'of Curtis', its manorial name. It is not quite certain at the end of which lane it lay. Lane End Farmhouse was on the site of what was the entrance to Holy Cross and has been demolished. The Combes held Lane End until 1770 when it was sold to Roger Shotter V (the last of the five Roger Shotters) of Pitfold.[15] By the 1770s there had been a number of entries in the rolls whereby various Combes applied for licences to demise (sublet) all their copyhold lands in the manor of Farnham generally and others in the tything of Tilford in the same manor.[16] Whether these were the local Combes with land other than their Shottermill holdings is not known.

The Thomas Combes of Curtis/Lane End who first purchased Allens Farm (described below) in the 1640s lived at Lane End and enrolled his will into the manor rolls in 1697[17] and, after leaving Lane End and Allens Farm to his son Thomas, laid down the precise conditions under which he should inherit. Thomas was to pay his mother Joan £10 a year and make sure that she had sufficient room to dwell at Lane End, sufficient fuel for her to burn and liberty to brew, wash, bake and dress her meals and also to have use of the herb garden. Thomas was also to pay his younger brother John £50 when he was 25.

In fact the son Thomas who inherited must have died early as in 1722[18] Lane End and Allens passed to *his* son Thomas. He too did not seem to have lasted long as in 1732 the farms passed to his brother John[19] and in 1765, John's two sons inherit.[20] It is at this date that some of the holdings of the Combes of Lane End were divided up. John the elder son inherited the Lane End and Allens Farms. Thomas the younger inherited the two closes in the Great Purpresture[21] which the Combes had purchased in 1712 from the Tamplins.[22] There are other lands which members of the Combes family held during the 1600s and 1700s, and these are dealt with below but by this time, the late 1700s, it is impossible to sort out the complex Combe family relationships. All that can be said is that by 1770 the direct line of the Combes holding Lane End ended and their lands were sold to Roger Shotter V.

Allens Farm *(The Farmhouse late Blossom Cottage now Church Lane House)* and Lees Cottage *(Farnham manor)*

Allens Farmhouse, known for many years as Blossom Cottage but now Church Lane House is a Grade II Listed Building. It lies, somewhat hidden, on the eastern corner of the junction of Church Road and the Hindhead Road (see Fig.13). Although much changed externally and extended, it was originally a small timber-framed mediaeval open hall house of two bays and probably dates to the late 1400s/early 1500s. There is within much exposed timber including a massive tie beam, inglenook fireplaces and the remains of bread ovens. There was possibly an earlier dwelling of some sort there, as a William and Richard Allayn are recorded as paying taxes in the Tything of Churt in the 1330s, although property taxed at that date cannot be identified, and there were Allayns elsewhere in the Tything, particularly over a long period at Whitmoor.

Allens comprised a messuage or farmhouse and half a virgate – about 16 acres or so – with a quit rent of 10s as was standard for a property of this size. The fact that the farm was there at least around 1500 suggests that possibly the Allens had managed, like the Pope family, to successfully weather the difficult period during and after the Black Death when the records are more often full of references to derelict farmhouses and vacant land. The Allen family is first recorded as holding the Allens Farm in Pitfold in 1560[23] by which date the manor rolls are beginning to comprise an orderly record, and various Allens are listed as holding the farm[24] until in June 1640 a John Allen is recorded in the Linchmere Parish Register as having been 'murdered by ye fall of his Mare' leaving another recently baptized Thomas, his son, as his heir.

Allens Farm/Blossom Cottage before its modern extension

There were other John Allens around at this time, and whether or no the John who fell off his horse was the holder of Allens Farm, at all events after this date no more is heard of the Allen family at the farm. Perhaps his infant son had died or widow Margaret had felt unable to cope on her own, as the property is next seen as being held by Thomas Combes of Lane End. The transfer from the Allens to the Combes seems to have taken place in 1646.[25] This entry is itself missing as this year fell within the period of the Civil War when many of the Farnham manor records are either missing or difficult to find, but the purchase is referred to in the entry in 1666[26] when Thomas Combes sold off an Allens Farm cottage. This 1666 entry describes the cottage as coming into the hands of Thomas Combes in 1646 along with Allens Farm proper comprising a messuage and half virgate, rent 10s. from which the cottage in 1666 is then divided off and awarded a quit rent of 1d.[27]

This was the cottage which is now known as **Lees Cottage** in Church Road, and which henceforth is always described as late parcel of Allens, ie conventional manorial jargon indicating that, although now a copyhold in its own right, it had originated as part of the holding called Allens. This description was necessary to identify it to the manor from the many other similar cottages, originally parcels of other ancient farms.

It was sold to William Tamplin, member of an iron worker family of Linchmere which had purchased other properties in Shottermill (see the

Tamplins further below). In 1673, when Jane Tamplin inherited it from her father, William, the cottage was described as being in the occupation of Thomas Billinghurst,[28] and in 1719 in the tenure of Thomas Kingett,[29] these two names remaining associated with the description of Lees cottage for many years and long after either Billinghurst or Kingett had ceased to have any connexion with it. Thomas Billinghurst was in fact Jane Tamplin's husband and typically her cottage was held in her right but in his name.

Lees Cottage (today its timber frame is again visible)

Lees Cottage is also a Grade II listed building but dated to the 1500s, being of typical post-mediaeval timber-frame construction. Like all these small cottages and unlike the farms which tended to remain in the hands of one family for generations, Lees was held by a number of relatively short-term tenants. After Jane Tamplin had sold it to James Stoneham in 1693,[30] he sold it almost immediately and between 1696 and 1710 the Cottage was held in turn by two Roger Shotters, the second selling it to John Shepherd.[31] Shepherd had been a hammerman at Pophole and would have been known to the Pitfold Shotters. However, these two Shotters may well not have been the two main Rogers of Pitfold, father and son, as the second Roger inherited Lees cottage on the death of his father in 1710 and Roger of Pitfold senior had died in 1701. There were other minor Rogers about.

The next inhabitant was Thomas Kingett who held it for about 40 years between 1720 and 1764.[32] It is just possible that Kingett may have been a paper maker at Sickle Mill during part of his tenancy. His son probably was as he is on record as a papermaker in the 1754 Haslemere Poll List by right of owning an undivided sixth part of some indecipherable property.

Lees Cottage takes its present name from the tenancy between 1765 and 1821 of two generations of the Lee family, one of whom, Christopher, was a mealman from Kirdford. He was buried in 1789.[33] From Christopher it went to his brother James and then to James's son also Christopher who was in 1813 described as a taylor.[34] After this in 1821 it came into the hands of John Harding who was a paper maker and worked for the Simmons family. This farm cottage had probably been built circa 1550. Its timber framing is of fairly modest quality.

The Combes family of Lane End held Allens Farm until 1770 but before selling the land, John Combes sold off the old Allens farmhouse, Blossom Cottage, when this parcel is also described for identification purposes as late parcel or part of Allens. John Combes sold Blossom Cottage in 1768 to John Morley the Younger,[35] possibly a glover like his father, after which there is a direct descent to Mary Petter who held it at Tythe Map time in 1839.[36] The farmhouse, Blossom Cottage, was sold to John Morley with its garden only, rent 6d. The remaining triangle of land around Blossom Cottage (Junction Place) remained part of Allens farm land so that in 1841 it was Edward James Baker (who then owned Allens land – the rest of this triangle being his hop garden) that James Simmons III had to approach when seeking a site for St. Stephens Church.

After this sale of Blossom Cottage to Morley, the rent of Allens Farm was reduced from 10s to 9/6d, which rent it continued to pay until the late nineteenth century, Blossom Cottage always being described as a messuage or the farmhouse from which the farm had originally been run. In 1768, therefore, the Combes were left holding only the old Allens Farm *lands*. Their own farmhouse of Lane End was only just across the road – a couple of hundred yards from Blossom Cottage – and presumably Blossom was no longer felt to be necessary to them, particularly as the sixteen or so Allens Farm's acres had long been absorbed into and become an integral part of Lane End Farm. Both these land parcels the Combes held until 1770 when they were sold to Roger Shotter V of Pitfold.[37] Shotter at this date was an Attorney at Law in Guildford and had probably not lived in Pitfold since the 1740s, but he continued to purchase property in Pitfold which he held until his death in 1781.

Sturt Farm (Farnham manor)

Sturt Farm was bought in 1665 by one of the Combes, in this case a John Combe who seems to have been a younger brother. The earlier history of Sturt Farm can be found in the chapter on the Wheeler Family who built the Hammer (later Sickle Mill) on part of its lands circa 1600 and its later history under the Combes is also given in the Wheeler Family section.

Part of the Great Purpresture – The Six & Three Acre Closes
(Farnham manor)

In 1712 a Thomas Combes also purchased two closes containing three and six acres respectively which lay on the central and western parts of the Great Purpresture where now the road from Haslemere turns down by Junction Place to Sickle Mill, being part of the 18 acres of the Great Purpresture.[38] These closes had been in the hands of the Tamplins and their history will be detailed under that family.

Brookbank *(Farnham manor)*

The last Combes holding, bought in 1734/5, was the house later to become known as Brookbank opposite Cherrimans. This is described in the chapter on the Surrey-side cottages. The next chapter follows the fortunes of the Payne family.

References in Chapter Ten

[1] PRO.E36/169
[2] Has.Mus.LD.5.258
[3] Has.Mus.LD.5.232
[4] Simmons Dy. 18 Jul 1848.
[5] Has.Mus.L.D.5.245.
[6] HRO.11M59/E1/126/1
[7] HRO.11M59/E2/153035
[8] HRO.11M59/E1/133/4
[9] HRO.11M59/E2/153017
[10] HRO.11M59/E1/133/3
[11] PCC 1740/33
[12] Has.Mus.LD.5.444
[13] Has.Mus.LD.5.261 & 5.258
[14] HRO.11M59/E1/131/2
[15] HRO.11M59/E2/153053
[16] Ibid 153152
[17] HRO.11M59/E1/131/2
[18] HRO.11M59/E2/153005
[19] Ibid 153015
[20] Ibid 153048
[21] Ibid 153048
[22] HRO.11M59/E1/133/4
[23] Ibid 111/6
[24] Ibid 111/7;117/4
[25] Ibid 126/2
[26] Ibid 126/2
[27] Ibid 126/2
[28] HRO.11M59/E1/158141
[29] HRO.11M59/E2/153002
[30] HRO.11M59/E1/130/4

[31] Ibid 130/4, 131/2 & 133/2
[32] HRO.11M59/E2/153002
[33] Frensham par.reg.
[34] HRO.11M59/E2/153093, 153047, 153072, 153092 & 153101
[35] Ibid 153051
[36] Ibid 153101
[37] Ibid 153053
[38] HRO.11M59/E1/133/4

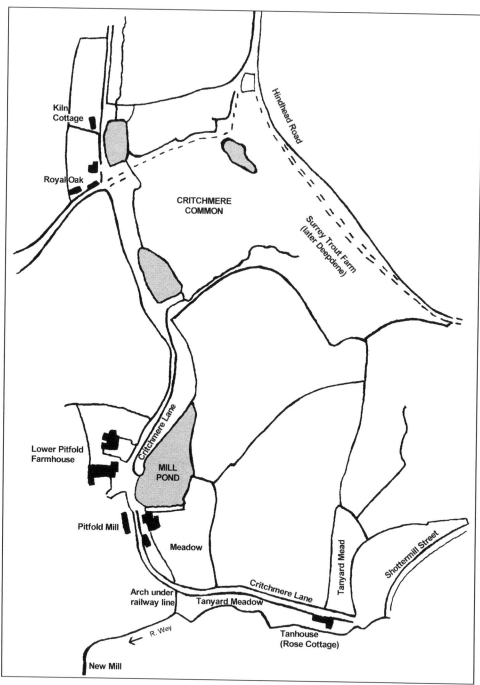

Fig.11: Pitfold Mill and surroundings

Chapter Eleven

The Landholding Families (2)

The Thomas Paynes at Pitfold Mill and Lower Pitfold and High Pitfold Farms; their other small Pitfold manor land parcels which the Benifolds grouped to form Middle Pitfold Farm; after the Paynes, the Bardens and Shotters (with local family tree) at Pitfold Mill and Lower Pitfold Farm; the Napper and Cherriman families at the Tanhouse; High Pitfold Farm thro' the Paynes, Benifolds and Bakers.

The Paynes, Benifolds & Shotters (also the Napper and Cherriman Families)

The second important family of Pitfold landholders was the Payne family. Members of the family appear in the records in the middle 1500s but have obviously been accumulating small local land parcels in both Surrey-side manors for some time. They continue in Pitfold until the death of Thomas the Elder in 1638.

Members of the Payne family held land both in the part of Shottermill belonging to Farnham manor and also in Pitfold manor. In Farnham manor they held Lower Pitfold Mill and Pitfold Farm and briefly the Tanyard Cottages (now Rose Cottage). In Pitfold manor they held the small land parcels of Hamlyns and Stevens and also High Pitfold Farm.

Although first appearing in the records in the early/middle 1500s, almost certainly they had been in Pitfold from an earlier date. In the 1593/4 Lay Subsidy, they headed the list of local tax payers. Nothing much is known about their origins but after holding properties in the area for about 100 years they appear to head in the direction of Elstead.

In the manor of Pitfold the first references are to a Henry and John Payne who had held High Pitfold Farm and Hamlyns from 1549 and probably before that. (In 1549, High Pitfold Farm was held by a William White but only through his marriage to the widow of John Payne.) They had also held the small land parcel of Stevens as it is seen to pass to the Benifolds on the death of the younger Thomas Payne in 1627.[1]

The first reference in the Farnham manor rolls is to Henry Paine in 1572 for holding on a long rent through an escheat one and possibly both of the

Tanyard cottages.[2] It sounds as though the Paynes were seriously into the process of accumulating whatever properties in the area they could lay their hands on and had been a family benefiting from the dislocation after the Black Death.

The second reference is to Richard Paine, about whom nothing is known except that he was of Thursley – probably the parish – who held Lower Pitfold Farm (Pope's or Popys) in 1537.[3] Thomas Paine his nearest kinsman and heir succeeded to the farm in 1571[4] and in 1579 bought Pitfold 'fulling mill' next door.[5] This was Thomas the Elder of Pitfold. He had several sons but only Thomas the Younger and James are relevant to Pitfold. The elder Thomas Payne lived until 1638, at his death living at Runfold near Farnham and instructing that he should be buried at Elstead. His eldest son Thomas predeceased him in 1627. They were both persons of consequence. They are described as Gentlemen and were undoubtedly the preeminent family in Pitfold. They held the lease of Shottover Mill from 1582/3 until some unknown date in the early 1600s.

Both Thomases served on numerous Grand Juries on the Home circuit as far afield as Southwark and Reigate. The Elder Thomas Payne appeared on several local wills as overseer or trustee, although oddly enough he appears to have made only his mark on his own will when he is described as 'aged and weak', and Thomas the Younger in 1623/4 held Courtshill and its 30 acres (in the Thursley part of Haslemere) when acting as trustee in the will of Richard Heath.[6] Thomas the Elder was the man seen in the Pophole chapter as having requested Viscount Montague in 1584 to maintain the banks of Pophole pond, presumably so that his mills upstream did not suffer. He was one of the local Gentlemen listed in the 1623 Visitation by the Heralds who were investigating people's claims to coat armour.

The early Stuarts employed a means called Distraint of Knighthood to raise cash whereby all suitable people owning land worth £40 a year (an amount set some centuries ago) were fined if they had neglected to be knighted. The revival of this custom in a period when knighthoods were clearly seen to be traded for cash gave great umbrage to the landed classes and in particular to the upper stratum of yeomen. Whether Payne paid the fine for refusal is not known, although it seems that the Heralds found his antecedents deficient and he is listed under the Disclaimers. The returns for this exercise[7] demonstrate its unpopularity. Local yeomen are entered as sick, visiting, gone away (leaving no forwarding address), being under age, or as just failing to appear. In Haslemere Matthew Cobden said he had £40 p.a. but refused to compound.

In 1608 when the last Valuation by the Crown of the remaining undisposed-of holdings of Shulbrede Priory took place, it was Thomas Payne the Elder who was nominated to report on any such in Frensham parish. It was Thomas the Younger who advanced to the Wheeler family the large mortgage on the Wheeler/Sturt hammer (see below), and lastly it was

Thomas the Younger who for a short period was joint Lord of the Manor of Frydinghurst with Peter Quennell of Imbhams. In addition, they also held High Readen in Thursley parish which they sold to Henry Wheeler in 1600[8] and other holdings elsewhere in Farnham manor.

Only the will of Thomas the Elder seems to have survived[9] but the will of Elizabeth widow of Thomas the Younger showed her to have been in very comfortable circumstances dispensing 50s to the poor, silver spoons in various directions, forgiving debts of £70 to her nephew Nicholas Harding and several other smaller debts, and leaving £5 to £12 legacies to a number of nieces, nephews, servants and friends. The family probably lived at Pitfold Farm, although as members of the upper stratum of yeomen, almost certainly their properties were sublet and they lived off their rents. The three younger sons of Thomas the Elder came into other family holdings in Farnham manor, in particular in Elstead, but the two Thomases seem to have lived in Pitfold.

The Benifold Family

When Thomas Payne the Younger died in 1627, his Pitfold manor properties passed to his aunt Agnes Benifold, his father's sister and member of the Bramshott yeoman family. Perhaps the most significant feature of Pitfold in the 1600s was the accumulation of small holdings in Pitfold manor by the Benifolds. These were Hamlyns and Stevens from the Paynes, and a few acres near Pophole, some waste on Woolmer Heath, and Brownes and Portbrewers from others.[†] These lands the Benifolds amalgamated into the farm which became known as Middle Pitfold and which was held by them until 1765 when they sold the farm to William Baker, second son of Richard Baker of Stilland Farm in Northchapel.[10] This was the start of the Baker association with Pitfold and Shottermill which lasted until the late 1800s.

Apart from their coming to constitute Middle Pitfold Farm, the individual location of these land parcels is not known (see Fig.5). There is a collection of deeds in the Haslemere Museum[11] which details the history of the Benifold family and their accumulation and eventual disposal of these holdings. The Bakers held Middle Pitfold Farm until the late nineteenth century.

When comparing the descriptions of some of these Pitfold manor holdings in 1549[12] with those in 1727, it is noticeable that some of these Middle Pitfold farmhouses have disappeared. In the 1727 Pitfold Manor Rental,[13] Stevens, Hamlyns and Brownes no longer have houses upon them and are described only as land. Brownes at that date is only meadow. It is possible

---

[†] Brownes came from the Hardings when it is seen to pass between the Roger Benifolds Elder and Younger in 1708 when it was a parcel of meadow; a few acres of moor near Pophole came from William Hayward [Has.Mus.LD 5.256]; Portbrewers and some waste on Woolmer Heath came from John Combes in 1668, [Ibid.LD.5.245] and Hamlyns and Stevens came from Thomas Payne in 1627 [Ibid.LD.5.243].

that these old farmhouses became barns or farm buildings only. There is a hint in the late accounts of James Baker of Stilland, Northchapel, that the farmhouse of Middle Pitfold may originally have been on the land called Portbrewers.

Pitfold Mill and Lower Pitfold Farm (Farnham manor)

After 1520 when Thomas Pope licensed the fulling mill at Pitfold to Thomas Bedyll under condition that he should repair it as it had fallen into decay, the assumption is that this was done.[14]   Afterwards the mill passed briefly through the Cooper family to Henry Marshe in 1578[15] who obtained in that year a licence to 'convert' the mill, and when in 1579 it was purchased by the elder Thomas Payne,[16] he also applied in 1594 for a licence 'to pull down and amend one close situated on his land to the extent that he could erect as many buildings on his premises as he could maintain.'[17]

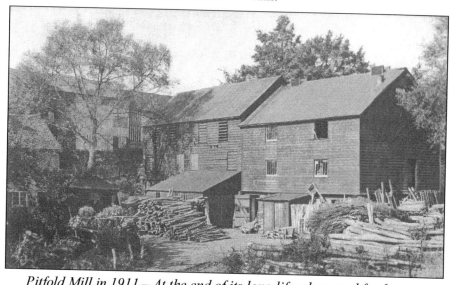

Pitfold Mill in 1911 – At the end of its long life when used for fencing by which time few hints of its past history can be seen

Something fundamental was going on it seems but precisely what is not made clear. Pitfold Mill retained its description as a fulling mill long after its use changed. It is therefore impossible to say precisely what its function was until it was known to be one of the Simmons' paper mills 200 years later. It may, however, have gone from fulling to the processing of skins at this time. With Pitfold mill Thomas Payne held the one acre mill pond (now gone) on the north side of the mill with a watercourse, and the small meadow south of the mill extending down to Critchmere Lane which meadow he purchased from Richard Baldwyn of the Tanyard Cottages in 1599.[18] The mill, pond and meadow went together as a unit almost until the end of the rolls. See Fig.11.

A twentieth century photograph of the mill shows it to have been built of wood (almost certainly the later Simmons rebuild) but there is no evidence to suppose that it had ever been of a more solid construction. Probably, during the course of its long life, it had been subject to constant patching and re-building.

Lower Pitfold Farm (the later Manor House) in 1876 from the south, when it had been part cannibalised and occupied for many years by farm labourers

Lower Pitfold Farm had been bought some time earlier than the mill by Richard Paine of Thursley in 1537[19] and this came to Thomas Payne the Elder in 1571.[20] In 1611[21] Thomas Payne the Elder passed both Pitfold mill and farm in his lifetime to Thomas the Younger with the proviso that if there were no heirs of the latter's body, they should go to a younger son James. This sort of proviso was not at all unusual but its inclusion in every reference to farm and mill possibly suggests that the likelihood of the younger Thomas lasting long or producing heirs was thought to be in doubt. In the event this proved to be the case.

After Thomas the Younger's death in 1627[22] without issue, his younger brother James inherited the Pitfold farm and mill and later retired to the Elstead area where he had other holdings left to him by his father. As was the custom, Elizabeth, Thomas the Younger's widow retained her rights in Pitfold Mill and Farm for the term of her natural life but in 1640 she forfeited these rights by cutting down and turning to her own use various trees suitable for timber without a licence from the manor.[23] On the death of Thomas Payne the Younger, whereas most of his Pitfold manor properties went to his kin the Benifolds, the Farnham manor properties went to the younger brother James and in 1631 James sold Lower Pitfold Farm and Mill to Roger Barden for £400 which is recorded as being paid.[24]   (James Payne is to be seen holding properties in Badshot and Elstead for some time after this, inheriting his mother's properties there).[25]

Roger Barden was a member of one of the original iron working families and he has been mentioned in the chapter on Pophole. There is nothing, however, to suggest that his iron interests were transferred to Pitfold Mill. After ten years he sold both farm and mill to Roger Shotter in 1641[26] and presumably moved away as there is no record of his burial locally. This was Roger Shotter I of Pitfold.[27]   Roger's wife, Elizabeth, was the daughter of Henry Figge and Figge's heir to two virgates in the tything of Frensham and another in the tything of Churt.[28]

Roger Shotter I was the middle son of old Roger of Shulbrede. As a minor and jointly with his elder brother William, he had been admitted in 1610 to Watts Farm (but excluding Pophole Hammer). He was also the Roger who by 1668[†] had built or possibly rebuilt the farmhouse at Pitfold which later became known as Pitfold Manor House and is remembered today in Manor Close on the bend of Critchmere Lane.[‡]

A digression is made from the history of the Payne properties to continue the history of Lower Pitfold Mill and Farm under the Shotters until their purchase in 1781 by the Simmons.

The Shotter Family

In 1662, Roger I surrendered both Pitfold farm and mill to his son Roger II with the provision that his son should make an annual payment of £20 to himself and Elizabeth for the term of the survivor.[29]   He also surrendered Watts Farm to his son. He was then 65, an age which seems to have had a long pedigree for retiring from the fray (although only where financially possible). The Shotters of Pitfold – all Rogers – were to hold Pitfold farm and mill for 140 years until 1781.

During the 1600s and 1700s Shotters are to be found all over West Sussex, Surrey and Hampshire – in places such as Haslemere, Pitfold, Linchmere, Churt, Frensham, Fernhurst, Bramshott, Farnham, Lurgashall, Verdley, Lodsworth, Chichester and Newton Valence – to name but a few. Many were landholders but some of the younger sons are found as mercers, tanners, cordwainers and butchers. In many cases they married profitably and were connected to most of the other prominent local families such as the Sandhams, Boxalls, Cherrimans, Osbornes, Rapleys, Uptons, Marshalls, Willards, Stillwells, Figges, Wakefords and Yaldens.

[†] Ponsonby's sketch of the house shows a date of 1668 but his text says 1669.

[‡] Occasionally this house is referred to as Critchmere Manor House, but there was no manor of Critchmere. This description indicated only its location on Critchmere Lane.

As mentioned above, Elizabeth Figge brought Roger I a considerable property. Roger and Elizabeth died in 1672 and 1676 respectively. Their son, Roger II, married Margaret Yalden of Lodsworth in 1662, when Roger II was admitted to his father's properties in his father's lifetime; and inherited his mother's properties on her death.[30] In 1662, he is described in the Linchmere rolls as 'Roger of Lodsworth' and may have been pursuing an independent livelihood there. There is a Shotter's Farm near Lickfold Bridge. However, on the baptism of his son, Roger III in 1663,[31] he is referred to as Roger of Pitfold. Roger II died in 1693[32] leaving a will dated 1689.[33]

In this will, Roger II describes himself as 'of Pitfold' and called his newly built house at Pitfold Farm (the later Manor House) 'Hillside'. (In the 1780 Land Tax return it is called 'Pitfield Place' and in the rolls in 1693 simply 'Pittfield'). It is in this Shotter will that the reference appears to his 'iron at Pophole', but there is no hint of his leaving any remainder of a lease of the hammer there which, if it had existed, would certainly have been mentioned. His connexion with the iron industry has already been commented on in the chapter on Pophole Hammer.

His two daughters were well looked after, receiving £200 apiece, and the will refers only to his houses and contents and lands insofar as their inheritance by his son Roger is conditional upon his paying out the specified sums to his brothers and sisters. There is no detailed reference to the disposition of his land holdings as the descent of these went automatically to the eldest son and these transfers are recorded in the Linchmere Rolls of 1693, and the Farnham rolls.[34] His two younger sons, William and John who appear to get little in his will, inherited his lands in Frensham tything.[35] It seems that in turn Roger II passed his lands to his eldest son in his lifetime (in 1687). Roger III was to pay his father £20 p.a. and son John (his brother) was to receive £250 when he was 21. If John died before he was 21, the £250 was to be divided amongst William and the girls, Mary and Margaret.

Failure by Roger III to continue to support his father as specified would mean that this surrender was void and Roger II laid down a number of requirements his son was to adhere to. These included a chamber for his father's use and also access in common to other rooms where his father could greet and receive guests; his father reserved to himself a locked room in the cellar; he was to have the use of means for dressing his meat, for brewing and baking etc, use of the fish pond and half the apples. Son Roger was also to provide him with fuel for the drying of malt and with the use of the stable, and pasture and oats and hay and the shoeing of a horse.[36]

The third Roger of Pitfold, baptized Linchmere 1663, died in 1701 at the age of only 38, leaving a widow Ann who survived him by another 37 years and who seemingly continued to reside in Pitfold. It is from this date that the fortunes of the Pitfold Shotters begin to go awry. Roger III produced two sons – Roger IV and John (bap. Frensham in 1689 & 1695 respectively) but the fourth Roger also died comparatively young, aged 46, in 1735,[37] leaving behind him an infant son, Roger V, born the previous year.[38] This caused complications in the rolls as Roger V's properties which in normal circumstances would have come to him from his father, had in fact never been formally held by his father as grandmother Ann was still alive and holding them for her bench. In 1743, a minor, he inherited from his grandfather[39] but in 1766, he had to re-establish his rights by virtue of a Recovery, a legal procedure.[40] It is for this reason that in the 1735 will of Roger IV[41] he left to his son, Roger V, only lands in the parish of Newton Valence, Hants, presumably acquired in his lifetime, possibly through his wife. He left his wife, Rachel, £30 p.a. according to the marriage settlement. Roger IV had married a Rachel James who after his death remarried John Batchelor. She, and her sister Margaret who had married one of the Neale family, left Roger V additional lands in Wrecclesham.[42]

Roger V, therefore in 1743[43] – being only 8 years old – was placed in the guardianship of his Uncle John, and as grandmother Ann had died in 1738,[44] he may well have left Pitfold somewhere around this time to go and live with Uncle John in Guildford. He is certainly there in the 1750s. Uncle John had been in Guildford since about 1712 when he was apprenticed to an attorney at law and later practiced there on his own account. He was apprenticed to Leonard Child of Guildford, Gent., for six years at a charge of £100[45] and is himself seen to take apprentices between 1735 and 1747.[46] In Trinity Church, Guildford, is a memorial to 'John Shotter of this Town, Gent, who departed this life 16th October 1761 aged 65. Several years Towne Clerke of this Towne'.[47] Young Roger V also became an attorney after attending Eton and Christ's College Cambridge.

The Shotters continued to hold their Pitfold properties until Roger V died in 1781, and even to increase them (dealt with below), although no longer resident in the area. Roger V died without a direct male heir. His heir was Anthony Beauchamp, yeoman of Chobham, his nephew.[48] On his death in 1781, Roger V's Pitfold lands were High Pitfold, Lower Pitfold Farm and Mill, Lane End and Buffbeards (including Allens), and Watts Farm in Linchmere parish, and they were all auctioned.

A family tree is given to facilitate an understanding of the local Pitfold Shotters and the John Shotters of Bridge, and also to clarify that of the senior line of Highbuilding and Northpark as there was (not unsurprisingly in view of the then absence of the rolls) some confusion in earlier family trees regarding the various Williams. The family tree has been restricted to these lines. The Shotter family properties described are only the local ones in Pitfold and Linchmere. They held others.

There is no doubt that until the advent of the Simmons family in the 1730s and then not until the Simmons acquired a large estate, the Shotters replaced the Paynes and Wheelers as the first family in Pitfold. In 1661 in response to the request to make a 'voluntary' contribution towards Charles II's debts on his restoration, Roger Shotter gave 40s (one of the largest sums) and in the 1664 Hearth Tax returns (which suggests his house at Pitfold was already built if not completed till 1668) he paid for a house with 6 hearths, by far the largest house in Shottermill. The Wheelers and Paynes are, of course, gone by this time and the Simmons not yet arrived.

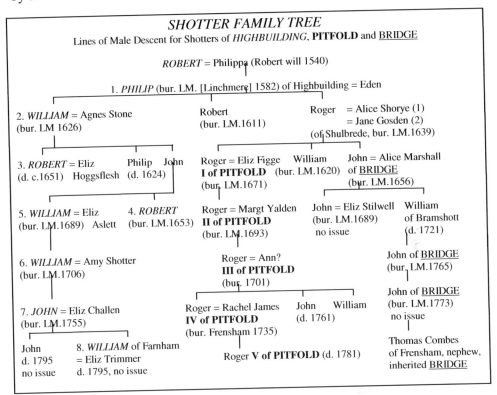

SHOTTER FAMILY TREE

Lines of Male Descent for Shotters of *HIGHBUILDING*, **PITFOLD** and BRIDGE

ROBERT = Philippa (Robert will 1540)

1. *PHILIP* (bur. LM. [Linchmere] 1582) of Highbuilding = Eden

2. *WILLIAM* = Agnes Stone (bur. LM 1626)

Robert (bur. LM.1611)

Roger = Alice Shorye (1) = Jane Gosden (2) (of Shulbrede, bur. LM.1639)

3. *ROBERT* = Eliz (d. c.1651) Hoggsflesh

Philip John (d. 1624)

Roger = Eliz Figge **I of PITFOLD** (bur. LM.1671)

William (bur. LM.1620)

John = Alice Marshall of BRIDGE (bur. LM.1656)

5. *WILLIAM* = Eliz (bur. LM.1689) Aslett

4. *ROBERT* (bur. LM.1653)

Roger = Margt Yalden **II of PITFOLD** (bur. LM.1693)

John = Eliz Stilwell (bur. LM.1689) no issue

William of Bramshott (d. 1721)

6. *WILLIAM* = Amy Shotter (bur. LM.1706)

Roger = Ann? **III of PITFOLD** (bur. 1701)

John of BRIDGE (bur. LM.1765)

7. *JOHN* = Eliz Challen (bur. LM.1755)

Roger = Rachel James **IV of PITFOLD** (bur. Frensham 1735)

John (d. 1761) William

John of BRIDGE (bur. LM.1773) no issue

John d. 1795 no issue

8. *WILLIAM* of Farnham = Eliz Trimmer d. 1795, no issue

Roger **V of PITFOLD** (d. 1781)

Thomas Combes of Frensham, nephew, inherited BRIDGE

There is during this whole period, however, still no firm evidence about what Pitfold Mill was engaged in although the mill and all the Shotter lands (and others elsewhere in Farnham manor) are continuously sub-tenanted, sometimes as a unit of farmhouse and land, sometimes as house and land separately. In 1686, Roger II took the mortgage surrender of 'all that messuage or tenement, barne, gardens, tanyards and two closes being near Pilewell in the parish of Haslemere' from John Bradfold tanner, son and heir of the late William Bradfold, for £247.[49] John Bradfold retained the Pilewell tanyard, perhaps just needing to raise some ready cash on the death of his father. There is nothing in the document to indicate whether he turned to Roger Shotter for the money purely on the basis of social acquaintance or because Roger, like John Bradfold, was also associated with the tanning/ skinning trade at Pitfold Mill. The Shotters made no attempt to purchase the nearby tanyard although there were opportunities.

201

The Tanhouse (Farnham manor)

To return to the Paynes' properties, they had a brief connection with the Tanyard Cottages (now Rose Cottage) opposite Shottover Mill. Tanning must have been one of the earliest industries as the requirement for leather for boots, belts, saddlery and so on together with the need for skins for parchment was ever present. A tanning industry on the Wey here might well have long preceded its first mention in the late 1500s.

Tanning required much water during the cleaning process and areas of a whitish deposit have been found in the garden of Rose Cottage which might well be remains of the old tanning pits in which lime was used. In James Simmons III's Particulars of the Sale by Auction of most of his farms and some of the mills in 1832 the two 'Tanyard Cottages', now Rose Cottage, are included. Rose Cottage is a Grade II Listed Building dated to the late mediaeval period. In the Farnham rolls, there are always two Tanyard Cottages, one with a garden and an acre of meadow running westwards along the north side of the Wey, the other smaller cottage with a half acre paddock running up behind the Staff of Life and Brookbank. For a long time it was thought that there were two separate cottages and certainly each of them has a separately recorded history in the rolls. It would seem, however, that the present building – Rose Cottage – incorporates them both.

Both cottages appear for the first time in the Farnham manor rolls in the late 1500s. In 1572 the rolls show them to have been in the hands of Henry Payne who had held them on a long lease by virtue of an escheat[50] after which, in 1581, John Baldwyn held the one (and probably both – the early records are not totally clear).[51] A will of John Balden of Frensham parish of 1595[52] shows him to have been a tanner and on his death he left the larger cottage to his elder son Richard and the smaller to his son Blaise.[53] The Baldwyns may well have been tanners for some time as, in 1568, a John and Thomas Baldwyn of Shottermill had been indicted for selling leather in contravention of an act forbidding its sale outside a corporate town or market[54] and in the Lay Subsidy of 1593/4, John Baldwyn was amongst the higher tax payers.

Blaise Baldwyn having died, in 1600 his brother Richard disposed of both cottages,[55] the larger to Thomas Payne the Younger[56] who did not use it but sublet it, leaving it when he died in 1627 to his aunt Agnes Benifold.[57] The smaller cottage Richard Baldwyn sold to Charles Barden, the hammerman at Pophole Hammer,[58] who was followed there by his son John. This smaller cottage passed through various hands including those of William and Robert Heyward, probably members of the bellows-making family[59] who no doubt were supplying bellows to both Pophole and Sickle Mill as well as making bellows for domestic use, until in 1693 it was bought by William Cherriman.[60] In the meantime the larger cottage which had gone from Thomas Payne the Younger to his aunt, Agnes Benifold, had been sold immediately by Agnes in 1629[61] to James Napper who describes himself in a

202

deed as a Haslemere tanner[62] and it was in the 1629 rolls entry that this cottage is described for the first time as 'now Le Tanhouse'.

The Tanhouse, now Rose Cottage opposite Shotter Mill

James Napper although he was twice married had no surviving male heir and willed in 1663 that his daughter Ann who had married Edward Stevens should inherit the Tanhouse but on condition that the Stevens should pay him £40 p.a. and that they should also pay his other spinster daughter Elizabeth £3.10s. in 1664 and a further £73.10s in 1665.[63] The Stevens, however, failed to perform these conditions and in 1666, through default, Elizabeth held the Tanhouse.[64] However a year later this ruling was overturned and the Stevens again gained possession of the Tanhouse (the Stevens and Elizabeth had come to some peaceful agreement) until 1674 when it was sold to William Cherryman.[65] It is at this point – the time of the Napper daughters' disagreement – that there appears in large manuscript in the margin of the rolls 'Omnia Vincit Amor' (Love Conquers All). Whether this was some comment on the resolution of the Napper family quarrel or whether the clerk in a moment of tedium was reflecting on a private concern, it is not possible to tell. By 1693, therefore, the Cherriman family of tanners held both Tanyard Cottages and continued to do so until bought out in the 1760s by the Simmons family of Sickle Mill. Further details of the Cherriman family are given below under 'Cherrimans' the house in Shottermill Street which they purchased in 1700 and to which they gave their name.

The report on Rose Cottage made by the Surrey Domestic Buildings Research Group in 1974 refers to a seventeenth century extension and this would seem to agree with its documentary history as having been built either by James Napper or the Cherrimans. Originally the oldest part of Rose

Cottage was a three bay mediaeval open hall house, with the addition of a new parlour bay with jetty to the north and a later three bay cottage or wing at the back. The jettied parlour bay is framed separately from the original old house and the jettied end faces north on to the old Liphook road (Critchmere Lane) which ran west immediately from opposite Shotter Mill. This old road surface is still obvious in the garden of Rose Cottage at the foot of the railway embankment. The Domestic Buildings Research Group refers to evidence (hooks etc) remaining of its use as a skinners, but it is likely that this belonged to such use in the late 1800s when Thomas Gent revived the leather-dressing industry in Shottermill.

High Pitfold Farm (Pitfold manor)

High Pitfold Farm is the last property which had an early connexion with the Payne family, which had held it prior to 1549. The Benifolds inherited it from Thomas Payne the Younger on his death in 1627,[66] but it was an exception to the transfer from the Benifolds to William Baker in 1765[67] of the lands comprising Middle Pitfold Farm. For how long after 1627 the Benifolds held High Pitfold Farm is not known, but according to the 1727 Pitfold Manor Rental, the Farm which included Wackfords (originally Wakefords) was by then in the hands of John Bicknold and it henceforward took a separate independent path.

It seems to have been let by Bicknold to Richard Roe of Pitfold for sixteen years in 1742[68] and was subsequently owned or occupied by William Marden[69] but Marden died in 1795 and in 1791 it is seen to have been held by the Bakers as James Baker of Stilland, Northchapel, surrendered it, amongst other properties, to the use of his will.[70] Some time before 1772, however, it had come into the hands of Roger Shotter V as an estate map of that date[71] shows it to have been in his possession. Probably James Baker had purchased it at the time of the Shotter Auction in 1781.

High Pitfold Farm is Grade II Listed and dates to the 1500s with the usual additions dating to the 16th, 17th, 19th and 20th centuries, and was originally a small two-bay timber-framed building. It has a smoke bay and inglenook fireplace and Tudor brick can still be seen in the infilling of the south wall. In 1976 the well, lined with brick for the first 10ft and in all 40ft deep by 6ft diameter was opened up. Sadly, however, the only items recovered were empty cinzano bottles. It has adjacent to it barns and stables designed by Lutyens in the early 20th century. [Personal communication from the owner].

References in Chapter Eleven

1 Has.Mus.LD.5.243
2 HRO.11M59/E1/111/4
3 HRO.11M59/B1/155880B
4 HRO.11M59/E1/111/2
5 Ibid 112/1
6 PRO.Ct.Common Pleas, 22 Jac.1. Mich. Term, roll 22
7 PRO E179 187/475
8 Has.Mus.LD.6.221
9 Probate Archdeaconry Court Surrey 21.8.1638
10 Has.Mus.LD.5.263
11 Has.Mus.LD.5.236–8; 5.241–6; 5.253–7; and 5.261–4
12 PRO.E36/169
13 Has.Mus.LD.5.258
14 HRO.11M59/B1/155866B
15 HRO.11M59/E1/111/3
16 Ibid 112/1
17 Ibid 113/5
18 Ibid 113/7 & 114/2
19 HRO.11M59/B1/155880
20 HRO.11M59/E1/111/2
21 Ibid 115/8
22 bur. Has 1627
23 HRO.11M59/E1/122/6
24 Ibid 120/7 & 120/9
25 Ibid 121/11
26 Ibid 122/8
27 bap. Linchmere 1597
28 HRO.11M59/E1/120/1
29 Ibid 125/6
30 Ibid 127/4
31 L'mere par.reg.
32 L'mere par. reg.
33 PCC prob.1694
34 HRO.11M59/E1/129/6

35 Ibid 130/4

36 Ibid 129/6

37 bur. Fren. 1735

38 bap. Fren 1734

39 HRO.11M59/E2/153026

40 Ibid 153049

41 PCC prob.1736 X/32/54

42 HRO.11M59/E2/153038

43 Ibid 153026

44 Linchmere par. reg.

45 Surrey Record Soc. Vol.10 No.2319

46 W.Sy Fam.Hist.Soc.Rec. Ser. 6, Nos. 4744–5 & 5210

47 Manning & Bray London, 1814, vol III, 55

48 GMR 115/3/1

49 Has.Mus.LD.6.221

50 HRO.11M59/E1/111/4

51 Ibid 111/7

52 Archdeaconry Court of Surrey, Prob.8.8.1595.

53 HRO.11M59/E1/13/2

54 PRO.Exch.K.R. Mem. R.East. 10 Eliz 234 and Mich.266

55 HRO.11M59/E1/114/6

56 Ibid 114/5

57 Ibid 120/1

58 Ibid 114/6

59 Ibid 130/1

60 Ibid 130/4

61 Ibid 120/2

62 GMR 56/6, 1649

63 HRO.11M59/E1/125/7

64 Ibid 126/2

65 HRO.11M59/E1/158142

66 Has.Mus.LD.5.243

67 Has.Mus.LD.5.263

68 Has.Mus.LD5.238

69 Has.Mus.LD.5.248

70 Has.Mus.LD 5.249

71 Has.Mus.LD.5.240

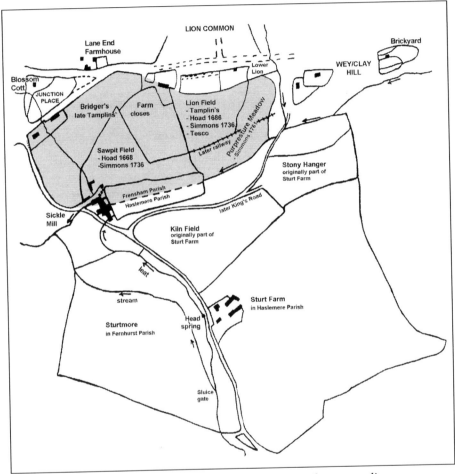

Fig.12: Sickle Mill, Great Purpresture and surroundings

207

Chapter Twelve

The Landholding Families (3)

Wheelers/Sturt Hammer, later Sickle Mill; Sturt Farm and the Great Purpresture; the Construction of the Hammer and its Early Years; the Various Early Names of the Hammer; the Hoads – Sickle-makers – at the Hammer; the Leat; Sickle Making; Sturt Farm its later History; Sickle Mill House; the Cherriman and Tamplin Families; the Tribe Family and Buffbeards.

The Wheelers & Hoads (at Sickle Mill), the Cherrimans, Tamplins and Tribes

The last of the important landholding families in Pitfold between the 1500s and the middle 1600s were the Wheelers, who were the builders of the hammer at Sickle Mill. This chapter also deals with the Hoads who followed the Wheelers at the hammer, and finally the families of the Cherrimans, Tamplins and Tribes.

The Wheelers were connected to the Paynes by marriage, were second to them in the 1593/4 Lay Subsidy for the amount of tax they paid, and held Sturt Farm, the Great Purpresture and the purpresture land on which Cherrimans was to be built. Early Wheeler wills of the 1400s and 1500s show them to have been at Guildford and other places on the North Downs but also and in particular at Elstead to which area the Pitfold Wheelers disappear in the late 1630s after living in Pitfold for about 100 years. There were also Wheelers in Haslemere but it is impossible to distinguish them at this early date and this latter branch continues for some considerable time. The Haslemere Wheelers in the late 1500s may, of course, have been the Wheelers of Sturt Farm which, a Farnham manor holding, lay in Haslemere parish. Members of the Wheeler family continue in the rolls in Elstead tything until the 1800s.

Sturt Farm and the Great Purpresture (Farnham manor)

The Wheeler family had held from at least 1546 the messuage and virgate of land called Sturts. They also held the Great Purpresture, an area of 18 acres abutting Sturt Farm on Sturt's north side and extending from the stream which ran E-W through the centre of the later hammer pond (now covered by the Industrial Estate and the Herons Sports Centre) northwards as far as the Lower Lyon Common, later the Lion Green Car Park, now Haslewey.[1] Fig.12 shows details of the lands of Wheeler's Hammer, of Sturt Farm and of the Great Purpresture.

Sturt Farm in 1876 – view from above showing the many barns

The first recorded Wheeler was William Wheeler of Haslemere parish and he is again described as having held his lands for a long time on a perpetual lease. The Wheelers also seem to have been a family which survived the period after the Black Death and benefited from it. These lands descended from William to Richard in 1546, to Henry in 1561, and then to Henry's son Richard in 1587. Henry of Sturt, Haslemere parish, yeoman, died in 1612 and left a will probated in 1613.[2] Son Richard of course inherited his father's lands but these had already been passed to him in his father's lifetime in 1587[3] with the usual provision for the protection of his parents' interests for the term of their natural life. It was, therefore either Henry or more likely son Richard who held Sturt Farm when the hammer was built there in the early 1600s. Henry's will also made provision for his two grandsons, Richard's children. Of the grandsons, Richard was left various house furnishings and the other, Henry, was left Heath Readen, the land parcel in Thursley parish (somewhere to the south of Hindhead) which Henry senior had bought from Thomas Payne.

It may have been this grandson Henry Wheeler, then tenant of Wakeners farm in Thursley parish, who was connected by Dr Rolston[4] with the reference in the Haslemere parish register in 1609 to Wheeler's hammer. This hammer connexion should, of course, have been to Richard Wheeler of Sturt. There is firm documentary evidence that the hammer was built upon Sturts land and, in any case, there was at that time at Wakeners Farm no

209

appropriate water supply. There was indeed a foundry there, which Dr Rolston mentions, and also a leat, but this was at a much later date.

Besides the Wheelers of Sturt (or as sometimes described 'of Haslemere') and the Wheelers who held property in the Tything of Elstead over a long period, there were also Wheelers of Thursley and another branch at Binsted (near Alton, Hants) who were related to the Sturt branch. In his will of 1612 old Henry of Sturt named Henry Wheeler of Binsted – his brother in law – as one of the overseers of his will, and left money to the church and bell ringers of Binsted. The Binsted Wheelers were obviously also a family of enterprising yeomen and between the late 1500s and 1800 are associated with various fulling and grist mills, and in 1779 Nicholas Wheeler of Binsted leased a spring opposite the Barford paper mill to Abraham Harding, a name associated in the early 1800s with the Simmons' paper mills.[†]

The Wheelers were also related to the Payne family. Constance, the daughter of William Wheeler (possibly a brother of old Henry of Sturt) had married John Payne, and in his will of 1657, a Richard Wheeler yeoman of Thursley appointed his nephew John Payne as sole Executor. Richard seems to have had no surviving issue and his lands were left to the children of his three sisters, but in addition to this he left innumerable small money bequests to a host of relatives and many godchildren. It is amusing but not in the circumstances surprising that a codicil was added to his will by which John Payne was left the use and profits of Richard's lands for a period of two years. This

BY THE STREAM, CAMELSDALE.

The stream flowing over the Sturt Road/Camelsdale Road junction

---

[†] Details of the Wheeler family can be found in the Wheeler Papers in the Hampshire Record Office [HRO 3M51] although most of these deeds concern the earlier Luffs of Hyde Farm who were succeeded there in about 1700 by the Binsted Wheelers through a female line.

may well have resulted from a hint from John Payne that he deserved some recompense for what obviously was going to be a strenuous financial exercise. Normally overseers were awarded a small sum to cover expenses.

To return to the Wheelers of Sturt Farm and the Great Purpresture. The land parcel of Sturt comprised a messuage or farmhouse and a virgate, in theory about 32 acres, although as usual the land was in fact somewhat larger than this. It was also always described as including two additional acres of purpresture the whereabouts of which are never detailed.

'Sturt' is a descriptive name indicating land between two streams. One stream was that flowing west from the Haslemere watershed being joined by others at Foster's (Railway) Bridge and at the Kingdom Hall of the Jehovah's Witnesses at the bottom of Wey Hill. This stream was Sturt's northern boundary flowing later through Sickle Mill pond. The second stream flowed from Blackdown through Sturt meadow behind the houses in Sturt Road. Much of these streams, now piped, can no longer be seen although a picture taken in 1908[5] shows the latter to have been flowing over the present Camelsdale Road (and which it was still doing during the floods in the winter of 2000/1).

The 'Great Purpresture' at the time of the Wheeler ownership was probably its nominal 18 acres but when in the middle 1600s it was divided up into various smaller parcels, its size and boundaries on occasion began to take on an elastic character. Purpresture land had originally been manor waste, cleared and eventually issued by the manor as copyhold land and, whilst in periods of expansion particularly in the 1600s many small parcels of purpresture were sought of the manor and granted – mostly parcels of between 2 and 6 acres – it is almost certain that the Great Purpresture represented a much earlier period of expansion and clearing. There were in Farnham Manor only one or two other similar purpresture areas of such large size. Purpresture land had carried with it no obligation of labour service to the manor.

It was on the stream which comprised the Sturt/Great Purpresture boundary, that Wheeler's Hammer was built, there being no problem with this as land on both sides of the stream were Wheeler-held and could be dammed and flooded to make the hammer pond.

Wheeler's Hammer – Its Construction and Early Years

On the whole, the circumstances of the construction of and early history of the hammer are not totally clear. The background history of the iron industry in the western Weald and also the technology has been described in the chapter on Pophole Hammer. At Pophole, because the entire land involved in its construction and operation – ie both sides of the Wey – were owned by the Viscounts Montague, manorial permission was no problem. In the case of Wheeler's Hammer, however, there is absolutely nothing in either the Farnham manor rolls nor in the Presentments to the Farnham Hundred Court, to indicate that the Wheelers either sought permission or were granted it by the Bishop of Winchester or his officials. The rents of neither the Great Purpresture nor Sturt Farm were affected until long after the hammer's construction. In none of the maps drawn throughout the 1600s was Wheeler's Hammer ever shown. The first indication of the existence of a mill there on maps is not seen until it is shown as 'Sickles Paper Mill' on Rocque's map of 1768.

It is well known that map makers often copied the information given on previous maps but if anyone had ever really looked, the hammer pond must have been fairly obvious. On the Tythe Map the pond occupied an area of about three acres. Possibly, however, if the early map makers had followed the kings highway from Haslemere to Liphook and beyond which went past Shottover Mill, then the Hammer and Pond on the site of the later Sickle Mill might have been easily bypassed. The absence of any record in the rolls to its construction is particularly curious in view of another entry found there in 1694 when a man in Bentley sought permission to dig a hole for a signpost for which he had to pay a new rent of 4s.[6]

The most likely explanation is that if the matter had been dealt with at the Farnham Hundred Court (as was the later mortgage arrangement) the relevant entry had appeared during the period around 1600 when there is a gap in the Court records. However, in the Haslemere parish register of 1609 there are two references to Wheeler's Hammer to prove it was in existence by that early date: the Baptism of Constance Hilman from Wheeler's Hammer, and the Burial of Richard Bartholomew at Wheeler's hammer.

These are the first two direct references to its existence and later evidence places its location firmly in the place now known as Sickle Mill. There is also, however, an additional allusion which, although not yet confirmed, might indicate that the hammer's construction date was around the earlier 1600s. This was referred to briefly under Pophole. In the Tythe Dispute of 1598 relating to Pophole Hammer, it was recorded that the occupier there was one Edward Tanner of Tillington who had refused to pay the prescribed tythe of 40s. In the King's Remembrancer Rolls of 1603/4[7] there is an entry stating that an Edward Tan*worth* of Tillington had been indicted for building a new blomary (hammer) in the parish of Haslemere in 1601/2 in contravention of the Statute of 27 Elizabeth which expressly forbade the construction of new iron works in places where they had not previously existed or where there was insufficient timber to support their demands for fuel (charcoal). Anyone providing information leading to a conviction was to receive half of a tempting £300 reward, the remaining half to go to the Exchequer.

It seems almost certain that this new blomary specified as being in the parish of Haslemere was Wheeler's Hammer. The boundary dividing the parishes of Haslemere (on the south) and Frensham (on the north) was the stream passing E-W through the centre of the hammer pond and the hammer is always described as being situated in Haslemere parish on Sturts land. There is, as far as has been discovered, no other hint of a hammer in any other part of Haslemere, nor any suitable water supply in that parish. The only other iron works which might have been indicated – that at Imbhams – was of course in the parish of Chiddingfold cum Haslemere, but this is usually described as being in Chiddingfold and was probably already working. In any case Imbhams was a furnace not a hammer.

Unfortunately, the Act of 27 Eliz. did not specify, as was often the case, in which court any infringement should be tried. In the early 1600s the appropriate records of the Surrey Quarter Sessions are missing and those of the Assize Courts, also incomplete for that period, contain no reference to Tanner/Tanworth's case. All courts recommended as possibilities by the authority on early courts at the Public Record Office have been searched without result. The Kings Remembrancer Rolls contain the names of people awaiting trial and Tanworth is listed there as he had pleaded not guilty and elected to go for trial. It will be seen that two renderings of Edward's name are given – Tanner and Tanworth – but in view of the fact that they were both Edward Tan... of Tillington, and were both obviously connected with local ironworking, the assumption has been made that these were two versions of the same personal name. The records of the trial, if ever found, would settle the matter comprehensively as they should contain depositions of evidence by local men of standing and these and reference to place names would certainly prove the matter one way or the other.

In 1587 Richard Wheeler of Sturt had married Constance Vice of Haslemere and the year after their marriage they were jointly admitted to Sturt.[8] According to information in the Woods Collection, Godalming, however, children of Richard and Constance were baptized in Wanborough between 1596 and 1600 so it may have been that Richard had farmed elsewhere until about 1600. In a will of Henry Johnsonne, clerk of Puttenham dated 15 March 1595, Richard is described as 'of Wanneborrowe'. Richard's parents, Ann and Henry died in 1607 and 1612 respectively and in 1612 son Richard and wife Constance applied jointly for a licence to sub-let the land of Sturt and the Great Purpresture.[9]

Almost certainly, however, they were by then actually living at Sturt as Richard appears from time to time in the penalty list of the manor of Linchmere rolls, usually for trespassing in some way on Linchmere lands. In 1615, for instance, it was ordered in the Linchmere Manor Court that six of the local tenants should investigate a nuisance committed by him on the nearby lands of Richard Boxold and the widow Hopkins and report at the next Court. Unfortunately no more is heard of this so that the nature of this nuisance will never be known. The widow Hopkins held Washers (later Rats Castle/New Mill land) so it might well have concerned interference with these lands where they touched the river Wey.

After quite an interval Richard Wheeler seems to commence another episode of transgressions and in 1631 and 1633 is reported on several occasions for abstracting alderwood and grazing his pigs on Linchmere Common, and digging clay and extracting gravel from the Linchmere waste, in none of which places he had right to do so, not holding land in Linchmere manor. On his death in 1636, he was buried at Haslemere when he is described as Richard the Elder of Sturte.

The greatest mystery, however, is the taking out of a mortgage on his lands of Sturt, the Great Purpresture and the few acres on which Cherrimans was to be built. This occurred in 1617 by which time any initial financial demands occasioned by the building of the hammer should have been met. Various speculative avenues have been explored but to no avail. There is, of course, absolutely no detail about the finances of the hammer and the connexion between the mortgage and the hammer has been assumed rather than proven. Almost certainly Richard Wheeler himself would not have been involved in the day to day running of the hammer. Iron working of any sort was a skilled and specialised craft and more than likely Wheeler would have leased the hammer out, but who took the financial risks is not known. As a yeoman farmer raised in the expectation of being primarily concerned with farming matters, it cannot be presumed that Richard Wheeler would have been lettered although it seems he was, according to his will of 1613.[10]

For whatever reason, however, in 1617 Wheeler needed money suddenly and badly. If reasonable evidence had not existed for the existence of the hammer in 1609 in the parish registers, it might have been thought that this need for a capital sum was connected with the setting up of the hammer. No evidence has been found that Richard Wheeler had been involved in expensive litigation. The hammer, perhaps, had suffered a catastrophe. As explained in the Pophole chapter, hammers were subject to a whole variety of hazards such as destruction by fire or flood and in particular to bad debts. Cleere & Crossley suggest that many small hammer businesses went to the wall in the absence of sufficient capital to see them through difficult periods. Richard Wheeler's mortgage money was supplied by Thomas Payne, the younger of the two Thomas Paynes who lived in Pitfold, and who both were yeomen entrepreneurs with an interest in many local financial matters and holders of much property. The Paynes and the Wheelers had intermarried so that the Paynes were the obvious persons for Richard Wheeler to turn to.

The mortgage agreement is not given in the rolls but as a presentment to the Jury of the Hundred Court of Farnham, as follows:[11]

Be it remembered that on the 18th day of March in the 15th year of King James [1617/18] to the first court of Charles Mountagu Knight, Seneschal of the whole of the Bishopric of Winchester, came Richard Wheeler and Constance his wife (the said Constance having been examined alone) and they surrendered into the hands of the Lord a messuage and a virgate of natural land called Stirte & ii acres of purpresture in the Tything of Churte to the use and behoof of Thomas Payne junior and his heirs etc according to the custom of the manor.

Under condition *that if the said Richard Wheeler and his heirs etc shall pay or cause to be paid to the aforesaid Thomas Payne or his heirs etc the full and whole sum of £171 and 15s of good and lawful money of England in the manner and forme following viz on the 15ᵗʰ day of April next to come, the sum of £10, in and upon the 16ᵗʰ day of July next following the sum of £10, and upon the feastday of St. Michael the Archangel next the sum of £141 15s, and in or upon the 20ᵗʰ day of October next the sum £10 in full payment and satisfaction, the aforesaid sum of £171 15s.*

And **Under Another Condition** *also that if the said Richard Wheeler, his heirs etc shall pay or cause to be paid to Thomas Payne junior annually each year during the whole term of 19 years the sum of £40 at the ends of four quarters [specified] at the dwelling house of Thomas Payne junior situated in Pitfold in the parish of Frensham in the County of Surrey, THEN this surrender shall be null and void.*

This agreement also included in addition to Sturt the 18 acres called the Great Purpresture and the six acres of purpresture (later 10 acres with Cherrimans).

In other words, if Richard Wheeler paid the above sums to Thomas Payne at the intervals specified, he would at the end of twenty years recover his property. If he did not keep up the payments, then the property would pass to Thomas Payne. As long as he kept up the payments, Wheeler would have use of the property in the normal way.

In a note in the margin Thomas Payne testified to the fact that the £171 15s. was paid on the day specified. Another margin note further identified Sturt by its rent in 1586/87 of 20/4d.[12]

These repayments over a period of 20 years and the initial £171 amounted to a sum approaching £1,000. There is not at this date a great deal of local information about the price of land, but this sum must have represented somewhere around the full value of all the three properties involved. In 1660 the value of Sturt was put at £424.[13] It is not, however, possible to say whether the price in 1617 was inflated to include the value of the hammer. The 1660 value did *not* include the hammer. Repayments apparently continued without problems until 1625/6 when there was a re-statement of the mortgage agreement in the rolls. It seems that the Wheelers had forgotten or had had difficulty with the repayment due at the Feast of St. John last gone.[14] In 1627 the Wheelers released and quitclaimed these holdings into the peaceful possession of Thomas Payne,[15] and a couple of years later Sturt and the Great Purpresture are found to have been transferred to William Billinghurst – the Haslemere attorney – along with the responsibility for the annual payment to Thomas Payne of the £40.[16]

In 1627, however, Thomas Payne the Younger had died and in 1630 Richard Wheeler is once more seen to hold his properties under the old mortgage conditions, having recovered them from William Billinghurst.[17] As

Thomas Payne the Younger – the supplier of the mortgage money – died in 1627 and as William Billinghurst was an attorney, and as Payne did not appear to have left a will, it is possible that the above hiatus was more legal than real. At all events Richard Wheeler continued to hold the mortgaged property until his death and burial in Haslemere in 1636. What happened to these Wheeler lands is moderately clear. Why it happened is less clear and will probably remain so. That they had possibly had trouble repaying the mortgage right from the start of the arrangement in 1617 might be indicated by the fact that the third small holding involved – the six acres of purpresture (later Cherrimans) – was sold off shortly afterwards in 1621 to Edward Fauchin.[18]

A final possible explanation for the need to raise cash might be that Richard Wheeler, making money from the Hammer, had decided to expand but no evidence for this was found. He must, however, have been confident at the time of raising this money that he would be able to repay £40 annually for the next twenty years, a no small undertaking. When he died in 1636, he seems to have been in a reasonably good financial state as he left a number of £50 legacies to sons, daughters and sons-in-law (and 1/6d apiece to the servants). Unusually, although not proved until 1636 he had made his will as long ago as 1613 when he was 'sick' and this remained unaltered.[19] He must have been one of the lucky ones to have recovered from some life-threatening episode of illness. His witnesses were Thomas Payne and William Yalden of Lodsworth.

From 1630, when Richard Wheeler recovered his properties, to 1636, there are under the Great Purpresture several rolls entries whereby he reserved his rights in the 'watercourse flowing across the Lords waste called le Lyon to his purpresture land in a certain place called Pitfold to a water meadow there'.[20] This is the watercourse flowing from Weysprings into the east end of the hammer pond (see map Fig.12) supplying water both to the Hammer and to the Purpresture Meadow which lay around the stream. In these entries the prior rights in this water supply were reserved to the Purpresture Meadow, and this possibly indicates that the Wheelers were not running the hammer themselves.

The Various Early Names of the Hammer (later Sickle Mill)

During the 1600s the Hammer is variously referred to as Wheeler's Hammer and Sturt Hammer and it was originally not known for certain whether they were one and the same. After the above references to 'Wheeler's Hammer' in 1609 in the Haslemere parish register, the Linchmere parish register refers in 1624 to 'Sturt Hammer in the parish of Haslemere' (bur. of Samuel Barden) and again in 1654, 1656 and 1659 to 'Sturt Hammer' (baps. of the daughters of John Hoad the Elder). The Haslemere parish register refers to 'Sturt Hammer' in 1635 (bur. of Samuel Blanchet). There is, however, little doubt that they were one and the same. The references to Sturt rather than

216

Wheeler's hammer may indicate that in the 1620s and '30s the Wheelers themselves might not have been personally involved in the running of the hammer, or it may indicate merely, from its location on land bearing the very ancient name of Sturt, that 'Sturt Hammer' came more readily to the local tongue. The 'Sturt Hammer' references in the later 1650s are totally comprehensible as by this time the Wheelers had cut their connexion with both the hammer and Pitfold.

After the death of Richard Wheeler the Elder in 1636, both Sturt and the Great Purpresture passed to his son Richard who sold them immediately to Edward Rapley of Linchmere.[21] Edward Rapley was at this date a yeoman farmer building up his holdings in Linchmere manor. Rapley died in 1651 and his will shows that he was already a man of some means, leaving four-score pounds sterling apiece to his two daughters and a son, and other smaller amounts to two other sons and also his house adjoining Linchmere cemetery.[22] To his wife and a fifth son Edward jointly, he left the Great Purpresture lying at Pitfold. He also left instructions that he should be buried in the chancel of Linchmere Church. There is no reference in his 1651 will to Sturts. At this point – the years of the Civil War and Commonwealth – the records of the manor of Farnham are incomplete. When they resume after the Restoration in 1660, an attempt was made by the manor officials to fill in the conveyances during the missing years which generally took the form of giving the date only of the last previous entry and change of tenancy, but no details.

The rolls do, however, show that Edward Rapley had surrendered Sturt Farm almost immediately after purchasing it but in this case in divided form.[23] Sturt was sold to the Launder sisters, Joan and Sarah, in 1640,[24] but in this case the farm and its lands only. Specifically excepted were *'ii cottages, i iron works (fabrica ferrea) ii gardens and a parcel of land called the hammer place with a pond and watercourse running thereto'*. This is the first explicit reference to the hammer on Sturts land and although this entry is dated 1640 it is stated that this division of farm and hammer had taken place in 1637, the rent of 20/4d for Sturts being henceforth divided into 20/- for the farm and 4d for the hammer. Rapley continued to hold the hammer until 1649.[25]

From this time on the history of the hammer begins to assume a more solid shape.

What happened to Richard Wheeler the Younger after he sold his Pitfold lands is not known. He may have been the Richard Wheeler who was buried at Elstead in 1653. At all events, as far as the Pitfold lands are concerned, the Wheelers take no further part in their history.

The Hoads (the sickle makers) at the Hammer

In the chapter on Pophole there were given a number of names of iron workers 'at ye hammer' which might have been either Pophole or Sturt.

There is, however, in 1635 an entry for the death of Samuel Blanchet a wandering boy specifically from *Sturt* hammer. One of the entries in the Linchmere register is for the baptism of the son of Thomas Hoade which, although again 'at ye hammer' unspecified, might well apply to Sturt, as in 1649 the Hammer was purchased from Edward Rapley by John Hoad the Elder and he and his son worked it until 1712.[26] Thomas Hoad[e] was probably the brother of John Hoad the Elder.

As the Frensham parish registers are illegible until the mid 1600s, the early history of the Hoad family cannot be traced, but Johns and Gregorys appear in the Farnham manor rolls in the 1600s and early 1700s for small holdings in the Tything of Churt near Hooks and at Diggetts Green. The daughters of John Hoad the Elder of Frensham parish (where Sickle Mill house stood as opposed to the hammer itself which was in Haslemere parish) Elizabeth, Dority and Margaret, were baptized in Linchmere in 1654, 1656 and 1659 respectively. When, however, the Elder John Hoad died in 1697 it is seen from the rolls where his widow was admitted to the hammer for her lifetime that John Hoad the Elder had purchased it from Edward Rapley in 1649.[27] (The actual purchase in 1649 is one of the missing entries). It may well have been, however, that the Hoads had been working Sturt hammer before their actual purchase, possibly from the division of the farm and hammer on Sturts land in 1637, or even earlier. It is unlikely that Rapley who bought the hammer in 1637 and held it until 1649 had operated it himself.[28]

Confirmation of the Elder John Hoad's purchase is given – although without dates – in the preamble to an agreement concerning the leat to the Hammer pond made between him and William Sadler of Chiddingfold, blacksmith, in 1662/3.[29] The Launder sisters who had bought Sturt Farm in 1637 both died in 1647[30] and the farm had passed from them to the Phillipp Bardens Elder and Younger with a mortgage from William Sadler. Phillipp Barden the younger had forfeited his inheritance as he was unable to pay his mortgage interest to William Sadler so that it passed into Sadler's owner-ship,[31] and the Hoad/Sadler agreement of 1662/3 concerning the leat[32] was drawn up to confirm a previous arrangement made between Hoad and the Elder Phillipp Barden on 11th February, 1655.

The Leat to the Hammer – The Agreement

This agreement concerns the rights of the two parties in 'all watercourses … running from … Styrt unto the pond of the said John Hoad called Sturt hammer pond and also the hammer land'. Whether the leat which is the subject of the agreement had been part of the hammer pond water supply from its inception or whether it stemmed only from the 1655 agreement, is not clear from the text. The watercourse referred to was the stream running down from Lowder Mill and then through Sturt meadow behind Sturt Road. It flowed along the back of the houses in Sturt road, joining the river Wey some way below Sickle Mill. The agreement concerned a leat taking water off this stream and directing it into the hammer pond at its west end, ie the pond head/hammer end[†].

In the agreement John Hoad was to enjoy the watercourse running into his pond called the Sturt hammer pond without hindrance from Barden. John Hoad was to renew and maintain a stone upon the side bay (bank) of the watercourse in Sturt Meade 'at the same height as it then was for a mark and bound to penne the sayd pond by and for a place for the water to runn over upon into the sayd Sturt Meade whensoever John Hoad should please to penne the sayd pond to its full height'. It is not known where this 'bound stone' was. The agreement also referred to the various maintenance obligations of Hoad and Barden as far as the *head spring* in Sturt mead. Phillipp Barden was obliged to lay and maintain a trough in the bay of the watercourse running through Sturtmeade 'in the place where *formerly* it hath beene layd for dividing the watercourse running from Lowdell Mill [so] that one half of the water thereof may runne to the sayd hammer pond'.

There are the remains of a sluice behind the houses at the south end of Sturt road near its junction with the Camelsdale road which would have diverted water into the mill leat. John Hoad was responsible for maintenance of the stream from the hammer as far as the head spring in Sturte mead. There is a large spring just to the south of Sturt Meadow House but the head spring referred to is almost certainly the major one emerging opposite Sturt Farm where it was later developed to provide the Haslemere water supply and is now channelled into the pumping station. This stretch of land along Sturt Road between the mill leat and Sturt Road from the hammer as far as Sturt Farm and the head spring was purchased by John Hoad in 1658,[33] and was retained by the Simmons family until the sale of James IV's land in 1903.

It is probable, therefore that there had been an arrangement for channelling water into the hammer pond from its inception represented by the sluice *formerly* operating near the Sturt Road/Camelsdale Road junction. This provision for dividing the water between the stream running through Sturt meadow and a leat running to the hammer pond is shown on the Tythe and later maps. It would seem to have been improved by the Hoads who utilized the better supply from the head spring near Sturt Farm.

John Hoad was to maintain the bays of the watercourses and to plant willows and alders upon the lower bay. Barden was to grant him at all times free ingress to amend, cleanse and scour the watercourse and to dig turves, earth, stone and gravell for the doing thereof. After 1660, the quit rent of

---

[†] Mr E E Orchard of Sturt Meadow House has since that time (with the agreement of the Haslemere Urban Council) reversed the flow of part of the leat and much of it now empties into the Wey below his house opposite Sickle Mill. It no longer flows across the road and into the hammer pond.

Sturt Farm was reduced from 20/- to 18/8d, the 16d reduction being thereafter for the strip of land containing the leat from the hammer pond as far as Sturt Farm and the head spring. This was known initially as Water Hatch Mead and later as Hatch House Mead.

During the Civil War the furnace at Imbhams which was producing guns was closed down by the Parliamentary forces. Nothing of this nature seems to have affected either Sturt hammer or Pophole neither of which, of course, was involved in the casting of guns. It is, however, possible that already at this date Sturt Hammer was involved in something a little different from the normal production of bar or wrought iron.

Sickle Making at the Hammer

In 1710 the Haslemere parish register refers to John Hoad the Younger as the 'sickelmaker'. For want of further information it had initially been assumed that it was under the younger John Hoad that the hammer had specialised in the production of sickles giving the mill the name by which it is still known today. However, in the returns of the 'Free and Voluntary Present' for Haslemere in 1661/2 the name of the Elder John Hoad of Sturts in the parish of Frensham appears for a contribution, when he describes himself as a 'whitesmith'. At that date the term whitesmith was used to distinguish from blacksmiths, craftsmen who dealt with white steel (and other non-ferrous metals) rather than black iron.[†] The elder John Hoad is also described as whitesmith in a deed of 1691.[34]

It seems likely, therefore, that the Hoads may have been specializing in the production of sickles and other edge tools from their initial official tenancy of the hammer in 1649, or even prior to that date if they were already working there before they purchased it. The technology of the production of soft wrought or bar iron has been described in the chapter on Pophole. The difference at Sturt Hammer/Sickle Mill may possibly have been that the process for the reduction of the carbon content of the cast iron would have been halted at a slightly earlier stage, leaving it harder and susceptible to being ground to a sharp edge. The carbon content of cast or pig iron was normally reduced in a hammer from its 3–4% to 0.1 or 0.2% but the process of decarburization could be stopped short with a carbon content of 0.3 to 0.4% to produce steel. The sickles probably had a steel edge, hammer-welded on to wrought iron, and then ground to sharpen. As with Pophole,

---

[†] The New English Dictionary on Historical Principles [Founded on Materials collected by the Philological Society] ed James A.H. Murray, Clarendon Press, 1893, gives a number of examples of the use of 'white-smith' between 1302 and 1886, all referring to a place where edge tools such as scythes, reaping hooks, etc were produced or ground. The last example comes from 'Patience Wins' by Alice Maud Fenn in which a character says 'I arnt a blacksmith. I'm a whitesmith, and work in steel'.

much of its product almost certainly would have been directed at the London market and it should not be visualized as supplying only local requirements.

The Voluntary Present was organised on the restoration of Charles II in 1660 as an attempt to free him from the substantial debt incurred during the period of his exile. Though 'voluntary' it was clearly politic to subscribe. The well-to-do yeomen such as the Shotters and the Benifolds contributed 40s. Lesser yeomen seem to have been content to pay 10s to 20s. Husbandmen and small craftsmen gave around 2s to 5s. with the odd enthusiast contributing more as a gesture perhaps of social one-upmanship. John Hoad the Elder struck a neat balance with a payment of 8s.[35]

Sturt Farm – The Later History

After the admission to Sturt Farm of William Sadler in 1659/60[36] the history of this property is no longer directly connected with that of the hammer but is briefly summarised here up to its acquisition in 1752 by the Simmons family. William Sadler of Chiddingfold to whom Sturt Farm had passed from the Bardens in 1659/60 did not hold Sturt for long but in 1662 decided to carry out some repairs and he was granted a licence by the steward of the Diocese of Winchester to 'demolish, remove and take away part of one messuage and one barn built on land called Sturt and to dispose of the material thence produced and to use it to repair another part of the aforesaid messuage and barn'.[37]

A Grade II listed building, the present Sturt Farm seems to be officially dated to the 1700s when it is described as having a tiled roof and tile-hung first floor. It is obvious from the documentation that there had been a farmhouse of some sort there from the 1200s at least and that Sadler above had made alterations to the buildings in the 1600s. Earlier, mention was made of the discovery during recent rebuilding of a tile dated 1733, possibly relating to improvements made by one of the John Combes holding Sturt Farm shortly after his marriage in 1729 to Dorothy Hoad of Sickle Mill, and this probably accounts for the building's official dating to the 1700s. The Listed Buildings description also refers to two barns and a granary, dating to the 1600s and 1700s respectively, but, one of the barns having been recently destroyed by fire, the insurance assessor commented that the method of some of the jointing of the beams pointed to a much earlier period.[38] A John Combes had purchased Sturt Farm from the heir of William Sadler in 1665[39] and various John Combes held it until it was sold to the Simmons in 1752.[40] By 1755[41] it would seem that John Combes, the eldest son of John and Dorothy (née Hoad) Combes of Sturt had moved to Bramshott, having either bought or inherited property there.

Sickle Mill

In 1697 John Hoad the Elder died and it is only then that his hammer property received its full description, when it was left to his widow Dorothy for her lifetime. Dorothy was admitted first to two cottages, an iron mill, two gardens and a parcel of land called the hammer with a parcel called the hammer pond and a watercourse belonging to the same, being late parcel of Sturts, rent 4d. She also was admitted to a pond called the hammer pond, the pond place and the pond head and a parcel of land called the Sinder Place near the pond, except the watercourse (referred to above) running from the Lyon to the Great Purpresture, being late parcel of the Great Purpresture.[42]

The reason for what might appear to be reference to two ponds etc is that each entry refers only to a half of the pond, the southern half late part of Sturts and the northern half late part of the Great Purpresture. It will be seen that the mill itself and also the two cottages are described as part of Sturts which is in the parish of Haslemere. In after years, however, Sickle Mill House and its inhabitants are always described as being of the parish of Frensham. In 1661 above, and in 1697, 1710 and 1712 when the two John Hoads, Elder and Younger, appear in the Haslemere parish registers, they are always described 'of Frensham parish'. It is just possible, therefore that the present Sickle Mill House which is dated to the middle 1600s was built in its present position by the Hoads, ie in the Frensham (northern) half of the hammer site and that the original 'two cottages and gardens' had been elsewhere. Any earlier housing for the workers at the hammer fifty years previously in Wheeler time might well have been of a less substantial construction and have been replaced by the Hoads with something better for their own occupation. Today Sickle Mill House is indeed a pair of cottages but during the occupation of both the Hoads and the later Simmons it was one dwelling house. The house was certainly on its present site in 1668 when Hoad purchased some land specifically described as adjoining it.

The many changes at Sickle Mill over the last 350–400 years make it fruitless to try to locate the precise location of the hammer itself. It can only be said that it must have been somewhere below and within the bounds of the pond head dam. The dam, only lately (1997) revealed to the eye when some parts of the mill and later buildings were demolished and re-built as flats, can be seen to have been much patched over the years. The date of the brick facing of the dam is not known.

Some few years ago, Sickle Mill House, a Listed Building, suffered vandalism resulting in a severely damaging fire particularly to the roof, after which it was restored. During this operation, massive pieces of hammer cinder were found at the back of the house, but this could have indicated repair of the dam itself as well as the location of the hammer house. The north wheel (one of two wheels) is situated immediately on the south side of Sickle Mill House and this, and also the later additions of the paper mill buildings extending further on the south side, suggests that the hammer occupied a place near but on the south side of the present House. The boundary separating Frensham and Haslemere parishes passed immediately below Sickle Mill House. Sinder Place, perhaps where the detritus was thrown, lay to the north of the hammer as it was part of the Great Purpresture and was not described as containing the hammer itself. Sinder Place now has on it the exit road from the Sports Centre.

During the years following 1649, John Hoad the Elder purchased small parcels of nearby land. In 1668, he purchased a 4 acre close 'adjoining his dwelling house', a triangular piece of pasture, part of the Great Purpresture, rent 10d, by Tythe Map time known as Sawpit Field, from Richard West.[43] In 1686 he bought another close of 3 acres, rent 7d, also part of the Great Purpresture (known as Lion Field) from the Tamplins.[44] He also purchased Hatchhouse Mead containing the leat in 1658 as described above.[45] These small closes remained associated with the Simmonses until the death of James IV in 1903. See map Fig.12.

In 1697, all the Elder John Hoad's property was left to his widow Dorothy for her lifetime[46] and her son, John Hoad the Younger, was admitted after her death in 1700.[47] John Hoad the Elder had obviously made a success of his business and it seems that he was also literate which must have been a help, as there is record of Thomas Burges, the curate of Haslemere 1627–1653, having lent him a 'Florus' [plant handbook?] in English.

John Hoad the Younger operated Sickle Mill until his death in 1712 and had four daughters but no surviving son, so that in 1712 the hammer and lands were left to his widow Mary as the four children were obviously under age.[48] These daughters were Elizabeth, Sarah and Anne, baptized 1703, 1705 and 1707 at Linchmere, and Dorothy baptized in 1710 at Haslemere. In his will enrolled in the manor rolls in English he enjoins his widow to keep the house, barns, buildings, mill, land, pond and pond place, etc in good repair so as to provide for the maintenance of herself, their four daughters and any other child of their begetting.[49] The Hoads were obviously both still quite young as the last daughter – Dority – was only aged two at her father's death. After Mary's death all was to go to the children. Widow Mary died in 1728 and the story of the daughters is continued[†] when in 1736 they sold the mill and lands to James Simmons I, papermaker.

Sickle Mill House

Mary's story ends with the inventory of her goods at Sickle Mill House, taken 16th February, 1729. There seem to have been ten rooms in the house including a number of utility rooms downstairs. The roof line shows that there was a rear range to the house of a similar period to the main building. The crops of wheat, hay and oats in the barn do not indicate that the Hoads did much farming but like everyone, had to have a couple of horses and oats and hay for them, and they kept a few pigs and a cow. The land, the 3 acre and the 4 acre closes of the Great Purpresture, were meadow and pasture.

There is nothing listed in the inventory relating to the mill unless the

---

[†] See *Shottermill its Farms, Families and Mills – Part 2*

entries under 'Ready Money' relate to this. In his will of 1712, which as usual with wills is in English, John Hoad the Younger refers only to the 'mill', but in the rolls entry (Latin) it is still described as a 'fabrica ferrea' or iron works. It is possible, however, from a different description of the mill in 1736 when it was bought by James Simmons I, that Mary Hoad, on her husband's death, beset about with four young children and not knowing one end of a sickle from another, had leased the mill to someone who had changed its use. In 1736, when sold to James Simmons I it was described as a corn mill.

Sickle Mill House was a timber-framed building although now faced and altered so that the timber framing is no longer obvious from the outside. The interior, however, revealed a great deal of patching, with the spaces between the timber verticals and horizontals filled in with bricks (some Tudor), stone and a mixture of both on occasions, giving the impression very much of a DIY history of repairs and alterations. During the 1997 alterations, in places the original wattle and daub infill could still be seen. In what had probably been the main bedroom at the front of the house were three layers of ceilings, the last being of elegant recessed wooden panels. There are no drawings of the hammer or house at this early date.

Mary Hoad's Inventory is given below.[50]

A true and perfect inventory of all and singular the goods and chattells ready moneys and creditts of Mary Hoad late of Frensham in the County of Surry Widow dated taken and Appraised by William Upton of the parish of Haslemere in the said County of Surry Glover and John Berry of Frensham aforesaid Yeoman the sixteenth day of February in the year of our Lord One thousand Seven hundred and twenty nine as followeth viz:

	£ = s = d.
Imprimis: <u>In her bedchamber</u> her wearing Apparell and money in her purse	*3=00=00*
It(em) One feather Bed one [?] Bed one coverlet two blankets one Bolster two pillows two Bedsteds matts and cords	*3=00=00*
One joynᵈ Chest and one old Box	*0=02=06*
In the inner chamber	
Two old Chests and one old Side Sadle	*3=10=00*
In the hall chamber	
One feather Bed one Bolster two pillows one coverlet three Blanketts Bedsted Curtains matt and cord	*3=10=00*
Item Two Chest four Chairs One firepann and one pair of Andirons	*12=00*
Item Thirteen pair of Linen sheets & twoe odd sheets	*5=00=00*
Item Nine pair of Linen sheets	*2=00=00*
Item Six table cloaths Sixteen Napkins fourteen pillow drawers and four more Table Cloaths	*1=17=06*

Item Six sheets more and Three hand Towells   0=07=06

In the Kitchen chamber
Item Two [?] Beds four old Blanketts one feather Bolster two   1=05=00
feather pillows One Bedsted mat & cords
Item Four chests & one old pannell   0=08=00

In the Kitchen
Twenty Six dishes of pewter Six Small dishes Seven pewter   2=05=00
Candlesticks one brass candlestick two porring*ers* and three
salts
Item Four Brass Kittles one warming pann one skimer & one   1=02=00
girdle
Item One Jack five Spitts one slice one [?] two cleavers one [?]   1=19=00
Knife two driping pans three Iron Girdles one Girdiron one
Box Iron one Iron candlestick one pair of Andirons firepan &
tongs one fender one pair of girdirons & two pot hooks
Item One pewter still   0=04=00
Item Four iron candlesticks   0=01=00
[line missing]
Item Cubboard one salting trough & other small things   0=10=00
Item One clock & one pair of Pillows   1=00=00

In the Hall
One table two Joyn'd stoolls & four chairs   1=07=00

In the Milkhouse
Seven dozen bottles   0=10=06

In the drink house
Thirteen drink tubs Six Truggs one funnell and four stanns   1=10=00

In the Brewhouse
Six Kivers Five tubs One Brewing vatt and other lumber   1=07=00
Item Two potts one Iron Kittle and two skilletts   0=14=00

In the Shooting Room
Seven bushels of wheat   1=06=00
Scales & weights   0=12=00

In the Barns
Hay and Oats   3=10=00
One Cart harness   3=00=00
Three prongs and one Rake   0=01=06

Goods without Doors
Dung and Ashes   1=07=00
Two hoggs and three pigs   9=10=00
One Cow   2=15=00
In ready money   26=03=00
Debts Sperate   41=00=00

Debts desperate[†]
Two horses
Sum total
Appraisers: William Upton, John Berry

41=06=02
8=00=00
171=14=08

Cherrimans (Farnham manor)

The last Wheeler land parcel mentioned above which became known as Cherrimans is detailed below. The first recognizable reference to this property is when, as a small piece of purpresture land of six acres, it was held by the Wheelers in 1574[51] when it was described as having been held for a long time in perpetual lease by Henry Wheeler from whom it descended in 1587 to Richard and Constance Wheeler of Sturt Farm and the Great Purpresture.[52]

The Wheelers parted with this six acres in 1621 as seen above, and it passed through various hands including the Fauchens and the Bardens. It was acquired by yeoman Phillipp Barden in 1629.[53] Cherrimans is one of the few properties in the area which can be located with ease and precision from its description in the rolls. In 1625 when there was already a house upon it, it was described as 'a messuage and ten acres of purpresture in the Tything of Churt in Pitfold between the king's highway from Shottermill to Haslemere on the north, the Sussex shire hedge on the south and a lane leading to Sturt on the east'.[54] (This is the second reference to the shire hedge, the first being on the occasion of its disappearance under Pophole Pond. Whether this meant that it was itself the shire boundary, or whether it merely described the hedge running alongside the stream which was the county boundary, is not known.)

During the Civil War and Commonwealth the missing Farnham Rolls meant that Cherrimans' documented history does not resume until after the Restoration, when in 1661 it is in the hands of the Hudson family about which nothing is known, then passing briefly through Pooles and Barlows,[55] until in 1700 it was purchased by William Cherriman,[56] and takes its name from its association with the Cherriman family who owned it with the Tanhouse at Rose Cottage until 1767. The Cherrimans probably resided there whilst running the tanyard. They seem to have needed a little additional land and in 1725[57] were in joint occupation with William Collen of the land of Stones (Mill Tavern land) just across the river. The Cherrimans were a family of tanners from Petersfield but with other land elsewhere. Edmund,

---

[†] The term 'desperate' when applied to debts usually indicated they were debts where all hope of recovery had been despaired of, ie bad debts. Whether the above £41 was really such or whether it referred to money owing and simply still outstanding, would probably depend upon the knowledge and sophistication of the assessors. [Isobel Sullivan, Archivist, Surrey History Centre, Woking].

the son of William who purchased the Tanhouse and Cherrimans, sold property in the manor of Kymer in 1681.[58] The Cherrimans may not have been strangers to this area as in 1668, widow Elizabeth Cherriman of Pulborough had married Henry Shotter, tanner of Haslemere[59] and William himself married Katherine Combes in 1675[60] at the time he bought the Tanhouse.

Cherrimans was bought by William Cherriman in 1700 and it passed on his death in 1728 to his son Edmund[61] and in 1761 to Edmund's grand-daughter Catherine.[62] After two generations working the tanyard and living at Cherrimans the family's lack of male heirs caused their presence in Shottermill to come to an end. Many of the Cherriman records are to be found in the Bramshott register and reference to the burials of two Williams there in the 1680s may have been sons who did not survive. Edmund only had one daughter, Catherine, who married a William Barnard but she predeceased her father and in her turn left behind her only a daughter who became the heir. However, this Catherine also died young (she had married a Richard Belchamber) so that in 1765 the sole remaining heir was Thomas Cherriman, Edmund's brother.[63]

By this date Thomas and his wife Anne were getting on – their children were baptized in Haslemere in 1715 and 1716 – and Thomas obviously did not want to start or at least continue longer in the tanning trade (if he had indeed been associated in the business with his brother) so that he either immediately sold Cherrimans and the Tanyard Cottages in 1767 to the Simmons family of paper makers, or alternatively, James Simmons I bought the property on his death.[64] Thomas and Anne both died in 1767 and are buried at Bramshott.

Cherrimans has been described elsewhere as a farm but as it never possessed more than ten acres of which one description in 1629 says that this included the house, garden, a haybarn and two orchards,[65] it was more likely to have been used by the Cherrimans, as it was later by the Simmons, as a meadow for hay and pasture for the animals which would have been necessary to their business. It is a Grade II listed building with its main range dating to the early 1700s but including also one bay of an earlier timber-framed house, and several later additions, this agreeing with its documented history.

The only picture of Cherrimans is the one taken in the late 1800s.

The Tamplin Family

Of less importance but of some interest was the Tamplin family, originally going by the name of Turke. The name change seems to have taken place in the mid 1600s when the Linchmere and Bramshott parish registers refer to a Turke alias Thampline. The Tamplins have already been referred to in the chapter on Pophole Hammer as one of the iron worker families. One of them, John Tourke, had been working at Brookland furnace at Wadhurst in

1534. They suddenly appear, however, on the Surrey side in the 1660s when they buy up parts of the Great Purpresture. There seem to have been three Tamplins, Nicholas, William and his son or brother Thomas, and Jane who was William's daughter and heir.

The last great parcel of land – the Great Purpresture, as distinct from the smaller parcels of purpresture land – had until the Wheelers sold it and left the area in 1636 comprised a single unit of 18 acres, for long tenanted along with Sturt Farm which it abutted. Its sale by the Wheelers to Edward Rapley yeoman of Linchmere has been described above. Details of the history of the Great Purpresture is shown in Fig.12.

In 1665 Edward Rapley's son sold it to Richard West.[66] Richard West was of Roundhurst and mentioned in Swanton and Woods, p.179 where his 'Porpister Meadow in the parish of Frinsham' is referred to in his will of 1673. When West had bought the Great Purpresture in 1665 it still comprised its 18 or so acres which roughly extended south from the Lower Lion to Sturt Farm land and from Junction Place eastwards to the Thursley parish boundary on Clay/Wey Hill. However, with the coming of the Hoads to the Hammer and also the Tamplins to that area, it began to be partitioned up until at his death in 1673 West retained only the Purpresture Meadow which was in the occupation of William Chitty who had a cottage nearby on Lion Common.

In 1668 John Hoad had bought 4 acres near his dwelling house (Sawpit Field) from West[67] and in 1668/9 the three Tamplins also bought from West three other parcels, one of six acres and another two each of three acres.[68] Richard West died in 1673, aged only 38, and the lands of the Great Purpresture or at least the remaining part – the Purpresture meadow – went to his daughter Elinore who had married Nathaniel Arnold, and from her to Francis Jackman of Thursley End in Haslemere town. From Ann Jackman, Francis's widow, it went to her brother Joseph Cornelius who sold the Purpresture Meadow to James Simmons I of Sickle Mill in 1761.[69]

The Tamplins were not around for long, having surrendered most of their properties by the early 1700s. The interesting question is, what occurred to make them apparently leave Linchmere and appear on the Surrey side in the 1660s. The furnace at Northpark where originally they might well have been employed is recorded as being ruined in 1664, this possibly the result of its having been dismantled by the Parliamentary forces who occupied the Montagues' Cowdray land during the Civil War. Had they moved into Pitfold as they were still associated with the iron industry and had they accumulated closes of land – much of it very close to Sickle Mill – because they were employed there by the Hoads? There is no proof of this but it is suggested as a possibility. The three iron worker families of Hoad, Tamplin and Briday were intimately connected through marriage. A Joanna Hoad was kin and heir to Thomas Tamplin. The Tamplins' departure in the early 1700s may also have been connected with the cessation of iron-working at Sickle

228

Mill on the death of the younger John Hoad in 1712.

Of the Tamplins' land parcels, one 3-acre close (Lion Field) was later (1686) bought by John Hoad the Elder, eventually going to the Simmons along with the other Hammer lands.[70] The Tamplin's six acre close and the other three acre close went to Thomas Combes in 1712[71] being sold by the Combes in 1777 to John Bull of Haslemere[72] and both ending up with John Bridger (a Bull/Hurst descendant) in the early 1800s when he had a farmhouse and about 12 acres of land (Frensham Tythe Nos. 1197, 1198, 1199 & 1200–1204). There were in 1839 on Bridger's farm, opposite the later St. Stephen's church, two cottages which may have been the forerunners of the ones still standing there, but there is nothing in the records about the dates of any of the buildings erected on this land.

John Bridger, baptised 1798, came from a Haslemere family but not from the same line as Charles Bridger,[†] the builder, who appears in James III's Diary, doing jobs for him at the mills and being churchwarden with James at St. Stephens. John Bridger the Elder came into this small farm in 1808[73] describing himself as a yeoman of 'Wheaten Down Common' (probably Weydown Common). He left a will in which he curiously referred to: 'Elizabeth who now lives with me and who goes by the name of my wife and is commonly reputed so to be, I having been in fact married to her but contrary to law'. It would seem that he had married first Ann Legg and then her sister Elizabeth who was within the prohibited degree. His son, John, inherited the farm in 1836.[74]

The Encroachment on the Lower Lion *(Farnham manor)*

There was, however, another plot of land – in this case common – which was annexed by William Tamplin. In 1663 William Tribe of Buffbeards (see below) had complained to the Farnham Hundred Court that: 'William Tamplin hath taken in parte of the Comon or waste soyle of the Lord of this manor to the great annoyance of the highway and the tenants. And if it be not throwen open to Comon againe before the 25th day of march next we peyne him in ffyve pounds'.[75]

The area which William Tribe complained about was in fact part of the Lower Lion just south of the present main road. This was Common Land and the Lord's property and Tribe was well justified in making complaint. However, this encroachment seems to have paid off as in 1667 under the heading of a 'New Grant' William was given the copyhold.[76] The subsequent details of this land parcel are lost. It may eventually have become part of

---

[†] Charles Bridger became a builder and around 1850 founded the first Estate Agent's business. He lived until his 91st year, playing an active part in the much later development of Hindhead and Shottermill. The picture of him clad in his woolly greatcoat is well known.

Bridger's small farm, or it may have comprised the later land holdings on the Lower Lion Common of James Harding and William Moorey who held copyhold cottages north of the highway near the later Co-op and whose lands seem to have extended over the road on to the Lower Lion with no documentation. It was on William Moorey's plat or meadow on the Lower Lion that he built Field End which he sold to James Simmons III for his retirement home in 1858/59. Later, some of this (originally) common land became the Lion Green Car Park and is now Haslewey.

The Tribe Family and Buffbeards Farm (Farnham manor)

The last family of interest is that of the Tribes who held property on the Surrey side between 1630 and the 1680s, and their heirs, the Sadlers until 1744. Their farm was Buffbeards, which lies to the immediate west of Lane End Farm.

Buffbeards Farm in 1876, at that time two dwellings

We had hoped to find some reason for its unusual name but, not unexpectedly, this was not the case. The manorial names took no notice of colloquial names as these changed and the purpose of the manor records was to maintain a descent of tenancy which was identifiable above all by descriptions of property which did *not* change. Buffbeards is a Grade II Listed Building dated to the 1500s. Like all these old buildings it has been considerably altered and in fact now faces the other way, but inside there can be seen many remaining early features such as the framing for a smoke bay with its wattle and daub filling and much smoke blackening, and an early staircase. Lying on the north side of the Hindhead Road just past the emergence of Church Road, it is today hardly visible, very different from the picture above.

It is first referred to in 1561, when the rolls start to become organised, as being held by the Baldwyns.[77] For a few years in the 1590s it was held by one of the iron fyners probably at Pophole, Blaise Bryday, and then passed from him to William Chawcroft[78] after which it passed into the hands of the Tribe family through the marriage of John Tribe of Pitfold to Elizabeth, William Chawcroft's [Chalcraft] heir in 1630.[79] In 1684 entered in the rolls is the will of William Tribe who describes himself as 'late of Bramshott Parsonage and now of Chiddingfold'.[80] The list of Bramshott rectors does not include William Tribe but he was obviously living there as he is listed under the Hearth Tax in 1665 for a house with 3 hearths. As at this time the two rectors of Bramshott are recorded as absentees, presumably Tribe was simply renting and living at the Rectory.

Tribe's will[81] left his lands of Buffbeards to his granddaughter Mary Stillwell, daughter of Anthony Stillwell, probably of Thursley or Chiddingfold as Mary married a Chiddingfold man – William Sadler the blacksmith.[82] However, William Tribe's will makes other dispensations besides his land and one of these is an annuity of 40s which was to be paid to his brother Henry at his house in Pitfold called Fynne House. Could this have been the original name of Buffbeards? In the 1332 returns of the Lay Subsidy for somewhere in the tything of Pitfold and Churt, there is listed a William Fynlegh.

There is for this farm a twenty year gap during the Civil War and Commonwealth after which, but not before, it is always described as comprising two separate parcels – one called Read & Readnetts and the other called Crouchmore. It has never been possible to ascertain which of these parcels was which except that the two of them seem to occupy the area to the east of Critchmere Common and around the house. (Later evidence suggests that, logically, Crouchmore was the southern portion).

In 1739, Mary (Stillwell) Sadler was involved in a Recovery (an impossibly complicated legal fiction often used to confirm a change of ownership) which also involved the Luffs.[83] It may be that the Luffs had been long-term occupiers of Buffbeards. They were certainly occupiers a hundred years later. William Sadler, Mary's son, sold this farm to Roger Shotter in 1744 and its lands, together with those of Lane End and Allens which were already combined, later became one farm known as Lane End and Buffbeards.[84] Because of this for much of its later history the farmhouse of Buffbeards seems to have been used to house farm workers, Lane End itself functioning as the farmhouse proper for Lane End and Buffbeards.

References in Chapter Twelve

[1] HRO.11M59/E1/108/5,111/6 & 112/5
[2] Archdeaconry Ct. Surrey Prob. 1.4.1613
[3] HRO.11M59/112/5
[4] Rolston op.cit.pp.29–30
[5] Has.Mus.P.2.194
[6] HRO.11M59/B1/155960
[7] PRO.E159/425.m.154. Hilary 1 Jac.I, 1603/4
[8] HRO.11M59/E1/112/6
[9] Ibid 116/3
[10] Archdeaconry Court Surrey, Prob.1636
[11] Ibid 149/3
[12] Ibid 149/3
[13] Ibid 125/2
[14] Ibid 119/4
[15] Ibid 119/6
[16] Ibid 119/9
[17] Ibid 120/5 & 120/6
[18] Ibid 118/6 and 119/3
[19] Archdeaconry Court of Surrey, Prob.14.4.1636
[20] HRO.11M59/E1/120/5; 120/6; 121/5;121/7
[21] Ibid 121/7
[22] Consistory Court Bishop Chichester Prob; Calendar vol 2. p497
[23] HRO. 11M59/E1/121/7
[24] Ibid 122/6
[25] Ibid 131/2
[26] Ibid 131/5 & 133/4
[27] Ibid 131/2
[28] Ibid 121/7
[29] Ibid 125/6
[30] Haslemere par.reg
[31] HRO.11M59/E1/125/2
[32] Ibid 125/6
[33] Ibid 125/3
[34] WSRO. Lucas & Albery papers
[35] WSFH Soc. Rec.Ser.No.2.1982
[36] HRO.1159/E1/125/2
[37] HRO.11M59/E1/158/1
[38] Personal communication from Mrs V.M Queen
[39] HRO.11M59/E1/126/1
[40] HRO.11M59/E2/153035
[41] WSRO. Lucas & Albery Papers
[42] HRO.11M59/E1/131/2
[43] Ibid 126/4
[44] Ibid 129/4
[45] Ibid 131/2
[46] Ibid 131/2
[47] Ibid 131/5
[48] Ibid 133/4
[49] Ibid 133/4

[50] PCC. Prob.1729, 3/29/46
[51] HRO.11M59/E1/111/4, 111/5 & 111/6
[52] Ibid 112/5, 112/6 & 112/7
[53] Ibid 151/5
[54] Ibid 119/3
[55] Ibid 125/3, 125/4, 126/1, 126/5, 126/6 and 131/6
[56] Ibid 131/6
[57] Linchmere manor rolls
[58] Feet Fines Trinity 33 Chas II 1681
[59] W.Ssx Marriage Registers 20.4.1668
[60] Fren. Par reg.
[61] HRO.11M59/E2/153011
[62] Ibid 153044
[63] Ibid 153049
[64] Ibid 153050
[65] HRO.11M59/E1/151/5
[66] Ibid 126/2
[67] Ibid 126/4
[68] Ibid 126/4 & 126/5
[69] HRO.11M59/E2/153044
[70] Ibid 153018
[71] HRO.11M59/E1/133/4
[72] HRO.11M59/E2/153060
[73] Ibid 153088
[74] Ibid 153142
[75] HRO.11M59/E1/160/1 Doc 134
[76] Ibid 126/3
[77] Ibid 110/5
[78] Ibid 114/3
[79] Ibid 120/5
[80] Ibid 128/9
[81] Archdeaconry Court of Surrey Prob.17.10.1684
[82] HRO.11M59/E1/128/9 & 128/10
[83] HRO.11M59/E2/153022
[84] Ibid 153027

Chapter Thirteen

Pitfold in the Courts

Some insight into the local goings on during the 1600s and later was gained from an inspection of the Calendar of Assizes and the presentments to the Hundred Court at Farnham, which indicated that the lives of the Surrey men were officially no more lively than their neighbours to the south in Linchmere. As often as not the Tythingman for Chearte/Churt would report to the Hundred Court that 'all was good and fair'. There were, of course, the usual complaints about the failure of tenants to clean ditches and maintain fences. Bartholomew Harding of Lane End was indicted for having fenced off a public well called 'Kerswell' probably originally 'Curtiswell' at Lane End.[1] Complaints were frequent about overloading the commons – in this case Churt and Hindhead commons – by people from Pitfold, Headley and as far away as Wishanger;[2] for cutting and carrying fern for animal bedding;[3] for cutting down trees etc – in fact the usual.

The odd reference taken from the Borough of Farnham shows town life to have been slightly more exciting. For instance John Hall of Seale was indicted for 'merdringe of his father in lawe William Michener and escaped away';[4] William Bicknell is ordered to immediately pull down a 'chimney very dangerous neare a barne' (not a problem in Pitfold's scattered community);[5] and there were several knife fights.[6] In the Assize Court records in 1564, Agnes, Thomas Quinnell's wife had her pocket picked by Matthew Willyam yeoman of Farnham who stole her purse worth 4d and its contents worth 16/5½d.[7] He was found guilty but pleaded clergy.

Sheep stealing seemed to be a regular hobby and two Haslemere labourers so accused were found guilty but also pleaded clergy, although the case of Henry Derford labourer of Pitfold who stole 29 sheep was left open as he appeared, wisely, to have fled and been still at large.[8] Theft of horses resulted in hangings as it was a capital offence. Juliana Collyn of Churt who removed from their owner a 6d shirt and a napkin got away with a whipping.[9] In 1612 Thomas Payne the Younger of Pitfold was accused of stealing a piglet worth 5s. at Chobham but, unsurprisingly, in view of his standing as well as the unlikelihood of the accusation, the case was dismissed.[10]

At the Hundred Court, which was held at Farnham twice a year, of the men who built illegal cottages on the commons (in this case Churt Common), the Newman family make a point. First indicted in 1621 and then 1623 and fined £10,[11] John and another Newman, Richard, were again presented in 1626 for building a cottage without licence.[12] In 1629 John was presented as having sold it for gain.[13] In 1630 John Newman the Elder was again presented for building a cottage and Richard for selling it to John Newman the Younger.[14] By 1633 the two John Newmans have *two* cottages built upon the Common[15] and in 1639 the manor is still complaining.[16] In 1641 it seems that both John and Richard Newman had taken in a further encroachment on the Common and 1642 is no different. At this point, after 20 years of complaint, somebody appears to be worn down and these entries cease. Either the manor gave up or the Newmans who in later years held the copyhold of this cottage, had settled to pay a rent. They were not the only ones to offend in this way, only the most persistent on record.

Another later series of presentments to the Hundred Court (in the 1700s) increasingly involved the illegal use of the products of the commons and selling them for profit . There are many presentments for the digging of stones and the cutting of turf and furze and heath to burn lime, to fuel brick kilns and to produce ashes for improvement of the land, and selling it out of the manor.[17] These items appear regularly with reference to anything up to 20 loads of turf, in spite of a fine of 10s per load, and these entries were only for the individuals who got caught. The Combes of Combes appear several times. The stripping of turf from the commons became a matter of serious concern. A further cause for concern was disease. In 1770 there had been an outbreak of rinderpest and in 1775 Thomas Page was presented for turning out 'distempered' cattle on to the commons, perhaps a hangover from this.[18] In the very late 1700s and into the early 1800s, probably when they were beginning to feel the pinch, the names of the Lion Green cottagers such as the Greenaways, Halls and Oakfords appear several times for undetailed encroachments.

There were also a few neighbourly spats nearer home. In 1613 William Chalcrofte of Buffbeards and John Bell of a cottage near the Shottermill Ponds were indicted for stopping up a watercourse that belonged to Thomas Payne's mill at Pitfold.[19] In 1641 Richard Tribe had not fenced his property against Thomas Combes' meadow.[20] In 1634 James Napper at the Tanhouse was ordered to make a fence between his property and that of Roger Barden then at Pitfold Mill,[21] and a year later Napper is again presented for encroaching upon Barden's land which presumably had been the reason for the previous complaint.[22] It would appear that these two small industrial establishments were perhaps not run on too friendly a basis, or at least were competing for space.

The Rolls show that occasionally things got a little more serious. In 1634 John Chandler applied to the manor for a licence to prosecute Thomas Payne of Pitfold Mill and Farm in any of the King's Courts he pleased, the customs of the manor not withstanding, although neither the reason for this nor the outcome is recorded.[23] On the whole, Pitfold does not seem to have been anything out of the ordinary.

References in Chapter Thirteen

[1] HRO.11M59/E1/146/5

[2] Ibid 146/6,147/2,154/1

[3] Ibid 147/4,148/2

[4] Ibid 150/2

[5] Ibid 154/3

[6] Ibid 147/2

[7] Cockburn, J.S.ed. Calendar of Assize Records, Surrey Indictments, James I,. HMSO, 1982.

[8] Ibid 2943

[9] Ibid 2098

[10] Ibid 426

[11] HRO.11M59/E1/150/2 and 151/1

[12] Ibid 151/3

[13] Ibid 151/6

[14] Ibid 152/1

[15] Ibid 153/4

[16] Ibid 155/6

[17] Ibid 155/6, 156/3 & E2/159589–96

[18] HRO.11M59/E2/195599

[19] HRO.11M59/E1/148/6

[20] Ibid 156/3

[21] Ibid 154/4

[22] Ibid 154/5

[23] Ibid 121/3

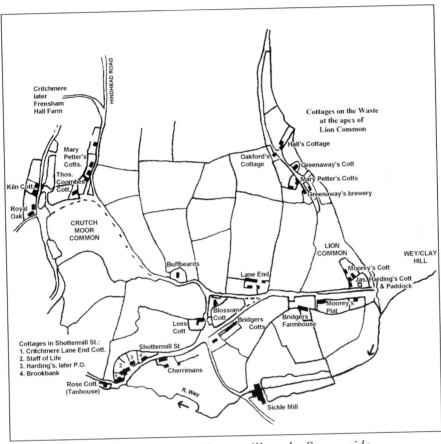

Fig.13: Cottages in Shottermill on the Surrey side

237

Chapter Fourteen

The Pitfold Cottages

The Cottages in Shottermill St. (now the Liphook Road) – the Critchmere Lane End Cottage, Brookbank, the Staff of Life, and Harding's Cottage late the P.O; the Cottages on Lion Green – Moorey's and Harding's on the SE corner; the Cottages above the Common in Lion Lane – now gone except for Bargate and Old Cottage; the Cottages on the Lower Lion, Clay Hill, and in the Nutcombe Valley; the Cottages on Critchmere Hill including the Royal Oak and Kiln Cottage; the Cottages in Wakeners Wells and on the Turnpike (Portsmouth) Road.

Like the Sussex side, there were on the Surrey side in the late 1500s apparently very few cottages. Some of these were in the Wey valley close to the mills and tanyard, and of these the Tanhouse, Cherrimans and Lees Cottage have already been touched upon. There was also a very early cottage opposite Shottover Mill, termed here the 'Critchmere Lane End Cottage', and probably also one at the south-east corner of the Lion Common to which there is a single passing reference in 1627.[1] As the 1600s and 1700s progress, however, more cottages begin to appear, some as a result of larger closes being carved up into smaller ones such as that along the west side of the road from Junction Place to Shottover Mill, which later became known as Shottermill Street; there were a couple on the Lion Common where the Co-op now stands; several on the waste in Lion Lane which started at the apex of the Common; a couple on the Lower Lion Common; three on Clay/Wey Hill in Thursley parish; and others around Critchmere Common and in the Nutcombe Valley.

These cottages, described here and shown on Fig.13, constituted the nucleus of the hamlet of Shottermill until the later 1800s. After this date, with the coming of the railway, the enclosure of the commons freeing much land for sale, and the influx of members of the wealthy middle classes into the area, there was a massive amount of new building of prestige and workmen's houses which changed Shottermill for ever.

The history of these cottages therefore, although many are now gone, is continued up to this time of immense change, as until that date they still represented Shottermill's historical extent and character. Some other cottages appeared in the middle 1800s but these, along with the illegal dwellings, particularly those of the broom-makers, are dealt with in the second book.

The Cottages in Shottermill Street

Critchmere Lane End Cottage *(Farnham manor)*

The earliest building at the bottom end of Shottermill Street (apart from the Tanhouse) was a house described as a Messuage with Curtilage, Garden & Close of Land Lying near Shottover Mill. This house is first referred to in 1562/3 as held by the Baldwyns.[2] Now gone, it lay just below the present entrance to Critchmere Lane. Reference to the Baldwyns and the tanning industry has been made above, and at this time they also held the Tanhouse and Buffbeards Farm. Probably in the late 1500s there was a thriving tanning industry hereabouts. After the Baldwyns, who round about the turn of the century fade out of the local picture, the Critchmere Lane End Cottage passed to their Bridger kin[3] until in 1662 it was bought by William Tamplin – one of the Tamplins mentioned above.[4] In 1712 it was sold to a 'John Glover alias Coales', probably a charcoal burner.[5] This Glover is the first-mentioned member of this family in this area and he had two sons baptized at Haslemere in 1711 and 1713. In 1718 the house passed to Ralph Hall by which time it is described as having half an acre.[6] It was probably set in a close of land extending up the west side of Shottermill Street and most of the other old cottages there were built on parts of its land.

In view of the nearby Hall's or New Mill, the presence of the Hall family so close by is possibly of importance. This house appears to have been the only one down Shottermill Street (except Cherrimans and Rose Cottage) until the late 1600s or early 1700s. In 1730 Ralph Hall divided his holding. He retained only his house and garden and sold the rest of the close of land extending (about 200 yards) up the hill, to Israel Hussey.[7] On part of this Hussey parcel, the house which is now Middlemarch and Brookbank was built.

In 1767/8 Ralph Hall's will was enrolled in which he describes himself as a husbandman.[8] His widow Joan inherited the house for life after which it was to pass equally to his children Roger and Mary. In 1667 widow Joan was indicted in the Linchmere rolls for illegally grazing her animals on Linchmere Common. Hall's elder son Ralph was described in the will as having been previously amply provided for and forgiven a debt to his father of £19. Had son Ralph been set up with the mill, later to become known as Hall's and later still as New (paper) Mill, and if so, what sort of mill was it? This is discussed in the next book in the chapter on the early Simmons.

Roger Hall, the younger son, obviously had no interest in holding his half of the property and surrendered it to his sister Mary who had married John Cobb, and the Cobbs held the house until 1788.[9] After this it was held by

John Bowles who was a paper maker and then from 1809 by the William Madgwicks Elder and Younger.[10] The last holder from 1815[11] was John Timms, later a shopkeeper, who still owned it at Tythe Map time in 1839.

When the railway came through Shottermill in 1859, the line passed immediately behind Rose Cottage and Critchmere Lane had to be moved a little way to the north to allow for the construction of the embankment. The old Critchmere Lane surface can still be seen in the garden of Rose Cottage running immediately behind, or probably originally past the front of the house. Timms' Critchmere Lane End Cottage was conveyed by him on 2nd December 1857 to the Portsmouth Rail Co. which demolished it. Members of the Timms family who were associated with James Simmons III's paper-making and with the Shottermill postal service are covered in the next book.

Brookbank (Farnham manor)

After 1730[12] when Ralph Hall sold most of the plot of land originally attached to his house to Israel Hussey, almost immediately in 1734 Hussey sold part of this land to Thomas Combes of Lane End who at the same court passed it on to his son William.[13] William was obviously on the point of marrying a Mary Read of Haslemere and this land was part of Mary's marriage settlement. The newly weds did not appear to have made use of this gift, as in 1735 they jointly disposed of it to Francis and Anne Jackman of Thursley End in Haslemere.[14] It is in the 1735 entry that for the first time this piece of land is described as having erected on it a cottage, ie the later-named Brookbank, although a cottage there may well have predated its first documentary mention.

This Cottage, now two dwellings, is Grade II Listed. It is described in the Listed Building account as of different periods, the older No. 24 or Middle-march being a two-bay timber-frame building dated to the late 1600s and No. 26 or Brookbank to the early 1700s. In fact, the two cottages were originally one dwelling, the later part being merely an extension. There is no documentary information describing the extension (not unusual) so that the architectural dating is the only evidence and the join can be clearly seen.

The Jackmans appear to have had no issue so the property passed to Ann Jackman's brother, Joseph Cornelius[15] who in turn left it to his two married daughters Mary, the wife of Peter Lambert, and Anne, the wife of Henry Jennings.[16] In 1764 the Lamberts surrendered their rights to the Jennings.[17] Henry Jennings was a Shottermill carpenter but was obviously not doing much more than scraping a living as when both the Jennings are dead in 1787, it can be seen that they had taken out a mortgage of £50 at 4½% interest but had not managed to keep up the interest repayments.[18] At this date, therefore, the Cottage passed by forfeit into the hands of William Boxall a tailor of Frensham parish, the mortgagee, and then to his 8-year old son and heir John Boxall. By 1801, young John Boxall was also dead and the Cottage passed into the hands of his sister, Mary.[19] It is this Mary Boxall who married Caleb Smith, a Shottermill paper-maker, who lived at the Cottage until 1860 when, on her death, it was bought by John Small of Petersfield, James Simmons III's son-in-law and husband of his daughter Charlotte.[20] It was bought by Small from William, Mary Smith's eldest son, who was a paper maker of Stoke next Guildford, and was subsequently let to Anne Gilchrist and George Eliot.

Brookbank in the late 1800s

The Staff of Life *(Farnham manor)*

When Israel Hussey sold some of the land (with Brookbank) to Thomas Combes in 1734, he retained the rest, and although there is nothing in the rolls to say so, it is probable that he had built on his remaining land the house which was later to become known as the Staff of Life. This house is referred to here by that name but its first description as the Staff of Life, a public house, does not appear until 1861.

The Staff of Life is again a Grade II Listed Building, but in part this grading is due to its prominent corner position. It is dated to the 1600–1700s (the earliest part at the north-east end) which would seem to confirm its building by Hussey, and has many later modifications.

The Husseys appear locally round about 1700 with several generations called Israel and they lived there until 1767.[21] The first local Hussey describes himself in 1714 as a hammerman when witness to his sister's marriage, and another in 1720 was a carpenter. Between 1750 and 1755 they held 15 acres in Heycombe Bottom and between 1750 and 1760 an Israel was rated for the Tanyard. Many of them lived long lives.

In 1767, the cottage was sold to William Marden but as the rates and the Land Tax show him to have been undertenant of Lane End and Buffbeards and then High Pitfold Farm it is probable that he was not the occupier. William died in 1795 intestate and an inventory made by his son George indicated that he had left something under £100.[22] Perhaps this was the value of this property. After this the Mardens are absent from the local records until the 1861 census when a George Marden is victualler and carpenter at the Red Lion. His father, also George Marden, was licensee of the Frensham Pond Hotel (also known as the White Horse) during the 1840–1860s.

Staff of Life, a Public House, around the late 1800s

After William Marden's death in 1795 the land was again divided, the part containing the Staff of Life passing from his son George to William White in 1804[23] and another part (further up the hill, later the post office site) going in 1799 to Stephen Harding.[24] In 1835 White's property was sold to Stephen Forey, a blacksmith of Thursley parish[25] and the Tythe map of 1839 shows Forey as owner but with William White still in occupation, although it is not certain in which house he lived. By Tythe Map time it is obvious that alongside the Staff of Life other small buildings such as the row of cottages running back from the road, and the large square house had been built. Later these were known as the Staff of Life Cottages.

When the land for the railway line was surveyed during the 1850s and it was decided that the line of Critchmere Lane would have to be moved, this affected the Staff of Life. To anyone standing at the front door of the Staff of Life, the steep fall to the road could inspire a feeling of vertigo. It is obvious from the comments and map in the rolls of 1858[26] recording the results of the Portsmouth Railway Company's survey that a considerable amount of land at the new junction of Shottermill Street and Critchmere Lane must have had to be cut away to provide for the construction of the embankment. The Railway Company undertook to 'construct and maintain proper and necessary steps out of the deviated roadway for access' etc Also a map showed that an L-shaped extension (now gone) on the south end of the house was purchased by the Railway Company and possibly demolished.[27]

At this time, 1855, the Staff of Life had been bought back from the Poultons (relatives of the deceased Stephen Forey) by William White the younger, who was gamekeeper to James Baker the Lord of Pitfold manor and holder of much other local land. He is described as of Frensham Hall Farm, his employer James Baker's residence, so presumably did not live there at that time. The William White who had owned the property in 1804 had presumably been his father. On the re-purchase in 1855, a mortgage of £200 was involved, this being furnished by John Rhoades of Haslemere who in 1871 was a corn merchant. By 1861 the building was a public house.

Harding's Cottage – lately the site of the Shottermill St. Post Office

The other part of the land sold by George Marden in 1799[28] to Stephen Harding was further up the hill but below Brookbank, and in 1805[29] Stephen left this cottage to his son James who was later a carpenter and timber dealer on Lion Green where he owned and lived in a house on the SE corner.

James, the Lion Green carpenter, was buried in Linchmere in January 1861. His will of 12th November 1856, enrolled in 1861[30] left his two houses in trust for all his children. It was on the Harding property in Shottermill Street which passed to his son James, that around 1880 the younger James's son, Henry, demolished the old cottage and built the red brick house which became the Shottermill Post Office which continued until 1996 in Harding hands. These Hardings do not seem to have been related to the other Harding family many of whom were James III's paper makers and who had been long associated with paper making in Shottermill and elsewhere. Both Harding families are commented on in the next book.

Cottages immediately North of the Staff of Life in Shottermill Street

Various O.S. maps show that these cottages were in existence by the 1860s. They are of no great age or interest and had probably been built in the early/ mid nineteenth century. They have no documentary history.

The Cottages on Lion Green

Even as late as 1839 as demonstrated by the Tythe Map, there were few cottages around Lion Green. There were two in the area of the Co-op, a small group at the apex of the Common on what had been waste beyond the Common, and a further two or three cottages on the Lower Lion Common. Nothing now remains of any of these except for two at the apex of Lion

Green, but a brief history of them will be given, starting with the two near the Co-op.

William Moorey's Cottage on Lion Green *(Farnham manor)*
– where the Co-op now stands – later the land occupied by Linton Cottage and the Red Lion

The Cottage belonging to William Moorey had been a new grant in 1667[31] of a small plot of land to Caleb Chitty whose son, William Chitty has been referred to above as working the Purpresture Meadow when it was held by Richard West.

Four generations of the Chittys held this cottage until in 1733 it passed into the hands of Hannah Bennett, the local midwife, whose family had the lease of Lane End Farm.[32] After Hannah's death in 1740, her son Peter sold it to Thomas Glasier[33] from whom it passed to Glasier's daughter, Mary Ford, when it is described in 1749[34] as a 'copyhold cottage with outhouses, gardens and orchards lying in the Common called the Lyon'. Mary Ford's father's will is enrolled and it leaves to his wife Mary Glasier for her natural life, 'the Room called the Best Chamber, the Hall, the Washhouse and Drinkroom and the piece of garden lying on the northeast as far as the Necessary House'.[35]

In 1771 the Fords sold the property to William Roe and his son William,[36] after which in 1809[37] it was bought by Richard Moorey, a broom-maker, passing in 1822 to his son William Moorey, then wheelwright of West Dean[38] but later wheelwright of Linchmere (near Arnold's Garage). The Mooreys also held a plat or meadow nearby on the Lower Lion on which William Moorey built Field End to which James Simmons III retired. The Lion Green cottage was sold in 1849 by William Moorey to Thomas Chuter of Weighdown[sic] Farm, Haslemere, and it was on this plot that Chuter built Linton Cottage which survived until the building of the Co-op.[39]

For some time, according to Sillick, this house was used as the village inn where Thomas Chuter brewed his own beer, and was the forerunner of the present Red Lion which was also erected on that land by Thomas Chuter for his son Henry. The Chuters are discussed further in the next book.

The Cottage of James Harding, Carpenter *(Farnham manor)*

The second cottage near the Co-op was James Harding's Cottage which lay on the corner of the Green and the Haslemere road. This property also had a paddock opposite on the Lower Lion. In 1781[40] this Cottage is described as having the cottage late of Mary Glasier (ie the above Moorey Cottage) on its North side and the Lyon Common on the other parts. It is also described as a new grant as the cottage which had formerly stood there had burnt down.

In 1781 this cottage was granted to Elijah Marshall as a new grant, being enclosed with a bank and quicksett hedge.[41] Although a new grant, it came to Elijah Marshall from his father John Marshall, so obviously it had already been rebuilt and occupied for some time. It is difficult to accept that such a site had remained unoccupied for any great length of time, although the only possible reference to the existence of the previous burnt-down cottage occurs in 1627.

In 1813 it was purchased by James Harding[42] but only on condition that Elijah and Sarah Marshall be allowed to continue living there for the rest of their natural lives – perhaps they were in-laws. This was the James Harding (1775–1861) who eventually came to live at this cottage, who was the carpenter and timber dealer mentioned above, on whose death there was a Coroner's inquest, and who also owned the cottage below Brookbank, later the Post Office. The Lion Green cottage, with carpenter's shop and land was still there in 1861 as it figures in his will[43] and it was divided between his son James who kept the carpenter's shop, and another son Thomas who kept the part facing the road where a house had been built and which Edward Dunce, a grocer, was occupying. It is probable that Thomas's part was where Bell's grocer's shop now stands.

Cottages on the Waste at the Apex of Lion Green *(Farnham manor)*

At the top of the Lion Common but on the waste and not on the Common itself there was a small group of cottages. It was never clear why the two houses on the Common itself described immediately above had the right to exist there. Although the tythe map shows many other buildings on this part of the waste, apart from the cottages described below, these were various outbuildings rather than habitations.

Bargate and Old Cottage – Lion Lane
(Farnham manor)

The first reference to a dwelling at the top of Lion Green was in 1661 when John Dickens was admitted to a cottage and adjoining acre of waste,[44] this passing in 1706 to John Chitty junior[45] and in 1717[46] to Edward Walker. The Walkers, an old local name, members of which family had held land in Nutcombe, and also down Linchmere Hill below St. Peter's, held this cottage and land until 1757[47] when it was first divided, after which date the land became increasingly subdivided and more cottages built upon its parts. The records in the rolls concerning these sub-divisions are something less than wholly clear but it seems that the original cottage is now two dwellings known as Bargate Cottage and Old Cottage. This building has been dated

William Oakford, Hannah's brother – he was a Shepherd and the last, apparently, to wear a Traditional Smock

245

to the 1700s but it may well have earlier origins.

From the late 1700s it was held by members of the Oakford family and one of them, Robert, was one of William Simmons' paper men,[48] being a witness to his will in 1801. At Tythe Map time (1839) it was owned by Samuel, Robert Oakford's son but occupied by William Kern as by that date Samuel was in living in Middlesex. By 1850,[49] although still in the occupation of a Mrs Rebecca Oakford, it had been sold according to the instructions in Samuel's will[50] and had been bought by Edward Hoad, a Haslemere wheelwright, one of the Haslemere people buying up small parcels of Shottermill lands at that time. Hoad also bought at this time some land opposite on the east side of Lion Common owned by Edmund Greenaway.

The Oakford family seem to have been late-comers to the area. The records for this small Shottermill family, which appear from the late 1700s in the Haslemere parish register, include Hannah (1819–1898) the well-known pauper water-carrier of Haslemere who was Samuel's granddaughter. A picture of Hannah's brother also survives.

Hall's Cottage *(Farnham manor)*

The track up the centre of the Common bisected this acre of waste and in 1797[51] a part of Oakford's land opposite on the east side, with a cottage on it, was sold off to Hugh Hall whose son Jesse (they were both broom-makers) was living there at Tythe Map time. This cottage has now gone. On the occasion of this purchase by Hugh Hall, Christopher Lee of Lees Cottage provided a mortgage.

Petter's Cottage(s) *(Farnham manor)*

A little to the south and on the western side of Lion Lane, Richard Petter in 1817 purchased another small part of the land and a cottage or cottages on it.[52] Richard Petter was a local cordwainer owning and living at Blossom Cottage and seemingly being in a position round about this time to snap up this small property and others at Critchmere. This cottage went in 1840 from the widow Petter to her son in law William Gill, also a cordwainer[53] who died in 1865 and then to his son.

This cottage or cottages are now gone, but Richard Gill, a descendant, owned four cottages on the same land in 1910. These Petters (sometime Pitters) were not a local family although the name appears in other parts of Farnham manor such as Seale and Tongham and Wrecclesham from the 1600s.

The Greenaways' Cottages *(Farnham manor)*

The last two parcels of this original acre of waste went from the Oakfords to the Greenaways in 1782[54] and 1813.[55] The one on the east side, bought in 1813, may still survive in the form of Mellow Cottage, as the Greenaways continued to own and occupy it throughout the 1800s. The other was a small piece of land not far above and on the same side as the (later) White Lodge.

Here William Greenaway bought or built a brewhouse in 1782[56] which still seemed to be operating in the 1850s.[57] Probably, prior to Thomas Chuter brewing his own beer at the Red Lion in the middle 1800s, the Greenaways may have supplied some of the local requirements. Certainly in the 1860s George Marden[58] who in the 1861 Census was the victualler at the Lion Public House, bought this Greenaway land and brewery.

The Greenaways, some of whom were broom-makers, and the Chuters are further described in the next book.

The Cottages on the Lower Lion and on Bridger's Farmland
(all Farnham manor)

Apart from the Moorey and Harding land on the Lower Lion Common, the remainder of the land running from Kingsdale round Junction Place and down to Sickle Mill was the land of John Bridger's small farm held of Farnham manor which was described above under the Tamplins. On this land and opposite the Church were a few small houses on the 1839 Tythe Map but they have no documented history. Now of brick, the end wall of one is partly of stone suggesting a nineteenth century rebuild. Other small cottages appear to have been built later near Bridger's farmhouse, for example Rapson's smithy.

The Cottages on Clay/Wey Hill

Originally the Lion Common had extended almost down to the valley bottom by the Jehovah's Witness Kingdom Hall. From what is now St. Christopher's Green and some way down toward the Railway Bridge stretched the industrial wasteland of Clay Hill in Thursley parish. In the early 1800s between the bottom of Wey Hill and St Christopher's Green there were only three cottages, one where the Ford Showroom now is at the bottom of Farnham Lane, which was the home of broom maker Daniel White, and another two behind the row of shops rising eastwards up the hill from the Public Library. One of these latter was the home of Edward the 'Royal' Moorey broom-maker, so called as he had supplied brooms to Kensington palace and advertised the fact on his cart.

Around Electra House and the 'Fair Ground' car park lay the brickfield and kilns. The last brick was fired here round about 1900, but bearing in mind that bricks may have been made on Clay Hill from sometime during the 1700s – if intermittently and on a small scale – it may well be that a considerable part of Clay Hill had been dug out and refilled. One of the later pits lay behind the row of houses above the Crown & Cushion. Edward Berry was making bricks on Clay Hill in the middle 1830s and on the 6th November 1839 James Simmons III, when about the mill, saw smoke arising, not as he thought from the kilns, but from Berry's house which was on fire.

It is difficult to visualise earlier landscapes but in the absence of buildings, trees and railway embankments, James III must have had a moderately clear view across to Clay Hill from home. Clay Hill cannot have been a place of much beauty and, until approaching 1900, had no houses on its eastern slope other than a few above the Crown and Cushion and the public house itself which were there in 1861.

The Cottages in the Nutcombe Valley

In the Pitfold Manor Rental of 1727, the two cottages in the Nutcombe Valley, one of which had 4 acres attached to it, were in the hands of Thomas Herne. These he held in right of his wife Elizabeth Walker. It is likely that these had been there from the 1600s. Land on both sides of Nutcombe Lane as it runs down from the A287 Hindhead Road to the point where it turns sharp left up the hill towards High Pitfold and the A3 belonged to the part of Lane End Farm in Pitfold Manor (Lane End Farm comprised land in both Surrey side manors) and was not therefore susceptible to being built upon.

From this junction, the land going in the direction of Hindhead had almost certainly at one time and in some part had been Common Land (see the comments on the boundary question). There are a number of houses along this lane today but only two are identifiable, one as having belonged in 1839 to Richard Combes – who lived near the site of the present Coachhouse – and the other to Stephen Combes – who was at Combes Cottage. The Pitfold Rolls and James III's Diary clearly show that Stephen Combes had first encroached on and then made his peace with Pitfold manor in the 1830s for the northern part of the valley. Above Combes Cottage there are no other field boundaries but there are a number of fleeting references, for example to members of the Lawrence family, to indicate that in the area of Upper Nutcombe broom-makers were active.

The Cottages on Critchmere Hill

Other than the nearby Pitfold Mill, there were no obvious employment opportunities to account for the group of cottages around the top of Critchmere Common and down Critchmere Hill in the early period. The most likely explanation for their presence is that it was one of the few untenanted parts of the waste (in a very wet area) where cottages could be built without incurring trouble from the manor or its tenants. It may also be that the stream coming down from Nutcombe, later a string of ponds, provided some sort of livelihood and this is discussed further below when describing Kiln Cottage which lies close to the Royal Oak.

Some of the cottages down the hill are now gone and others that remain, being in Pitfold manor, have little or no documentation. There were in fact two groups of houses with two different histories. The first were the three cottages on the slip road to the Hindhead Road. These had been built on the waste round the edge of Critchmere Common and at Tythe Map time were all owned by widow Mary Petter of Blossom Cottage. These cottages are all dated to the 1700s. 'The Cottage' now one dwelling had originally been two and the filled-in second door can be clearly seen.

In the second group were the houses at the bottom of Critchmere Hill – the Royal Oak and Kiln Cottage which lies behind it. These had been part of the Combes family's Critchmere Farm, lying at its extreme southern end.

Kiln Cottage *(Pitfold manor)*

The first reference to this cottage is on the 1727 Pitfold Rental where William Bridger is seen to hold a tenement and acre of land called Combers, a cottage which is identifiable by its description and quit rent as the house now known as Kiln Cottage. At some time after 1727 it must have been bought back from the Bridgers by the Combes, and on the death of Thomas Combes of Critchmere Farm in 1826 it was sold to Stephen Pannell of Haslemere for £160.[59] In 1839 it was occupied by William White.

In 1876 The Royal Oak at the bottom of Critchmere Hill and to its right Kiln Cottage showing the roof line incorporating the Kiln

It has never been Listed but has been examined by the Surrey Domestic Buildings Research Group as, not only is it of some great age but it contains within the building a kiln structure, the use of which could not be determined. A photograph dated 1876 shows the heightened part of the roof structure incorporating the kiln which is not traditional. The date suggested by the SDBRG was around 1800 or later and one of the possible uses put forward was for drying fish taken from the ponds.

The dates of the ponds on the Nutcombe valley stream are not known except that they were there in 1839, and their position and extent has been altered since that time. An alternative suggestion was that the kiln was for malting barley, but as the drying area was very small and malting was a process requiring a good deal of floor space, the SDBRG discounted this. The original building suggested a 3-bay open hall cottage constructed around 1600.

The Royal Oak *(Pitfold manor)*

This also had been part of the land of the Combes' Critchmere Farm and on the death of the last Thomas Combes in 1826 it was part of his estate bought by Edward James Baker. At tythe map time in 1839 Richard Moorey had the licence of the Royal Oak, and there is much additional detail about his family and the alehouse in the next book.

Woolmer Common

Apart from a reference in the 1727 Pitfold Manor Rental to John Berry's house on Woolmer Hill containing about 2 acres, having an orchard and being near Benefolds, absolutely nothing is known about Woolmer Common, how it was used and who, if anyone, lived there until the late 1800s.

Cottages in Wakeners Wells
and near the Turnpike (Portsmouth) Road

These were all on Pitfold manor land or on the Bishops Commons and have, therefore little documented history. They were, in any case, nearly all squatters' illegal cottages inhabited by broom-makers and are commented on further in the next book.

From the account of the Surrey-side copyhold cottages, it can be seen that in nearly all cases they were held by small craftsmen such as carpenters, cordwainers, tailors, husbandmen, paper-workers and the like, and also broom-makers some of whom in the late 1700s and early 1800s were without doubt a step above the agricultural labourer. The latter, who less and less tended to be retained by farmers as live-in farm servants, may well have been occupiers but few if any of this low-status group held property.

References in Chapter Fourteen

[1] HRO.11M59/E1/119/9
[2] Ibid 110/3
[3] Ibid 112/2, 120/7, 122/4, 125/2–4
[4] Ibid 125/6
[5] Ibid 133/3
[6] HRO.11M59/E2/153001
[7] Ibid 153013
[8] Ibid 153050
[9] Ibid 153054 & 153070
[10] Ibid 153089
[11] Ibid 153095
[12] Ibid 153013
[13] Ibid 153017

[14] Ibid 153018
[15] Ibid 153043
[16] Ibid 153047
[17] Ibid 153047
[18] Ibid 153069
[19] Ibid 153082
[20] Ibid 153141
[21] HRO.11M59/E2/153050
[22] Admons. Archdeaconry Court Surrey, 30.10.1795
[23] HRO.11M59/E2/153085
[24] Ibid 153080
[25] Ibid 153115
[26] Ibid 153138
[27] Ibid 153140
[28] Ibid 153080
[29] Ibid 153095
[30] Ibid 153142
[31] HRO.11M59/E1/126/3
[32] HRO.11M59/E2/153016
[33] Ibid 153023
[34] Ibid 153032
[35] Ibid 153032
[36] Ibid 153054
[37] Ibid 153089
[38] Ibid 153102
[39] Ibid 153129
[40] Ibid 153064
[41] Ibid 153064
[42] Ibid 153093
[43] Ibid 153142
[44] HRO.11M59/E1/125/5
[45] Ibid 132/5
[46] Ibid 134/3
[47] HRO.11M59/E2/153040
[48] Ibid 153112
[49] Ibid 153130
[50] Prob.Commissary Court Surrey 1.11.1849
[51] HRO.11M59/E2/153078
[52] Ibid 153097
[53] Ibid 153120
[54] Ibid 153064A
[55] Ibid 153094
[56] Ibid 153064A
[57] Ibid 153156
[58] Ibid 153149
[59] Has.Mus.LD.5.231

Index

255

John held Pond and Corner Cottages early 1700s, 111

married into Sadlers of Chiddingfold, 230–31

TRIMMER James, heir of William Shotter of Highbuilding, took Shotter name, 86

TROTTER, W.R., author of *The Hilltop Writers*, 19

TURKE/TOURKE. *see* Tamplins

TYTHE DISPUTE 1598. see Pophole Hammer

TYTHE MAP
Frensham 1839, 154, 164, 177
Linchmere 1846, 23, 58, 148

TYTHING. *see under* Pitfold Tything

UPTON
bought Deanes and Sturtmore 1670s, 64, 82
maltsters, glovers, mercers, 82, 167

VALOR ECCLESIASTICUS. see also Dissolution of Monasteries
late 1608 Valor, 26
lease in late 1608 Valor of Shottover mill, 99
Shottover mill not included in Priory lands, 99
Thomas Payne the Elder acted re Frensham parish in 1608 Valor, 194

WAGGONERS WELLS
corruption of Wakeners, 21, 46
in Pitfold manor boundary problems, 176–77
inhabited by squatter broom-makers, 178, 250

WAKEFORD
at High Pitfold farm 1200s, at early Saxon corn mill 1300s, 43
at Sturt Farm 1200s, 39

WAKENER Isabel, held Headley land in 1309, 46

WALKER, held Bargate/Old Cottage 1717, 245

WASHERS ALS WATCHERS [Linchmere manor land parcel, now Rats Castle]
bought by Joseph Mills, 62
decayed late 1500s, 83
ironworkers Bardens and Pelhams 1571–2, 127
monetary value 1600s, 64

present building dated 1700s, descent through Hopkyns in 1537, various investors, 1699–1781 Maidmans, land divided in 1700s, part bought by William Simmons for New Mill, southern part absorbed into Maidmans' Springhead farm, leased to Pelham & Barden ironworkers 1571–2, Allen attempted purchase 1651, unusual name changes inc. Coldwashers, by clerical error became Watchers 1699, present house Watchers [Dexam] by rights Watts farm, William Simmons bought remaining part 1788, 78–79

Walshes original name, 23

WATERHOUSE [Linchmere manor cottage], granted to Roger Seale 1622, 112

WATERHOUSE [Linchmere manor land parcel]. *see* Bridge Farm

WATERMEADOWS, Rapley indicted 1682 for illegal use, 76

WATTS FARM [Linchmere Wattmans & Elliots in Linchmere manor]
details of Watts Farm and Hammer from Persons/Roger Shotter of Shulbrede/his son Roger of Pitfold, and Hammer to Montague, perpetual compensatory annuity from Montague to Watts holder, 136–39
copyhold of Hammer and lands to Jas Simmons III for relinquishing of annuity to holder of Watts, 147–49
Pophole hammer built on land late 1500s, 77, 92
Pophole hammer rolls entries under Watts not Pophole, 118
Theyre and Person families 1533–1610, bought by Roger Shotter of Shulbrede 1610 for sons but excluding Pophole Hammer, Roger Shotters of *Pitfold* held 1610–1781, possible tenant Chilsum family, new farmhouse built, probably now Watchers [Dexam], Simmons bought 1781, 92–93
Thomas Person indicted 1609 for illegal lopping, Roger Shotter of Pitfold added Shottover Fields 1618, 61

WAVERLEY ABBEY, 50

Made in the USA
Charleston, SC
13 January 2016